AF572371

Desktop Publishing with PageMaker 3.0

IBM PC AT, PS/2, and Compatibles

Tony Bove
Cheryl Rhodes

John Wiley & Sons, Inc.

New York • Chichester • Brisbane • Toronto • Singapore

Editor: Therese A. Zak
Managing Editor: Ruth Greif

Library of Congress Cataloging-in-Publication Data

Bove, Tony, 1955-
Desktop publishing with PageMaker 3.0: IBM PC AT, PS/2, and compatibles / Tony Bove and Cheryl Rhodes.
p. cm.
Rev. ed. of: Desktop publishing with PageMaker. c1987.
Bibliography: p.
Includes index.
ISBN 0-471-51537-X
1. Desktop publishing. 2. PageMaker (Computer program) 3. IBM Personal Computer--Programming. I. Rhodes, Cheryl. II. Bove, Tony, 1955- Desktop publishing with PageMaker. III. Title.
Z286.D47B68 1989
686.2'2544536--dc20 89-14836
CIP

Printed in the United States of America

89 90 10 9 8 7 6 5 4 3 2 1

Trademarks

Adobe Illustrator is a trademark of Adobe Systems, Inc.
Aldus FreeHand is a trademark of Aldus Corp.
Apple, LaserWriter, LaserWriter Plus, Apple LaserWriter II, and AppleTalk are trademarks of Apple Computer Inc.
AST and TurboLaser are registered trademarks of AST Research, Inc.
AST Premium 286, AST Rampage, AST TurboScan, and AST TurboLaser/PS are trademarks of AST Research, Inc.
AutoCAD is a registered trademark of Autodesk, Inc.
ConoVision 2800 is a trademark of Conographic Corp.
Crosstalk is a registered trademark of Digital Communications Associates, Inc.
dBASE II and dBASE III are registered trademarks of Ashton-Tate Corp.
Dataproducts LZR-2665 is a trademark of Dataproducts
DisplayWrite 3 is a trademark of International Business Machines Corp.
Document Content Architecture (DCA, also known as the IBM Revisable-Form Text) was developed by International Business Machines Corp.
Epson FX-80 is a trademark of Epson America Inc.
Ethernet is a trademark of Xerox Corp.
Gallery Collection is a trademark of Hewlett-Packard Corp.
GEM Paint is a trademark of Digital Research, Inc.
The Genius is a registered trademark of Micro Display Systems, Inc.
HALO DPE is a trademark of Media Cybernetics Inc.
Hercules is a trademark of Hercules Computer Technology
Hewlett-Packard, H-P LaserJet, H-P LaserJet Plus, and H-P Vectra are registered trademarks of Hewlett-Packard Corp.
HPGL is a trademark of Hewlett-Packard Corp.
HotShot is a trademark of SymSoft
IBM, PS/2, and Proprinter are registered trademarks of International Business Machines Corp.
IBM DisplayWrite 3 is a trademark of International Business Machines Corp.
In*a*Vision is a trademark of Micrografx, Inc.
InBox is a trademark of Symantec
INTEL and Intel Above Board are registered trademarks of Intel Corp.
Linotronic is a trademark of Linotype Corp.
Lotus, Freelance, Freelance Plus, Symphony, and 1-2-3 are registered trademarks of Lotus Development Corp.
MacDraw, MacPaint and MacWrite are trademarks of Apple Computer, Inc.
Macintosh is a trademark of McIntosh Laboratories, Inc. and is licensed to Apple Computer, Inc.
MacLink Plus is a trademark of DataViz, Inc.
MacMemories is a trademark of ImageWorld, Inc.
MacPaint is a trademark of Claris
MaxiMITE is a trademark of Mycroft Labs
Micrografx Windows "Draw!", Micrografx Windows "Graph!", and Micrografx Graph Plus are trademarks of Micrografx, Inc.
Micrografx Designer is a trademark of Micrografx, Inc.
Microsoft is a registered trademark of Microsoft Corp.
Microsoft Chart, Microsoft Excel, Microsoft Windows, Microsoft Windows Paint, Microsoft Windows Write and Microsoft Word are trademarks of Microsoft Corp.
Mirage is a trademark of Zenographics
The Missing Link is a trademark of PC Quik-Art, Inc.
MS-DOS is a registered trademark of Microsoft Corp.
MultiMate is a registered trademark of MultiMate International Corp., an Ashton-Tate Company
MultiMate Advantage is a trademark of Ashton-Tate Corp.
Multiplan is a registered trademark of Microsoft Corp.
NetWare is a registered trademark of Novell, Inc.
Olitext Plus is a trademark of Olivetti
PageMaker is a registered trademark of Aldus Corp.
PC AT and IBM PagePrinter 3812 are trademarks of International Business Machines Corp.
PC Mouse and PC Paint are trademarks of Mouse Systems
PC Paintbrush is a registered trademark of ZSoft Corp.
PC Talk III is a trademark of Headlands Press
PC Write is a trademark of Buttonware
PostScript is a registered trademark of Adobe Systems, Inc.
ProComm is a trademark of PIL Software Systems
ProIndex is a trademark of Elfring Consulting
PublishPac is a trademark of Dest Corp.
Publisher's Paintbrush is a trademark of ZSoft Corp.
Relay is a trademark of VMPC
Samna Word and Samna Word III are trademarks of SAMNA Corp.
Scan-Do is a trademark of Hammerlab Corp.
SideKick is a registered trademark of Borland, International
Symphony is a registered trademark of Lotus Development Corp.
Timeline is a trademark of Symantec
TOPS is a registered trademark of TOPS, a division of Sun Microsystems
TOPS Network, TOPS PRINT, and TOPS Translators are trademarks of TOPS, a division of Sun Microsystems
Turbo Lightning is a registered trademark of Borland, International
Varityper VT-600 is a registered trademark of AM International
Viking 1 is a trademark of Moniterm Corp.
Volkswriter is a registered trademark and Volkswriter 3 is a trademark of Lifetree Software, Inc.
Webster's NewWorld Spelling Checker is a trademark of Simon & Schuster, Inc.
Word Finder is a trademark of Writing Consultants
WordPerfect is a trademark of WordPerfect Corp. (formerly Satellite Software International)
WordStar, WordStar 3.3, WordStar 2000, and MicroPro are registered trademarks of MicroPro International Corp.
XyWrite III is a trademark of XyQuest, Inc.

Acknowledgments

We would like to thank the following people for their support:

Paul Brainerd, Laury Bryant, Steven Carlsen, Jeff Halpern, Elaine Rickman, Gail Rice, and Mike Solomon (Aldus), Doedy Hunter, Ric Jones, and Keri Walker (Apple), Tom Yuen (AST Research), Jim McNaul (Xerox Imaging Systems, Datacopy Div.), Judi Kidwell and Ginny Pyle (H-P), Sara Scharf and Marty Taucher (Microsoft), and Bill Gladstone (Waterside Productions).

This book stayed on schedule thanks to the efforts of: Sanjay, John, Lars, and Krishna Copy (San Francisco, CA), who provided quick and accurate typesetting, and thanks to our indefatigable editors, Ruth Greif and Teri Zak (John Wiley & Sons, Inc.).

Dedicated to our parents and families.

Contents

Preface

This book provides a step-by-step approach to setting up publication files and templates for typical office documents, technical manuals, marketing literature, books, newsletters, and magazines. It assumes only a basic knowledge of word processing, so that anyone with a need to publish documents (but without training in page makeup or production) can use the book to produce the documents.

Each chapter introduces a different type of publication. This book also introduces the most basic concepts of design and typography. The intent is not to bog you down in details, but to show you some of the tried and true elements of good design. In some cases, examples of real publications are used. Other cases use simulated publications.

Here's a breakdown of the chapters and what you can expect to find in them.

Chapter One: Preparing for Desktop Publishing

The first chapter provides a brief description of the desktop publishing process, including word processing, graphics creation, text and graphics scanning, page makeup, laser printing, and typesetting. It provides a brief overview of Microsoft Windows and the use of a mouse and keyboard controls, plus how to perform simple file operations.

This chapter also explains in detail why certain word processing and graphics programs are better than others for working in conjunction with PageMaker. It also recommends spelling checkers and thesauri, various utility programs, and other programs that generate or manage information to be published (mailing lists and other data bases, spreadsheets, business charts, and graphs).

The chapter concludes with descriptions of the similarities and differences between the various laser printers, scanners, typesetters, and other output devices that work with PageMaker.

Chapter Two: A Newsletter Tutorial

This chapter takes you step-by-step through the process of producing a four-page newsletter, from starting PageMaker and designing a publication file from scratch, to producing and printing a sophisticated newsletter and saving templates for future issues. The instructions are suitable for starting up any design and production effort, and serve as a basis for understanding techniques used in subsequent chapters. This chapter can also serve as an impatient user's tutorial because it covers nearly everything that PageMaker can do.

Some highlights are step-by-step instructions for creating a newsletter title, placing formatted and unformatted text, using graphics with text, scaling and cropping graphics, sizing and resizing text, changing type styles, placing formatted and unformatted text files, changing column widths, changing the entire layout, and setting up automatic page numbers.

Chapter Three: Business Reports and Manuals

This chapter discusses how to put together a company annual report that features spreadsheets, charts, graphs, the company logo on the cover, and a designed interior. Special effects include a custom column layout, pouring text with the Autoflow option, adjusting hyphenation, adjusting word spacing to fix any widows or orphans, wrapping text around images, creating master page elements, and creating templates. Spreadsheets and graphs are enhanced with boxes and drop shadow effects.

The chapter applies the steps presented earlier in the book to produce a typical technical manual and a book (using the page design for this book). It also explains how to set up style sheets so that global changes can be made automatically. The use of templates, master pages, and style sheets allows a production group to work efficiently, sharing master page designs and graphic elements.

Chapter Four: Graphic Design

This chapter offers techniques for customizing pages and adding design touches and special effects. It shows how to mix column layouts, wrap text around irregularly shaped graphics and enlarged initial capital letters, spread headlines and titles, control word spacing and letterspacing, and perform manual and automatic kerning. The examples illustrate the use of special effects, such as enlarged initial capitals, reverse type, boxes, rules, and borders.

The examples include pages from magazines, newsletters, manuals, and books. This chapter also discusses how to prepare electronic pages with separate color overlays for handling spot color and four-color separations.

Chapter Five: Tips and Techniques

This chapter is a summary of the tips and techniques that can shorten your production time and keep you from constantly referring to manuals (although the Aldus manuals are quite good—you should read them!). You could use this chapter as an impatient user's summary, together with the laminated *PageMaker Quick Reference Guide* from Aldus.

Appendixes

The appendixes include instructions on how to prepare text and graphics from word processing programs, painting programs, and drawing programs for use with PageMaker. The appendixes also contain a list of special characters that can be produced, plus hints about how to transfer PageMaker publication files between PCs and Macintosh computers. Appendix E is a bibliography, and the book concludes with an index.

* * *

This book has been fun to produce, thanks to PageMaker. The entire book was written and edited on several PC AT-compatible computers (a Hewlett-Packard Vectra PC and an AST Premium 286) and placed onto PageMaker pages. The PageMaker pages were printed first with an AST Research Turbolaser/PS or an Apple LaserWriter IINT, and then printed with a Linotype Linotronic 100 typesetter (all are PostScript devices). Microsoft Word was used (on both PC AT computers and Macintosh computers) to prepare text files and to produce the index for this book. After placing the Word text files onto PageMaker pages, the Word files were edited to include last-minute changes (made in PageMaker) and PageMaker page breaks, as well as index entries and the table of contents entries. HotShot (SymSoft) captured "shots" of the screens that were used throughout the book as examples. HotShot can save images as TIFF (Tag Image File Format) files, which are universally recognized.

The entire project took less than three months for writing, editing, and production. This book is an example of what can be accomplished in a relatively short time and with little cost by using a desktop publishing system and PageMaker.

Aldus Manutius, the "patron saint" of publishing, would be proud of Aldus Corporation for its efforts to advance the state of the art.

Tony Bove and Cheryl Rhodes
Gualala, California

Introduction

Talk of nothing but business, and dispatch that business quickly.
—Aldus Manutius (placard on the door of the Aldine Press, Venice, established about 1490)

What do Northwestern Mutual Life Insurance, Boeing, 3Com Corporation, the U.S. Congress, Hesston Corporation, Lawrence Livermore Laboratory, RTE Deltec Corporation, and the Queen Elizabeth II have in common? These organizations use PageMaker to produce publications. Hundreds of small- and medium-sized commercial publishers use PageMaker (which is to be expected), but it is significant that *companies that are not commercial publishers* are doing desktop publishing.

Many people are involved with publishing, whether or not they see themselves as publishers. If you produce sales literature, marketing brochures, flyers, newsletters, advertisements, operating manuals, or other business communications, you may be able to save time and money—and have a great deal of control over the production process—if you use a desktop publishing system. A page-makeup program such as Aldus's PageMaker plays the central role in any desktop publishing system.

For example, Northwestern Mutual switched from conventional methods of production to PageMaker for an in-house technical newsletter, and cut the production time in half. The company also found PageMaker useful for producing advertising flyers and transparencies for speeches.

3Com Corporation, Lawrence Livermore Laboratory, and Hesston Corporation all use PageMaker to produce large manuals. Livermore Lab also uses PageMaker to produce research reports and papers for publication in scientific journals. Hesston also uses PageMaker to produce parts catalogs, department forms, and other instructional material.

The Queen Elizabeth II uses PageMaker to produce a daily world news bulletin. The news pages are put together into a PageMaker publication file in London, then transmitted by satellite to the luxury liner where a laser printer prints 1,200 copies for the ship's passengers.

Newspapers such as *The State Journal* (Charleston, West Virginia), *Behind the Times* (Corinth, Vermont), and *Roll Call* (weekly newspaper for the U.S. Congress), plus magazines such as *Publish!, MacUser, Macworld, Personal Publishing, Chartering Magazine*, and *Balloon Life* use PageMaker because the desktop publishing equipment shortens the production cycle and saves money.

Graphics experts and consultants can now focus on the design task and perform that work much more quickly and inexpensively with desktop publishing equipment, or else let their clients perform their own production work. Small publishers have the ability to produce commercial publications with the same quality look and feel as publications from the large publishers. Corporations can cut down on the cost of designing forms, brochures, and marketing literature, and technical publications departments can produce manuals and data sheets very quickly.

The desktop publishing phenomenon started when laser printers, which offer near-typeset-quality text and graphics printing, were introduced to work with personal computers. As a result, inexpensive publishing tools became available and made it easier for people to perform publishing production tasks without resorting to typesetting services and graphic design houses.

Desktop publishing tools became useful for commercial and corporate publishing purposes when they were made compatible with typesetters and higher-resolution devices (such as film recorders and plate makers). The industry-wide acceptance of a common language of typesetting, called PostScript (developed by Adobe Systems and used in printers first by Apple and then by Digital Equipment Corporation, IBM, Sun Microsystems, Texas Instruments, QMS, AST Research, and Wang) made it possible for desktop publishing software to produce typeset-quality text and high-quality photographs.

A page-makeup program plays a central role in a desktop publishing system, and is used as a finishing tool for preparing text and graphics for presentation and publication. A word processing program and a graphics program are used to create the text and graphics, and a page-makeup program brings the elements together on a page. The page-makeup program lets you adjust the design of the page at the same time that you place the elements.

Electronic page makeup offers many benefits over conventional manual page makeup and design methods. Because the electronic elements can be easily moved, cut, copied, resized, edited, and repasted on the page, your elements do not get lost. There are no cut marks where a sharp knife has slipped, and you do not have to wait for images or type to be reproduced at a new size or for new typesetting to replace a misspelled word found in a typeset galley.

PageMaker is the quintessential electronic page-makeup program because it simulates the procedures that artists and designers use in conventional page makeup. Text and graphic images are pasted onto an electronic page and cropped with an electronic "knife." Master page elements are created and duplicated automatically for all or some of the pages. Blocks of text can be moved on the page to fit around graphics, and you can wrap text around irregular shapes automatically. Columns of text are linked so that changes made to a column cause a ripple of reformatting to occur automatically. You can experiment with minor editing changes in order to shorten or lengthen a block of text, or change the size of the text block itself. You can even pour text onto multiple pages automatically and quickly in order to see how many pages the text will fill.

With this metaphor in action on the screen, designers, artists, and graphics-oriented people can feel the power of the computer and relate immediately to its use in desktop publishing. The metaphor of text threading is very close to the physical task of threading typeset galleys through a layout. Designers and graphic artists have no trouble understanding how PageMaker works; the precision of PageMaker's rulers and various page displays make it very easy to line things up (without the need for a T-square and a fluorescent light table).

The metaphor works with beginners as well, providing a real-world model for the activity of mixing text and graphics on pages. Coupled with Microsoft Windows, which handles file and disk management as well as program execution, PageMaker fits neatly into the desktop environment and is therefore easy to learn. The "menus" from which you select options look just like the "menus" in Microsoft Windows.

The Macintosh version of PageMaker has been used for applications such as magazines and books, even though it was really designed for newsletters. The authors of this book used PageMaker to produce a magazine *(Desktop Publishing,* now called *Publish!)*, and now use both versions of PageMaker to produce books, a monthly newsletter, and a variety of other publishing tasks. PageMaker has been used to produce tabloids and oversized brochures and flyers, even though the program supported only A4, 8 1/2- by 11-inch, and 8 1/2- by 14-inch pages on the LaserWriter. PageMaker's tiling techniques allow the printing of tabloid size pages in sections, and you can then paste the pieces together to match up the elements and create a page wider than 8 1/2 inches. If you use a typesetter such as the Linotype Linotronic 100 or 300 imagesetter, or a printer such as the DataProducts LZR 2665 (all of which support a larger page size of 11 by 17 inches), then you can print the tabloid page in one piece without tiling.

The latest versions of PageMaker (version 3.0 for the PC and version 3.02 for the Macintosh) are revised in accordance with customer feed-back. The newest features in PageMaker were added in response to the claim that PageMaker did not have enough typographic refinements for producing commercial-quality publications.

Aldus added automatic pair kerning (as supported by the different font manufacturers) and manual kerning, as well as automatic letter spacing and word spacing (for justified text only). PageMaker now offers para-graph spacing, typographic fixed spaces, leader tabs, additional line styles, the ability to size and resize columns at will, and hand-scrolling of an image within the space reserved for it on the page. The program also offers automatic hyphenation based upon a 110,000-word dictionary from Houghton Mifflin, as well as a supplementary dictionary (with up to 1,300-words), prompted hyphenation (the program displays words not found in the dictionary and lets you hyphenate them and add them to the supplemental dictionary), and manual hyphenation (discretionary hyphens).

With these features, Aldus improved PageMaker so much that it is now an excellent tool for producing commercial publications, as well as newsletters and marketing literature. The program is now capable of producing so many different publications that entire books about how to use PageMaker (such as this one) are needed.

Will desktop publishing foster a renaissance in the printed word and image? Some believe that poorly designed results from desktop publishing will prove that publishing should be left to the experts who have design skills. The enthusiasm for desktop publishing is infectious, however, and people can learn design skills by reading books, consulting with experts, and taking design courses.

In an era when automation is making information workers more productive, the ability to self-publish is a valuable asset for the smallest communications service company and the largest corporation, from the individual writer to working partnerships and government organizations. If you can present the information in a professional style and publish it for your customers without incurring variable costs or costly delays, you are using desktop publishing for what it was intended: to make you more productive in your business.

1 Preparing for Desktop Publishing

To produce a publication, even a very small one, you invariably have to go through the major steps of (1) designing the publication, (2) creating the text, photographs, and graphics, (3) making up the pages by combining the text, photos, and graphics with design elements, and (4) using a prepress shop or print shop to prepare film negatives, from which plates for the pages are made. The plates are then used with a printing press.

The goal of desktop publishing is to automate as many of the repetitive tasks in the production cycle as possible. A major advantage of desktop publishing is greater flexibility in design and layout, and easy accommodation of changes right up to printing time. Page design can be easily performed using personal computers, and sample pages can be printed with laser printers. Comments and editing changes are more easily incorporated when the manuscript is stored in electronic form. Line art that is stored in electronic form can be precise and revisable, and the process of electronic page makeup is faster and more revisable than the process of manual paste-up.

Text and graphics information should be in electronic form as early in the process as possible. The information can be *created* electronically with a personal computer, or else *converted* into electronic form through such techniques as the use of a scanner. Text and graphics information can be created on any type of computer, from a mainframe to a portable, and then stored in files on floppy disks, hard disks, erasable CDs, magnetic tape cartridges, and other digital storage devices. To convert information stored on paper into electronic form, typewritten text and hand-drawn line art can be scanned with a desktop scanner that costs less than $4000 (and perhaps as low as $1500).

Why is it so beneficial to store text and graphics in electronic form? For one thing, text that is stored electronically can be sent to a typesetting machine without being retyped. Also, graphics can be included with the text without the need to perform manual paste-up, and pieces of graphic elements can be used again in other illustrations without the need to redraw those elements.

The PageMaker screen displays almost the same image you can expect to see on paper, so check the screen carefully for any errors before printing your work. After you finish making all of the changes that you want, the typesetting machine or laser printer can print entire pages of camera-ready copy that can be used for volume printing without the need for further mechanical processes (wax, glue, etc.).

Where to Start

If you're new to publishing or production work, you may be surprised to find that there are so many steps to climb before you reach the finished, published work. At the top of the stairs is the volume printing process—the method by which mass quantities of the publication are printed.

Even if you need only ten copies of your publication, you must start with an idea about what the final printing process will entail. Will you use a copier or laser printer to produce 10 or 20 copies? Will you need more than 200 but less than 500 copies? More than 1000 copies? More than 10,000? You must answer this basic question first, and then plan the production effort for the publication.

For example, a newsletter or business report may require a clean, polished look, but because they are inexpensively printed in small quantities (less than 500), they do not require the extra production expense of the use of a 1000 dots-per-inch (dpi) typesetter—a laser printer

Figure 1-1. The Premium AT 286 computer and other products from AST Research.

could do the job. For these applications, you can use almost any desktop laser printer (at 300 or 150 dpi), and not worry about compatibility with a typesetter.

However, a book, magazine, marketing literature (such as a page advertisement, flyer, or brochure), or instruction manual might require typeset-quality text and photographic-quality images. For such production requirements, compatibility with a typesetter could be critical. The surest way to maintain compatibility between your laser printer and

Figure 1-2. The Hewlett-Packard Vectra PC (another PC AT compatible).

higher-resolution typesetters is to use a PostScript-compatible laser printer. PostScript is the most popular page description language used in both printers and typesetters, as well as in high-resolution film recorders and display systems.

In some cases, a desktop publishing system needs to provide the speed of laser printing, flexibility, and compatibility with typesetters. PageMaker offers the best of both worlds because it supports virtually every type of laser printer, as well as PostScript typesetters and printers. You can also add printer and typesetter drivers to Microsoft Windows at any time and recompose your publications for those devices. You can proof the file on a laser printer, and then provide the file on disk (or via modem) to a typesetting service bureau that will produce final typeset pages.

Consider also the type of system that you will use: Are all pieces of the system available now? Is retraining necessary? Can you purchase enough systems to handle the project? Will the same computer be used for writing text, editing text, creating graphics, and composing pages? How much time should you allocate for volume printing? All of these factors contribute to the process of defining a timetable for production efforts.

As you start to put together equipment suitable for running PageMaker, it may help to consider the equipment that was used to produce this book. Two different computers that are compatible with the IBM PC AT standard, known as ISA (Industry Standard Architecture) were used. One computer was the AST Premium 286 from AST Research (shown in Figure 1-1). This computer was used with the AST TurboScan desktop scanner, the Mouse Systems PC Mouse, and the AST TurboLaser/PS laser printer. The second computer was the Hewlett-Packard Vectra PC (Figure 1-2), which was used with the Hewlett-Packard LaserJet Plus printer and the Xerox Datacopy desktop scanner. An Apple LaserWriter was connected to the HP Vectra's second serial port, a LaserJet Plus was connected to the first serial port, and the AST TurboLaser/PS was used with the Premium system in order to test the PostScript and LaserJet Plus drivers and fonts.

To produce the final camera-ready pages of the book, PostScript was used as the target printer in order to print proof pages on the AST TurboLaser/PS. The final pages were typeset on a PostScript-based Linotype Linotronic 100 typesetter at a service bureau.

Learning Windows

If you and your production staff have no experience with Microsoft Windows on an IBM PC AT or compatible computer, you should set aside time to become familiar with it. To run PageMaker on the PC AT or compatible computer, you need either the full version of Microsoft

Figure 1-3. A Windows application starts as a window with a working area, an icon area, and a system menu box. The disk icon is the MS-DOS Executive part of Windows that lets you copy, rename, and delete files, as well as use other operating system commands.

Windows (preferred), or the run-time version (supplied in the PageMaker package for AT users who do not want to run the full version). PageMaker is compatible with the 286-based and 386-based versions of Microsoft Windows.

If you are familiar with the PC's operating system, you already know how to use system commands to format disks, copy or delete disk files, add or remove printers and other devices, print files, and run programs. Microsoft Windows (the full version) is a level of software that lets you use the operating system without the need for you to know specific commands. You can format disks, copy or delete files, add or remove printer control software, print files, and run programs—in short, you can do everything that the operating system lets you do, but you do not need to memorize commands. You operate Windows by pulling down menus with a mouse and then choosing commands, options, and filenames.

The run-time version of Windows (which is what you are using if you installed PageMaker without installing the full version of Windows separately) gives you most of the functions available in Windows, but does not let you start more than one application in a window, or condense a running application's window into an icon.

When you run an application with the full version of Windows, the application occupies a window on the display (Figure 1-3). The system menu box appears above the working area and controls the application window.

To use Microsoft Windows and most Windows applications, you must become familiar with the mouse. All of PageMaker's functions can be used with a single-button mouse. Double- and triple-button mice can provide helpful shortcuts because the left-most button can function as the main mouse button (unless you reconfigure the mouse—see the mouse device manual or the Windows Control panel).

Six basic actions are performed with a mouse:

1. *Point.* When the mouse is moved, a pointer moves across the display. This pointer appears as either a point or a crosshair (or a similar object). To point, move the tip of the pointer to the desired area on the display.

2. *Click.* To click, quickly press and release the mouse button.

3. *Double-click.* To double-click, quickly press and release the mouse button twice.

4. *Drag.* To drag an object (such as a graphic object, a block of text, or an icon), point the mouse, hold down the main mouse button (usually the left-most button), and move the mouse so that the pointer (or object) moves to a new position. Then release the button.

5. *Select.* To select a menu option or command, drag down a menu (which drops down farther on the screen in order to display the options or commands) until the command or option that you want is highlighted, and release the mouse button. You can also select a menu option or command by clicking the menu title, moving the pointer to the option or command, and clicking again. (Keyboard shortcuts are available for many commands.) To select text, double-click a word, or else drag across one or more words or paragraphs.

6. *Flow.* To use this PageMaker variation of Click, point and click a text placement icon. The icon will "pour" the text down the column.

Windows and PageMaker employ drop-down/pull-down menus specific to the application, plus a special menu, called the System menu, that drops down from a horizontal bar icon above the File menu (Figure 1-4). You can launch the Control Panel application from the System

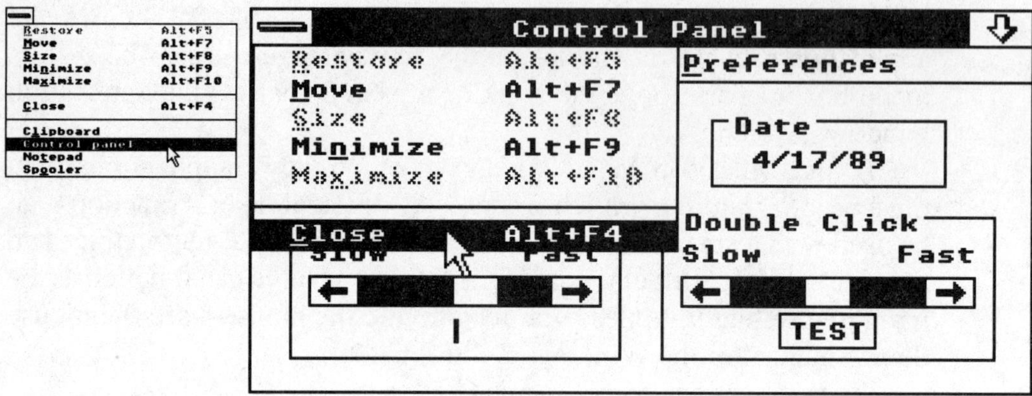

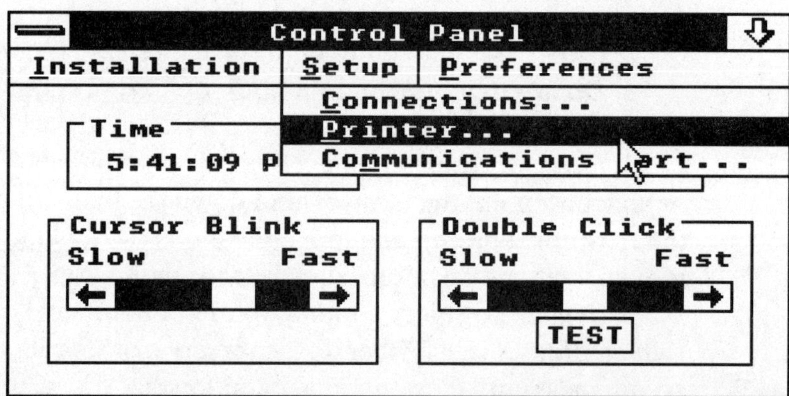

Figure 1-4. The System menu drops down to reveal a command to launch the Control Panel application. You can select from menus in the Control Panel, and then Close the Control Panel application using the System menu again.

menu, and then use the Control Panel to set the printer connections and other settings for Windows applications. (For example, you can use this method to adjust the speed of the mouse and to change the time and date.) Use the System menu to Close an application, such as the Control Panel. Other applications, such as PageMaker, can also be closed by choosing the Exit command from within PageMaker.

Figure 1-5. The Open dialog box displays filenames and directory names, plus a pathname and filename entry box for specifying the name of a PageMaker file.

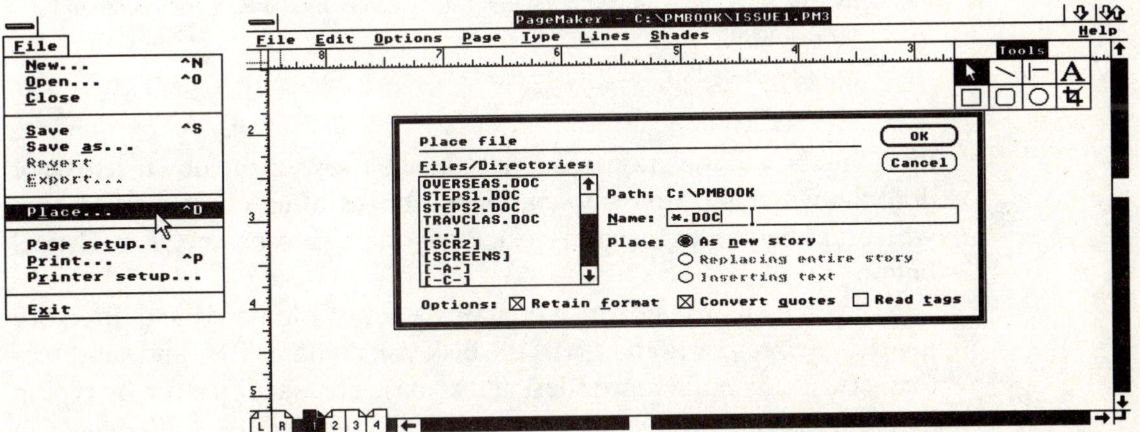

Figure 1-6. When an asterisk is substituted for the filename, but the extension is specified, the list box displays all files in the current directory that have that extension.

Applications typically have menu commands that display a dialog box where filenames are selected or typed, or choices are made. For example, when the Open command in PageMaker is used, a dialog box for selecting a file is displayed (Figure 1-5). To select items, click the boxes or buttons displayed in the dialog box. If scroll bars are displayed, you can scroll the items in a small window. To operate the scroll bar, click below

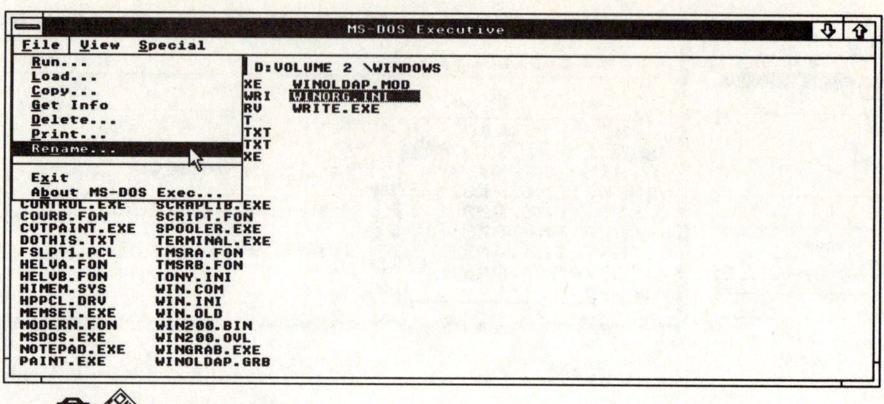

Figure 1-7. Windows offers the MS-DOS Executive window for file management functions. For example, you can rename a file by selecting the Rename command from the File menu.

the white box in the gray area, click the up arrow or the down arrow, or drag the white box up or down. Dialog boxes often contain text boxes where numbers or text can be typed. Every dialog box has an OK or Cancel button.

The Open dialog box also contains a list of filenames and directory names. A *directory* is an area of the disk that contains files and subdirectories (which contain more files, and so on). You specify a file by typing its filename in the filename entry area of the dialog box. A *filename* can be up to eight characters long (such as ISSUE1), followed by a period, followed by a three-character extension (PageMaker publication files have the extension .PM3, as in ISSUE1.PM3). When you search for a file, you can substitute an asterisk for the eight-character filename in the filename entry area. In this case, the list box displays all of the files that match the three-character extension, as shown in the Place dialog box in Figure 1-6. (This dialog box is used to place text or graphics files.)

To search in other directories, double-click the \ symbol in the *pathname*, which starts with \, followed by the directory name, and then followed by the subdirectory name, if any. (Subdirectories can be placed within subdirectories, with each name separated by the \ symbol.) A list

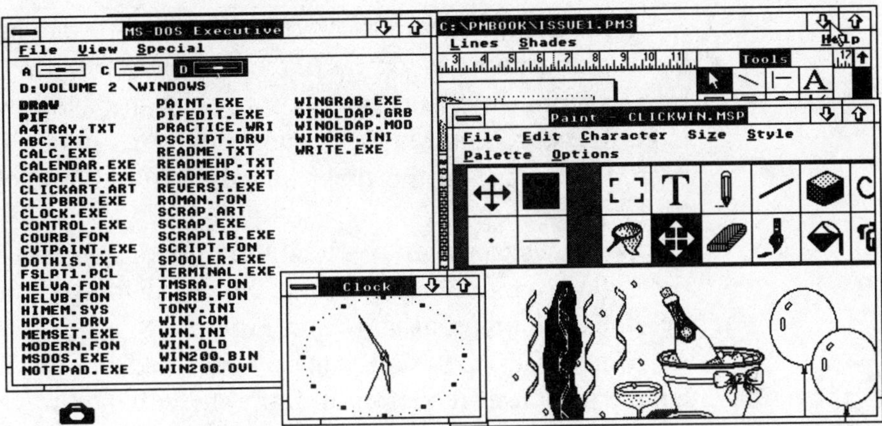

Figure 1-8. Several overlapping Windows applications can display at the same time.

of directory names appears in the list box. To switch to a listed directory, click a name and click the Open button, or just double-click the directory name. Instead of typing a filename, select a file for the filename entry area by clicking the filename in the list box and then clicking Open, or by double-clicking the filename.

When you first activate Windows (by typing **WIN** from the Windows directory), a window that displays filenames with the title MS-DOS Executive appears on the screen. File selection and basic file management functions, such as renaming files (Figure 1-7) are performed in the MS-DOS Executive window. To navigate from one subdirectory to another, click the \ symbol in the pathname displayed next to the icons for disk drives. You can also select other disks by clicking the disk drive icons.

To run PageMaker from Windows, double-click the PM.EXE file in the PM directory, or double-click a publication file that has the extension .PM3. PageMaker displays a new window that overlays the MS-DOS Executive window.

PageMaker, as with nearly every other Windows application, has a set of up arrows and down arrows in the upper right corner of the window. If the down arrow is clicked, the application turns into an icon at the bottom of the display. The application is not closed—it is merely hiding so that you can display other windows.

You can move a window by dragging its title bar, or resize the window by dragging from the corners of the window. Any window can be changed into an icon. To change the icon back to the window, double-click the icon. Thus, you can launch many programs under Windows and then switch from one to the other simply by double-clicking icons for the programs.

Windows can overlap each other, but only one window is active at a time. Two window applications can be displayed side by side, or can overlap each other, as shown in Figure 1-8.

Many other operations can be performed with Windows applications, but the most useful operation available with the full version of Windows is the ability to use the Cut, Copy, and Paste commands (which are in the Edit menu of most Windows applications) to transfer text and graphics from one application to another. For example, this feature can be used to transfer business graphics or a spreadsheet from a program (such as Microsoft Chart or Multiplan) to a PageMaker page.

This book will not attempt to provide a complete description of Windows, because a complete description is available in your *PageMaker Reference Manual* from Aldus, as well as in the Windows manuals from Microsoft. If you are not familiar with PCs in general, plan to take a considerable amount of time learning about files, filenames, pathnames, and the MS-DOS (or PC-DOS) operating system commands. It does not take nearly as long to learn about Windows features, such as how to switch applications by moving icons; how to use the built-in Notebook, Calculator, and Clipboard; and how to change screen colors (if you use a color monitor), country settings (which changes currency symbols and provides foreign formats for numbers, times, and dates); printers; and communications settings. Plan to allow a week to learn about PCs in general, and then to allow about a day to learn Windows.

Project Planning

The best tool that you can use to schedule the publishing process is a project planner. You can plan the process with paper and pencil, or use a software package such as Timeline (from Symantec). A basic critical path chart or a schedule that shows task completion dates would be useful.

Think of the publishing process as consisting of four steps:

1. Develop an idea into a written and edited manuscript.
2. Create and collect illustrations and photos.
3. Design the overall look and the individual pages.
4. Produce the master pages for printing.

Personal computers can be used in all of these steps. PageMaker plays an important role in the third step (design), and is responsible for the last step (production).

Figure 1-9 shows a project plan for producing a technical manual, and Figure 1-10 shows a plan for producing a newsletter. In both cases, the step of page design occurs early in the project so that the writers and artists have an idea about how the final publication will look.

Page Design

The step of page design cannot be finalized until the designer knows the length of the manuscript, and has information about the illustrations and photos. The manuscript stage for text, and the rough stage for illustrations and photos (Figure 1-11), are the starting places for production. Manuscripts and roughs are then changed into formatted text and final artwork, which are combined in PageMaker to make the final pages.

You can get an early start on the production process by using PageMaker to plan the overall look of the publication. Once you have an estimate of the number of pages, you can determine the page size, image area, page orientation, and perhaps even the number of columns per page. You can print thumbnail sketches of the pages, using gray boxes to represent text, black boxes to represent images, and white boxes to represent line art. You can also experiment with titles, headlines, logos, and rough graphics (scanned or created on the computer), and even produce full-size sample pages—all before placing actual manuscript text and final graphics and images on the page. PageMaker offers line-drawing, box-drawing, and circle-drawing tools, with 17 line styles (as well as reverse/none options for each) and many patterns, plus the ability to use graphics from a variety of programs.

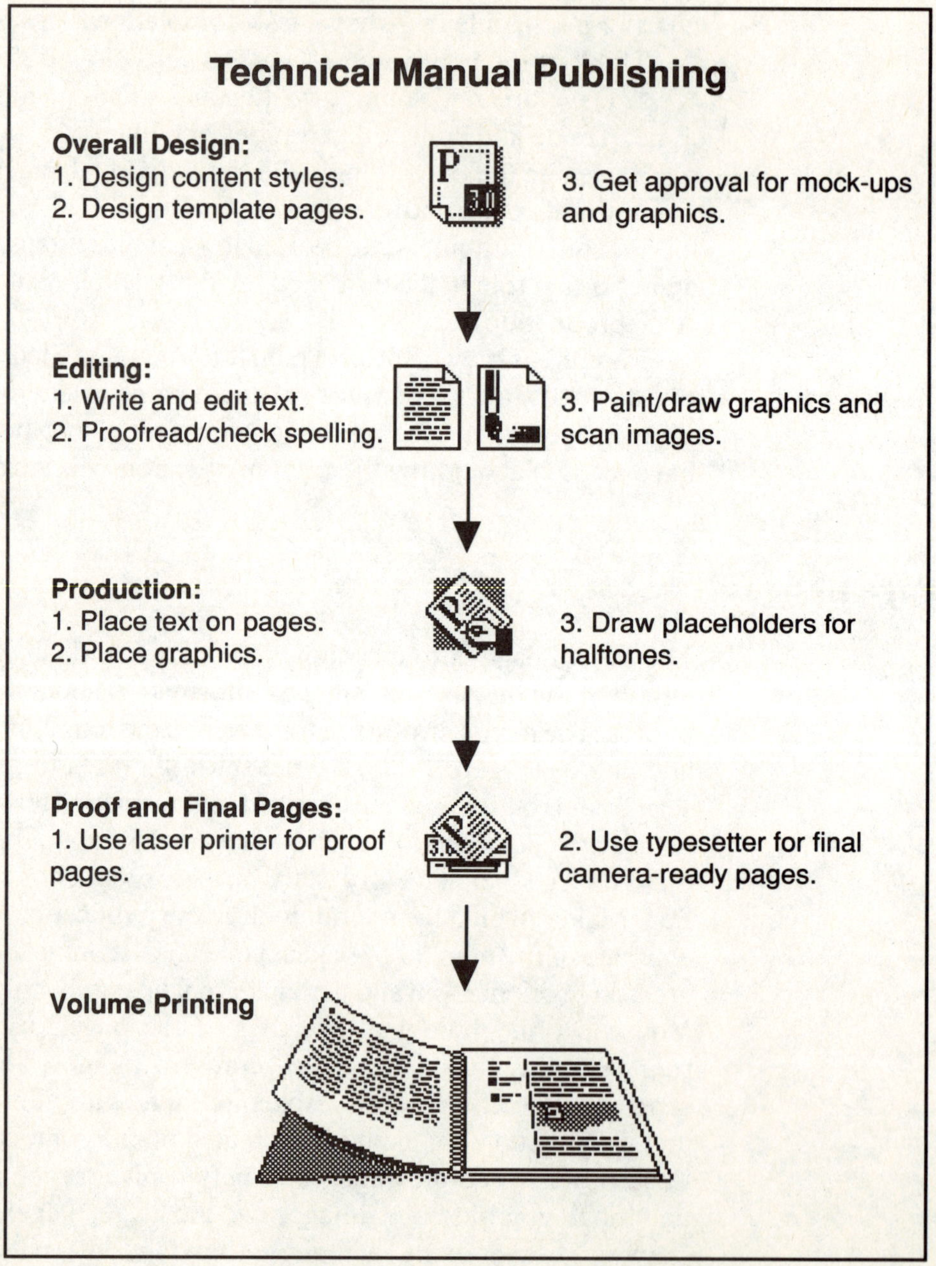

Technical Manual Publishing

Overall Design:
1. Design content styles.
2. Design template pages.
3. Get approval for mock-ups and graphics.

Editing:
1. Write and edit text.
2. Proofread/check spelling.
3. Paint/draw graphics and scan images.

Production:
1. Place text on pages.
2. Place graphics.
3. Draw placeholders for halftones.

Proof and Final Pages:
1. Use laser printer for proof pages.
2. Use typesetter for final camera-ready pages.

Volume Printing

Figure 1-9. Project plan for producing a technical manual.

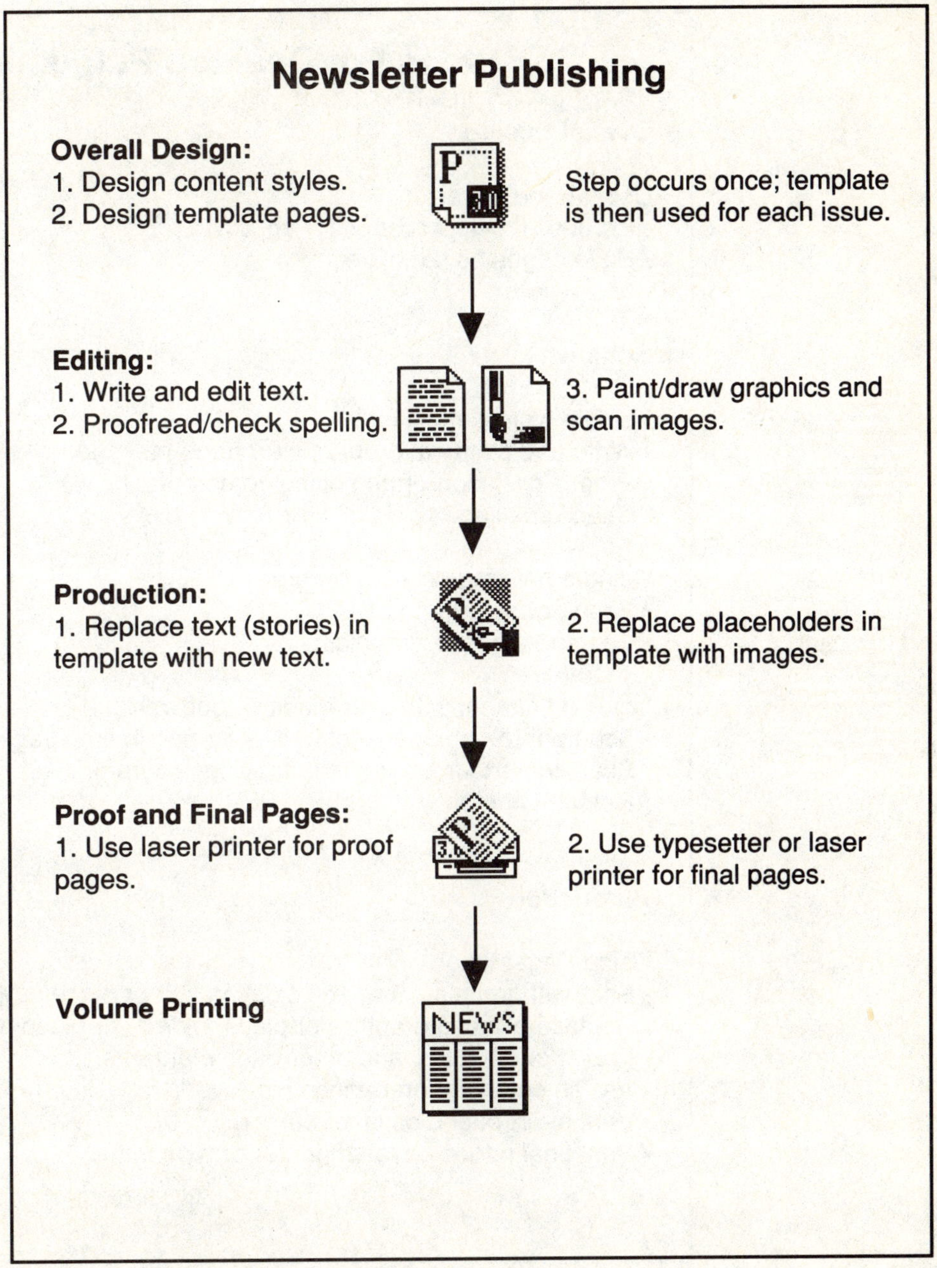

Newsletter Publishing

Overall Design:
1. Design content styles.
2. Design template pages.

Step occurs once; template is then used for each issue.

Editing:
1. Write and edit text.
2. Proofread/check spelling.

3. Paint/draw graphics and scan images.

Production:
1. Replace text (stories) in template with new text.

2. Replace placeholders in template with images.

Proof and Final Pages:
1. Use laser printer for proof pages.

2. Use typesetter or laser printer for final pages.

Volume Printing

NEWS

Figure 1-10. Project plan for producing a newsletter.

Steps For Desktop Publishing

Overall Design

Using PageMaker:
- Produce mock-up pages for approval.
- Save pages as template.

Editing

Using a word processor:
- Write and edit text, prepare it for page makeup.
- Proofread, incorporate editing comments.
- Check spelling.

Using a painting/drawing program:
- Paint or draw graphics.
- Edit and improve graphics.

Using a scanner with image editing software:
- Scan photos (for placeholders or for use in final pages).
- Scan line art for tracing in a drawing program.
- Retouch photos.

Production

Using PageMaker:
- Start with template: replace existing text or place new text.
- Replace existing graphics or placeholders, or place new graphics.
- Draw boxes, rules, and other page elements.
- Assign colors for preparing color overlays.
- Print proof pages on laser printer.
- Print final pages on laser printer or typesetter.

Figure 1-11. Production stages in desktop publishing.

Writing and Editing a Manuscript

Nearly every popular word processor for the PC can create text for use with PageMaker. You can use PageMaker to type and edit words on a page, but that process is much slower than the speed available with a word processing program. You should always use a word processing program if you write more than a page of text, or if you write text that will be used with different programs or in other publications.

Word processing programs are designed for the process of writing and editing text, and formatting controls (which determine how the text is presented on the page) were added almost as an afterthought. Sometimes it is very difficult to use word processors to create special formatting effects, such as the use of a different font for page numbers (if you have a choice of fonts at all), or drawing boxes around text and drawing vertical lines (called *column rules*) between columns.

Page makeup programs, however, specialize in formatting, even if they include word processing functions. PageMaker lets you edit text, but it does not offer a complete range of word processing features. PageMaker is designed as a finishing tool, so it accepts text from a variety of word processors and gives you complete control over page layout.

You should use the word processor that you are already familiar with when you prepare your text. If you have never used a word processor, you may not need to purchase one—the full version of Windows includes Microsoft Windows Write, which is easy to learn and use (Figure 1-12). In addition, Microsoft offers Word for the PC, a more sophisticated word processor that is compatible with both Microsoft Windows Write and PageMaker. Microsoft Word on the Macintosh is also compatible with the PC version of PageMaker, through Word's Save As command options.

PageMaker can *import* (bring into the page) and *export* (send out to a file) a variety of word processing files, depending upon which *filters* you install for PageMaker. (The import and export filters are described in PageMaker's installation handbook and release notes.)

Built-in filters that do not need installation include filters for Microsoft Word, Microsoft Windows Write, MultiMate (Ashton-Tate), WordPerfect (WordPerfect Corp.), WordStar 3.3 (MicroPro International), and

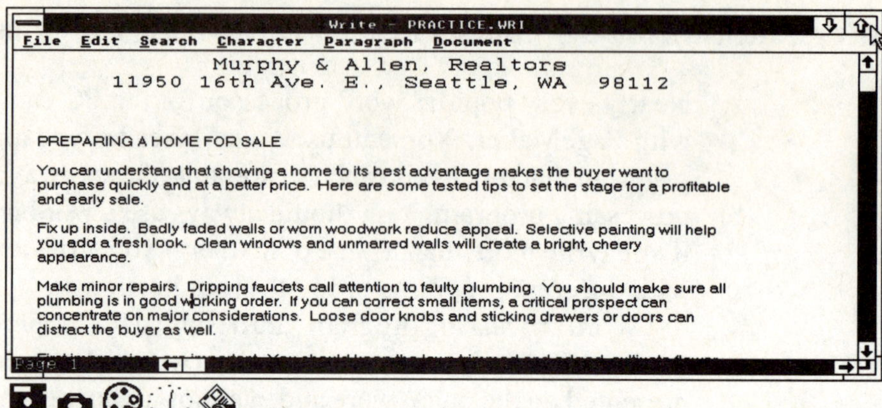

Figure 1-12. Microsoft Windows Write displays text using Windows screen fonts. You can collapse the window to an icon while using PageMaker, and bring back the Write window as you need it.

XyWrite III (XyQuest, Inc.). You can also install filters for PC Write, Olitext Plus, and any word processor that can save a file in the Document Content Architecture (DCA, also known as the IBM Revisable-Form Text), such as DisplayWrite 3 (IBM), Samna Word (SAMNA Corp.), Volkswriter 3 (Lifetree Software, Inc.), and WordStar 2000 (MicroPro).

All of these programs can produce preformatted text for PageMaker. *Preformatted text* already has some of the characteristics (font, type style and size, tab settings, indents, and paragraph endings) that are needed in order to determine the text's eventual appearance on the final pages.

If your word processor can produce files in simple ASCII form (American Standard Code for Information Interchange), which is a standard among all personal computers, you can also use that text with PageMaker.

PageMaker can export the text on its pages into ASCII files and Microsoft Word files (if you install the Word export filter). When PageMaker exports a Word file, it also exports style sheet definitions in the Microsoft Word format.

You do not need to know anything about PageMaker in order to write and edit text for PageMaker pages. Editors and writers can use different computers in different offices—or even in different countries—and still prepare text for use with PageMaker. Large manuscripts can be sent from one computer to another over the telephone or through network connections, and PC disks are easy to exchange.

Writers and editors can use word processing commands to prepare text for printing without regard to PageMaker. Margins, footnotes, page numbers, headers, and footers created by word processors are not used by PageMaker. Settings in word processors for these functions can be changed at will, without any consequence to the PageMaker production effort.

Proofreading a Manuscript

Once a large manuscript is in electronic form, it can be checked for spelling in just a few minutes. After the words are typed, they never have to be retyped, and editing changes can be added or deleted in an instant.

Built-in spelling checkers are available with some word processors, such as DisplayWrite 3 (IBM), MultiMate Advantage (Ashton-Tate), Word 3.1 (Microsoft), WordPerfect 4.2 (WordPerfect Corp.), and WordStar Professional 4.0 (MicroPro International).

Other word processors work with memory-resident proofreading programs, such as Turbo Lightning 1.02 (Borland International), Word Finder (Microlytics), and Webster's NewWorld Spelling Checker (Simon & Schuster).

You should use a spelling checker on the final draft of a manuscript before you use the manuscript with PageMaker, simply because errors that are not caught make a publication look less professional. Another reason to check the manuscript first is that changes made to the text on a PageMaker page may not be transferable back to the text file. Changes must be made in both files, or else your text file will not match the text on the PageMaker page.

If you prefer to proofread printed manuscripts, consider using a word processor such as Microsoft Windows Write, Microsoft Word, or another program that shows different fonts on the screen. Print the manuscript using a well-spaced sans serif font in a large size (such as 12-point Courier) with extra leading (or double-spaced lines) to allow easy reading and room for corrections between the lines.

Formatting a Manuscript

Although you can change text fonts (styles and sizes) and faces in PageMaker, you can save time by selecting font styles and sizes in the word processor as you write and edit the text. (This is possible only if the word processor is supported by PageMaker—see Appendix A: Word Porcessing Programs for details.) Next, format the text for placement onto a PageMaker page. This method lets you place text on many pages at once without stopping to select fonts.

Remember, PageMaker does not use the right margin setting, footnotes, page numbers, headers, footers, or special formatting features created by word processors. However, PageMaker does recognize the following features:

1. Fonts (type styles and sizes), line spacing (leading), and upper- and lowercase letters. Special characters that can be typed will be recognized. Windows ANSI and PC characters are allowed.

2. You have the option to retain keyboard-style single and double quotes (', "), or to instruct PageMaker to substitute open and close typographic quotes (‘’, “”). Double hyphens (- -) can be converted to an em dash (—), and a line of hyphens can be turned into a thin rule that comprises a row of em dashes.

3. The left margin is the basis for indents, but only if the word processor has a separate setting for the left indent. PageMaker breaks lines to fit its columns.

4. Left and right indents are measured from the corresponding edges of the PageMaker column. If the text file has a 1-inch indent from the left margin, PageMaker measures 1 inch from the left edge of the column when placing the text file.

5. The first line indents of a paragraph are recognized as regular, indented to the right, or as a hanging indent to the left of the left margin.

6. Carriage returns (produced by pressing the Enter or Return key in most word processors) are recognized as paragraph endings and as a forced end of a short line.

7. Tabs are recognized and used to align text or numbers in tables. You can use PageMaker to change tab settings to fit the column width, and to specify the position, alignment, and leader pattern (such as a dot or dash leader to fill the tab space). End each line of a table with a carriage return.

PageMaker will remember the font that you chose, even if the printer that is selected as the default printer does not print that font. PageMaker substitutes the closest font printable by your printer, and then remembers the actual font when you switch to another printer that can print that font.

Many writers and typists have the habit of adding two spaces after each sentence. Typeset copy should not contain two spaces, so all instances of two consecutive spaces should be replaced with one space using your word processing program's search/replace or formatting controls, before using the text with PageMaker.

Here's a tip: Before you place your text with PageMaker, remove from the text all of the captions, footnotes, and other independent elements that will be positioned separately. To save time when placing text on pages, store the headline or title, captions, and footnotes in one file, and store the body of the manuscript (including subheadings) in another file.

Here's another tip: Break up very large text files into smaller files of less than 64K in size, so that PageMaker will place the files quickly. (Some word processors also have trouble working with text files that are larger than 64K.) The Windows Clipboard is limited to 64K, but PageMaker can safely place files well over 2MB in size.

In many instances, you may have preformatted text but you may prefer to use PageMaker's formatting features and work with ASCII text. For example, you may want to override the word processor font and other settings and use PageMaker default settings, or you may want to use records from a database that are in a text format. In such cases, you can choose to *not* retain the format of the word processor file, and thus import that text as ASCII-only text.

Tabs, carriage returns, and spaces are recognized in ASCII-only files, but no formatting settings from the word processor are used. You can bring tables and paragraphs of text into PageMaker without retaining formatting settings (in other words, import the text in ASCII-only form), and still retain paragraph endings and table column positions (as long as each table row ends with a carriage return).

PageMaker's paragraph default settings apply to ASCII-only text files. If you first change the default values (with the pointer tool and no text selected) and then place your ASCII-only text file, the new settings are applied. You can choose new settings before placing a formatted text file, and ignore any existing formatting in the text file, by placing the file as an ASCII-only text file. (To place a formatted text file as an ASCII-only text file and use the default settings (or to use new default settings you chose from the Type menu), click to place an x in the Retain format option box in the Place dialog box before placing the formatted text file.)

The default settings (unless you change them) consist of the default font (usually Times Roman) at 12 points, automatic leading, automatic hyphenation, pair-kerning for all text larger than 12 points (for PostScript printers; no pair-kerning is available for PCL printers), no left or right margin, no first line of paragraph indents, no spacing between paragraphs, and flush-left alignment of text in columns with ragged-right margins.

PageMaker does not transfer last-minute text changes that were made on the PageMaker page back to the word processor files. Any changes made during page makeup should be made to the original text using the word processor, so that the text file and the publication file coincide. You can export the publication file (up to 64K at a time) from PageMaker back to Windows Write. To do so, use the Windows Clipboard to Select all, Copy, then Paste into Windows Write. Save the text as a Write file, a Text-only file, or as a Word file. For details on how to use PageMaker with text files from popular word processors, see Appendix A.

Special Characters

Although your chosen printer or font may not be able to print all of the special language characters and symbols in the PC character set, you can type all of these characters and symbols in PageMaker (and also in Windows-based word processors, such as Microsoft Windows Write). To type any character in the Windows ANSI character set, hold down the Alt key, type a zero on the numeric keypad, and type the ANSI code (with the Alt key still depressed). To type the special language characters, hold down the Alt key and type the three-digit IBM PC character code on the numeric keypad.

Special symbols include trademarks, copyright notices, section and paragraph marks, open and closed quotes, em dashes, and foreign language punctuation symbols. If you can't type them with your word processor, you can leave place holders (a character or a note to the production person) and then replace the place holders when you use

PageMaker. For a list of special symbols you can type in PageMaker, see Appendix C.

Some characters are placed automatically on the page by PageMaker. For example, PageMaker automatically changes a double quote (") that is preceded by a space into an open quote (“), and changes a double quote that is followed by a space into a closed quote (”). The program also changes a single quote (') in the same manner, so that contractions, possessives, and quotes-within-quotes include the properly slanted symbols. PageMaker changes a double hyphen (- -) into an em dash (—), and transforms a series of hyphens into half as many em dashes (a solid line).

Because PageMaker makes all of the above changes, and special characters and punctuation symbols are not available in most word processors anyway, most writers and editors do not need to think about those characters and symbols. You can use typical word processors plus the ASCII character subset available on all PC keyboards for the writing and editing steps of the publication production process, and save the special characters for the formatting and page-makeup steps.

Creating and Editing Graphics

There are two kinds of graphic images: *paint-type* (also called *bit-mapped)*, and *draw-type* (also called *object-oriented*). Painted images consist of dots that correspond to screen pixels. The resolution of these images is limited to the resolution of the display that is used to create them. Drawn images consist of a series of drawing commands that describe the image, and are usually not limited in resolution except by the printer or typesetter.

Painting programs (Figure 1-13) are popular with freehand artists and amateur artists. These programs are easy to learn and very flexible—you can touch-up the dots to improve images, and paint intricate patterns and shapes.

Drawing programs (Figure 1-14) are popular with commercial artists, designers, illustrators, architects, and engineers. These programs offer precision tools, perfect geometric shapes, and movable (and cloneable) graphic objects.

Figure 1-13. Microsoft Windows Paint is bundled with Windows and can create paint-type graphics.

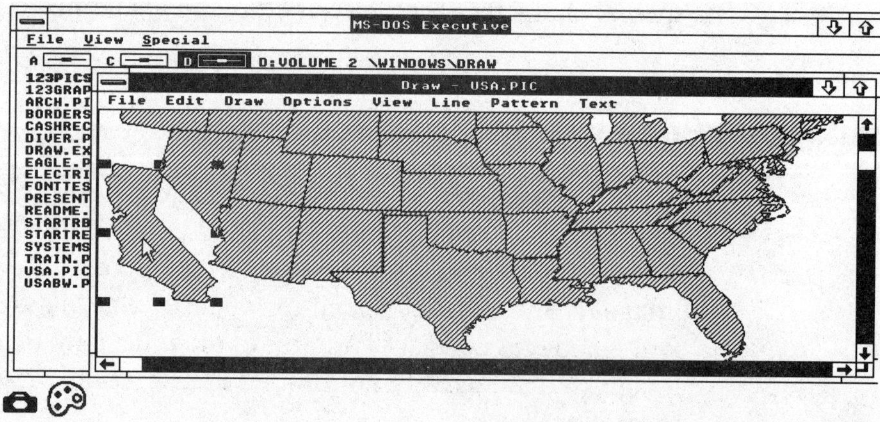

Figure 1-14. Micrografx Windows Draw is available for Windows and can create draw-type graphics; each state of the United States is a separate movable object.

Both types of programs are popular with desktop publishers, who use drawing programs for logos, line drawings, business charts, graphs, and schematics. Painting programs are used to create intricate designs and freehand art. The highest resolution can be achieved with drawing programs because these programs can produce *resolution-independent images* (which are described not by dots, but by graphics commands).

Paint-type Graphics

PageMaker recognizes graphics created by Microsoft Windows Paint, PC Paint (Mouse Systems), PC Paintbrush and Publisher's Paintbrush (both ZSoft), and MacPaint (Claris). PageMaker also recognizes paint-type graphics stored in the Tag Image File Format (TIFF).

Pixel sizes in paint-type graphics are fixed in resolution. If you use one type of graphics display device on a PC when you create a graphic, and you use another type of display with PageMaker, the graphic image will appear distorted on the PageMaker screen even though it will print properly. Because it is difficult to resize images by hand to proportions that print properly, PageMaker's built-in resizing feature automatically selects the best proportions for your printer. To use this feature, hold down the Control key while you resize the image. Chapter 5 offers tips and techniques for placing and resizing graphics.

When you place a paint-type graphics file that is larger than 64K on a PageMaker page, PageMaker creates a lower-resolution version of the image for display on the page. At the same time, PageMaker establishes a link to the original, higher-resolution version of the image, so that the program can use the higher-resolution version when printing. PageMaker uses the lower-resolution image for display purposes in order to increase the speed of the program. Most paint-type graphics files are less than 64K in size, but some files (especially files that contain scanned images) can be larger.

In order for the link to work automatically when graphics are printed from files larger than 64K in size, the original graphics file must be left in the subdirectory where it was located when you placed it—do not move or delete the publication file or graphics file from that subdirectory. If the publication file or any graphics file is no longer in that subdirectory, you must type the pathname for the graphics file when PageMaker requests that information during the printing operation (as described later in Chapter 5).

When you move, resize, and crop any type of graphic image, PageMaker applies those changes to the original image file when the publication is printed, but does not change the original image file. The pixels of a graphic image cannot be edited in PageMaker (except to enhance the contrast and brightness in a scanned image, as described in Chapter 4). Also, parts of an image cannot be erased in PageMaker, but the image can be *cropped* so that only a portion of it shows. Use your painting program to clean up an image before placing the image on a PageMaker page.

Programs that create color graphics usually do not match the standard color systems that are used in printing plants, and are not very useful for commercial publishing. Most laser printers do not print in color, and if you print a color graphic image on a black-and-white printer, the color areas are replaced with patterns that may not look exactly as you intended.

You can steer clear of problems by composing graphics in black and white, and by selecting patterns and shades, rather than colors, for filled areas.

PageMaker accepts color images, but you will probably not use color printers for a while. For details on how to use PageMaker with graphics files from popular painting programs, see Appendix B.

Draw-type Graphics

PageMaker recognizes graphics files created by Windows "Draw!" and "Graph!" (Micrografx), In*A*Vision and Designer (Micrografx), AutoCAD (AutoDesk), and programs that save files in the Windows Graphics Device Interface (GDI) metafile format. PageMaker also accepts files that use the Encapsulated PostScript (EPS) format.

Other programs are supported by filters that you can install. These include filters that support Computer Graphics Metafiles (CGM), Hewlett-Packard Graphics Language (HPGL), Lotus 1-2-3 and Symphony charts (PIC files), Videoshow (NAPLPS) graphics files, and Zenographics Mirage files.

Drawing programs provide precise tools for drawing geometric shapes. Usually, the drawing tools emulate drafting tools such as a compass, a T-square, a ruler, and a grid, and extra tools are included for quickly drawing perfect squares, circles, and geometric shapes. Amateur graphic artists and professional artists may find the drawing tools more difficult to learn than the painting tools, but the drawing tools produce precise shapes and perfectly proportioned squares and circles. In addition, the programs save graphics in a format that is independent of the resolution of the display and drawing device. When you print the graphics, PageMaker uses the highest possible resolution that is available with the printing device.

Draw-type graphics are described with a command language, rather than expressed as a series of dots. These graphics do not have the limitations of paint-type graphics, and can be resized freely. They can even be stretched or compressed with very little or no distortion. If you want to create graphics that must be a certain size on the final page, create the graphics with a drawing program—the graphics can then be resized to precisely the measurements that you want, not just to the measurements that PageMaker builds in for printing paint-type graphics.

In many cases, you can transfer text used in the graphics into PageMaker with excellent results. In other cases, you may have to delete the text from the graphics first and then use PageMaker to replace the text after the graphics have been positioned on the page. For details on how to use PageMaker with graphics files from popular drawing programs, see Appendix B.

Business Charts and Graphs

Programs that generate charts and graphs (bar and pie charts, x-y graphs, scatter plots, and combinations of these forms) usually save the result in a graphic file that is compatible with one of the graphics programs already mentioned. For example, Lotus 1-2-3 and Symphony create business graphics and store them in .PIC files. Micrografx Windows "Graph!" is another excellent chart and graph program that can automatically create business graphics from spreadsheets, and then save them in Micrografx .PIC files that can be used with PageMaker.

Usually, no graphics experience is required in order to use these products, because their function is to generate graphics automatically for business-minded people who are not skilled in graphics. Programs such as Micrografx Graph Plus, Microsoft Chart, Lotus 1-2-3, Symphony, and Freelance Plus can save charts and graphs as draw-type graphics that can be scaled to any size. All of the rules that govern the use of draw-type graphics apply to business graphics that are saved in draw-type graphics format.

Image and Text Scanning

Most publishing operations require the use of existing information, but how can you put existing text and graphics into the computer? Expensive text and image digitizers are used by large publishers and the government, but inexpensive desktop models can handle many of a desktop publisher's needs.

The technology of scanning text—called *optical character recognition* (*OCR*)—has not caught up with the technology of typesetting. Today's desktop scanners only have high accuracy rates with typewritten text or text that is printed in the Courier font on a laser printer. The scanners store text in simple ASCII format, which can then be edited with a word processor.

The process of scanning text works best with clean, crisp original documents that were printed using a Selectric-style typing element or daisy wheel with carbon-film ribbons, or else with clean copies of the originals.

If characters are broken or a bad photocopy is used, the software cannot automatically recognize the characters. The text-scanning process is fastest when a clean original is placed flat on the glass platen so that the lines of text are parallel to the top of the platen. The OCR software reads slanted text when the paper is placed askew on the platen, but the scanning speed will be slower than usual.

Desktop scanners also sense images that contain up to 256 different shades of gray, but many personal computers cannot handle the immense file storage space that is required in order to save these images in digital form. PageMaker accepts images stored in two versions of the Tag Image File Format (TIFF and compressed TIFF), which are supported by most desktop scanner manufacturers. (Compressed TIFF provides a method for compressing the image data into a file of a manageable size.) One version of TIFF can describe an image that contains 256 shades of gray, and another version of TIFF has the ability to store color images that can be displayed on PageMaker pages.

Scanner manufacturers, such as Xerox Imaging Systems (Datacopy), Microtek, and Hewlett-Packard, offer painting programs or image editing programs along with their scanners so that you can improve a scanned image. A black and white scanned image (without shades of gray) is similar to a paint-type graphic but offers higher resolution (the image is usually displayed with less resolution than the resolution of the printed image). Images that contain shades of gray are called *gray-scale images*, and can be edited only with image-editing programs that support gray scales.

When Scanning is Cost-effective

A desktop scanner can scan typewritten pages faster than the fastest typist can type, and will continue at top speed all day long. If you want the most efficient method, however, there is no substitute for writing and editing by computer. Even future versions of inexpensive text scanners will probably not match the efficiency of creating the data electronically in the first place.

Scanners are most useful for scanning pages of text that will be processed or filed by computer, and for scanning line art and sketches that will be improved with drawing software. Laser printers are not capable of reproducing a photograph with the same quality as a photographic halftone, so most desktop publishers use page makeup software to reproduce everything in the publication except photographs. A black-filled box is placed on the page in the location where a halftone will be dropped in before the publication is sent to the printing press. The cost savings are still tremendous, even if a graphics service produces the halftones.

Many publications, however, can use scanned images, especially scanned line art. Real estate listings can be updated frequently by scanning the photographs of new houses and preparing the listings with PageMaker. Personnel reports can contain scanned photographs of employees. Architectural studies can include scanned drawings of building plans, along with scanned photographs of the landscape. Scanned images are finding their way into art and design magazines as well as into newspapers, newsletters, and business reports. Subsequent chapters in this book show how to use scanned images in publications as final artwork, and also as temporary placeholders that allow the design of text and page elements around halftones that will be dropped into the publication later.

Halftones

PageMaker can print scanned images at actual size, or even at reduced or expanded sizes, with excellent results if you use the automatic resizing feature. (To use this feature, hold down the Control and Shift keys while you resize an image.) PageMaker also has an Image control feature that lets you change the lightness (brightness) and the contrast in an image. This feature also permits you to change the type of line screen and the screen frequency that will be used when a halftone is created.

A *halftone* is a continuous tone image converted to dots, or *halftone cells*, that simulate gray shades on a black and white printer. Photos and other continuous tone images must be converted by either a digital device or a photographic device into halftone cells. Photographic equipment produces halftones through the use of a line screen at a particular density. The *screen density* determines the size of the halftone cells in the image. (This size can make the difference between a muddy reproduction and a clear reproduction.) Density is measured by the number of screen lines per inch, and the method of printing determines the lines per inch measurement. Newspapers typically need either a 65-line or an 85-line screen. Advertisements, commercial work, and magazine pages, require screens with 120, 133, 150, or more lines per inch.

You can mix conventional photographic methods with desktop publishing methods for cost-effective production. PageMaker lets you draw a black-filled box on the page to represent a window for a negative. Camera services and print shops can produce halftones either as negatives to be stripped in by the printer, or as screened prints that you can paste onto artboards. A screened print is usually less expensive to produce, but a negative produces better results because the image is photographed only once. Unless you need to create a special effect, do not produce a halftone of a halftone, because when dots are overlayed upon dots, a *moirè effect* (a wavy pattern caused by the repetition of one pattern on top of another pattern) can result.

With the introduction of standard graphics file formats (such as TIFF), PostScript typesetters, and inexpensive hard disks for mass storage, the ability to use PageMaker to place scanned images on the page is an excellent opportunity to cut costs. At the very least, the scanned image can serve as a placeholder for a conventionally produced halftone. At most, the image can serve as a substitute for the halftone and eliminate the need to use the photographic halftoning process.

When the printer uses digital data to make the equivalent of a halftone cell, several small dots are combined into one halftone cell dot. Thus, printers with a resolution of 300 dots-per-inch (dpi) can produce the equivalent of a 60-line to 65-line screen (newspaper-quality) halftone with gray scales. You can raise the resolution of the image, but the result is a denser image with less gray scales. The typical 300-dpi laser printer can print some halftones better than others, but commercial publications need higher resolution devices.

The Linotype Linotronic 300 Imagesetter (with a resolution of 2540 dpi) can reproduce a commercial-quality halftone and is a PostScript printer. Thus, you can use a PostScript laser printer to print proof pages, and then send the output to a high-resolution Linotronic in order to produce a high-quality halftone on the page.

PageMaker's Image control command gives you control over the density (frequency) and the angle of the line screen for producing halftones, and over the values that determine lightness and contrast. Remember, however, that the more gray levels you specify (the higher the frequency), the more slowly the publication will print. The Image control command is introduced in Chapter 4.

Laser Printers and Typesetters

The motivating force behind desktop publishing is based on two factors: the availability of inexpensive laser printers, and the ability to transfer pages to higher-resolution typesetters.

You may start your publishing efforts by using scanning and word processing, but the quality of the results is directly related to your printer or typesetter. Laser printers have grown in popularity because they offer fonts and image printing at medium resolutions in comparison to the conventional resolutions available with dot-matrix and letter-quality printers. Most laser printers offer near-typeset quality results with a resolution of 300 dpi by 300 dpi, although some laser printers produce 400 dpi by 400 dpi resolution, or even 300 dpi by 600 dpi resolution. Laser printers are also capable of emulating both daisy wheel and dot matrix printers at much better resolution and print quality, although some printers offer only partial-page graphics at 300 dpi resolution.

The Apple LaserWriter is the recognized leader in desktop publishing applications because it was the first printer to use the PostScript page description language, developed by Adobe Systems and now used in laser printers from IBM, Texas Instruments, Digital Equipment Corporation, and many other manufacturers. PostScript laser printers are compatible with each other and with higher-resolution laser typesetters from Linotype, Varityper, and Compugraphic. For example, a PostScript-type laser printer such as the Apple LaserWriter IINT (300 dpi) is entirely compatible with the Varityper plain paper typesetter (600 dpi), and with the Linotype Linotronic class of PostScript-type typesetters, including the Linotronic 100 (1270 dpi; priced at about $35,000) and the Linotronic 300 (2540 dpi, and considerably higher in price).

Typesetters are still out of the price range of most businesses because the machines are expensive and are not suitable for the fast printing chores that are part of business computing. Typesetters produce output of such high quality that most businesses would only want to use a typesetter for the final typesetting step. Also, the paper used with the typesetter has to be developed by a chemical-based processor, so a ventilated room (preferably a darkroom) is needed to house the processor.

For desktop publishers who need both the speed and the flexibility of laser printers, plus the high resolution of typesetters, PostScript typesetters are available as output devices in copy centers and typesetting services. You can prepare text for these typesetters directly or else use a PostScript laser printer to proof your pages inexpensively before using the typesetter. The combination of a PostScript laser printer and a typesetter was used to produce this book.

To use a printer with Microsoft Windows, software that communicates with and controls that specific type of printer must be on disk and available to the system. This software is called a *printer driver*. PageMaker uses Microsoft Windows printer drivers and provides a few enhanced drivers for Windows that you can install quickly. Nearly all of the major laser printers available on the market support Windows, including page printers from IBM, Digital Equipment Corporation,

Hewlett-Packard, AST Research, QMS, Qume, Cordata, Texas Instruments, and Epson. Windows can drive any PostScript printer, and any printer that can emulate an Epson FX-80 dot-matrix printer or an HP LaserJet.

Most laser printers print only on standard page sizes (8 1/2 by 11 inches or smaller). The Dataproducts LZR-2665 and some other laser printers can print tabloid-size pages (11 by 17 inches).

PageMaker can control collation, the use of input paper trays, page orientation, and different resolution factors with certain printers (such as HP LaserJets and Apple LaserWriters). PageMaker can also set its pages to use a certain font cartridge for HP LaserJet printers.

When you add a printer to your Windows system, be sure to add both the fonts supplied with the printer on disk, and the screen fonts that display representations of the printed fonts. Dot-matrix fonts display on the screen exactly as they print and may be useful for decorative purposes, but look more jagged at the edges than higher-resolution laser printer fonts. Fonts are easy to add to Windows using the Control Panel's Installation menu.

Windows uses one printer as the default printer. You can change the default printer at any time. When you use PageMaker, choose a printer for a publication before you start to make the pages. (To choose a printer, use the Printer setup command in PageMaker's File menu.) If you change the printer selection after the text and images are placed in the publication file, PageMaker has to recompose all of the pages in order to adjust the fonts and images for the new printer. Line endings may change, so you will have to go back and check all of the pages for undesirable changes. The recompose operation does not take long with a short file, but it can take a few minutes with a 128-page publication.

When you print a publication from PageMaker, the program uses the Windows Spooler (unless you installed PageMaker to not use the Spooler option) so that control comes back to your computer quickly, and the computer handles the task of spooling the pages to the printer. You can control the spooling operation by double-clicking the Spooler icon (which appears as soon as you elect to print something). You can interrupt or cancel printing operations from the Windows Spooler.

You can also have PageMaker create a *print file* of the pages on disk, rather than create printed pages. You can then transmit that print file to another computer over a network, via a modem, or else transfer the file by disk. The receiving computer does not have to run PageMaker in order to send the file to the printer, but the receiving computer must have the same type of printer (such as a PostScript printer), even if the receiving computer's printer resolution differs. You can copy the print file directly to the printer by using operating system commands or Windows commands. For more information, see the discussion about printing tips and techniques in Chapter 5.

Complete Systems

The rest of the hardware and software that you need depends upon your application. Most writers and newsletter publishers need enough disk storage space to accommodate a year's worth of text (a 40MB hard disk is usually appropriate). Since it only takes a few seconds to copy files from a floppy disk, you can use whatever hard disk storage you have —but you must *always* copy files to floppy disk or tape cartridges for backup in case your hard disk fails. Gray-scale image files are usually too large to fit on standard PC XT floppy disks (at 360K per disk), so be sure to get a computer that has high-density floppy disk drives, such as any AT-compatible computer with 1.2MB floppy drives.

To run Windows and PageMaker, you need at least 640K of RAM in an IBM PS/2, IBM PC AT, or AT-compatible computer (that uses an Intel 80286 or 80386 processor). In order to speed up operation, you should get expanded memory (such as an Intel Above Board or AST Rampage board) for your AT-compatible computer. Windows and PageMaker can be installed to run with LIM (Lotus-Intel-Microsoft) expanded or extended memory. It is also possible to run Windows very slowly on a PC XT or compatible computer, but it is not recommended, and the computer may be incompatible with future versions of Windows.

You also need a graphics adaptor. Choices for color display include the Video Graphics Adaptor (VGA) standard used in the high-end IBM PS/2 computers, the MCGA graphics standard used in IBM PS/2 Model 30 computers, and the Enhanced Graphics Adaptor (EGA) and compatible adaptors. For black and white display, you can use VGA, EGA, or the Hercules Monochrome graphics board (or a compatible board). You can connect a high-resolution monochrome (black-and-white) monitor to all of these adaptors except MCGA (which is not high resolution). Higher-resolution full-page monitors are also available for Windows from Wyse Technology, Micro Display Systems (The Genius VHR monitor), Moniterm (Viking), and Conographic (ConoVision 2800).

Desktop Design

Many of you who are not designers by trade should prepare yourselves by reading books about design and production. A few good books are listed in Appendix E. There is no substitute for a good designer, but desktop publishers càn learn good design techniques and put them to use without paying top dollar for a professional designer. Your research will also help you know what to evaluate when a top designer provides thumbnail sketches and finished artwork for your approval.

The purpose of this book is to show you how to use PageMaker to produce general types of publications. The book's secondary mission is to teach a few design skills. All of the desktop publishing software in the world cannot save a badly designed publication. The best approach is to practice using PageMaker, and then read some good design books and seek advice from a professional designer. Finally, use this book to refresh your memory on how to use PageMaker.

2 A Newsletter Tutorial

This chapter introduces PageMaker and provides a few layout and production tricks that can save you time and money. Although you may not be interested in producing a newsletter, the process of designing a newsletter format provides a straightforward demonstration of PageMaker's features. This book and the Aldus manuals were produced with PageMaker, and show off the program's features for book design and production. You should keep the *PageMaker Quick Reference Guide* from Aldus at hand while you complete the examples in this book, in order to become familiar with PageMaker in the shortest possible time.

This book is not a crash course in design, because there are many excellent books that provide such information. (See the Bibliography for a sample list, but note that the publication dates of some of these reference books predate the introduction of desktop publishing tools.) This book uses examples to describe many basic production techniques, typesetting and printing terms, and design considerations.

In order to acquaint yourself with the limitations of PageMaker, as well as with the conventional constraints of typical printing presses, start with a simple design effort. Before beginning any publishing project, find out how the presses work. The number of copies that you want to print (which is the size of the press run), the page size (which partially depends on your choice of stock), the number of pages, and the use of color can all be factors that determine which printing presses and binding machines are appropriate to use for your job. You should read *Pocket Pal* (see Bibliography) or some other reference in order to learn printing and production procedures and terms. Next, provide a written description of your job to several printers, or to a print broker, who can help you determine the mechanical specifications for your job and then offer you price quotes for the paper, ink, printing, binding, and other services. The use of PageMaker could quickly reduce your production costs enough to pay for upgraded printing, such as the additional use of color, a better grade of paper, or other services.

Always start with an idea about how big the publication will be (the number of pages and the size of each page) before you design the pages. The example in this chapter is a typical 8 1/2- by 11-inch, four-page newsletter (Figure 2-1). PageMaker's default settings are used for the image area.

Starting Up PageMaker

PageMaker for the PC is supplied on disks and is ready to be installed to run under Microsoft Windows. PageMaker uses your Windows configuration for the printer and display, but also includes enhanced drivers for alternative printers and displays. Check the installation section of the PageMaker manual for details about how to install the enhanced drivers (the process is simple).

First, make a backup copy of the PageMaker disks before you use the supplied Install program to copy the programs to your hard disk. Store the backup disks in a safe place—they may be needed if your hard disk is damaged, or if Aldus supplies an update to PageMaker. The DOS command for copying a disk is DISKCOPY. On most systems, you can insert an Aldus-supplied disk in drive A, a blank disk in drive B, and then type **diskcopy a: b:** (and press Enter) in order to make a backup copy of a disk.

Before you start PageMaker, first start Microsoft Windows by typing **win** while in the \WINDOWS directory of your hard disk. Next, move to

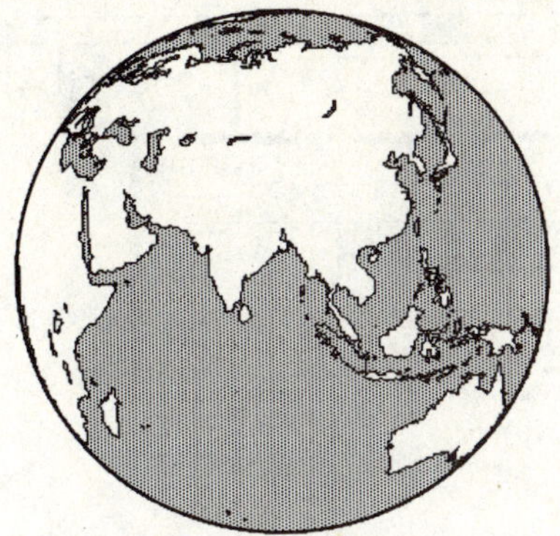

WORLD Explorers News

Learning From Marco Polo

There is no sea innavigable, no land uninhabitable.
— Robert Thorne, merchant and geographer (1527)

Too far East is West. — English proverb

We open this issue with an excerpt from the first printed travel guide of Western Society on how to travel to the Near and Far East. This guide was written 70 years after Marco Polo embarked on his historic visit to China. The following text is from a handbook written in 1340 by Francesco Balducci Pegolotti, agent for the Bardi banking family in Florence:

In the first place, you must let your beard grow long and not shave. And at Tana you should furnish yourself with a dragoman. And you must not try to save money in the matter of dragomen by taking a bad one instead of a good one. For the additional wages of the good one will not cost you so much as you will save by having him. And besides the dragoman it will be well to take at least two good men servants who are acquainted with the Cumanian tongue. And if the merchant likes to take a woman with him from Tana, he can do so; if he does not like to take one there is no obligation, only if he does take one he will be kept much more comfortably than if he does not take one. Howbeit, if he do take one, it will be well if she be acquainted with the Cumanian tongue as well as the men...

Whatever silver the merchants may carry with them as far as Cathay the lord of Cathay will take from them and put into his treasury. And to merchants who thus bring silver they give that paper money of theirs in exchange. This is of yellow paper, stamped with the seal of the lord aforesaid. And this money is called; and

with this money you can readily buy silk and other merchandise that you have a desire to buy. And all the people of the country are bound to receive it. And yet you shall not pay a higher price for your goods because your money is of paper...

(And don't forget that if you treat the custom-house officers with respect, and make them something of a present in goods or money, as well as their clerks and dragomen, they will behave with great civility, and always be ready to appraise your wares below their real value.)

Figure 2-1. Sample newsletter page.

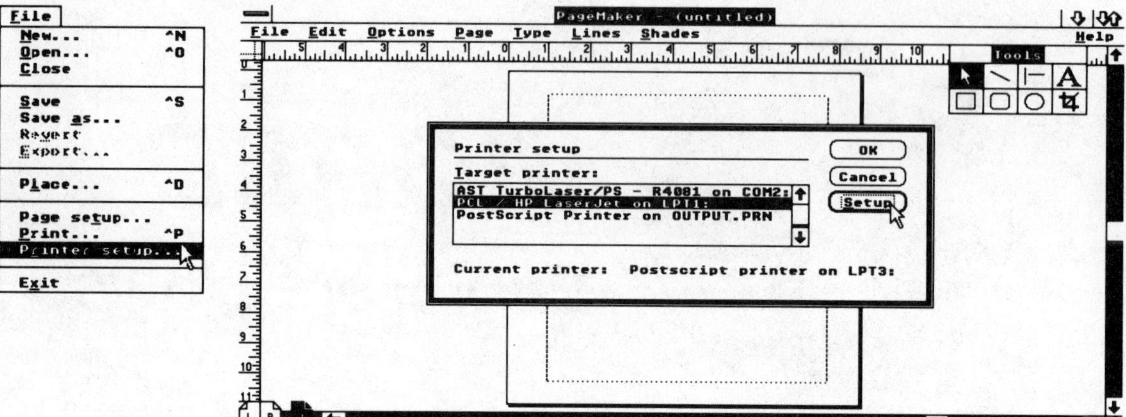

Figure 2-2. To display this dialog box, in which you can select a Windows printer driver, select Printer setup from the File menu.

the parent (\) directory by clicking the first \ symbol in the pathname at the top of the MS-DOS Executive window. The display should change to show the names of the subdirectories in the root directory. PM should be one of those subdirectories (unless you changed this default setting when you installed PageMaker).

Double-click the PM subdirectory, in order to view its files, and start PageMaker by clicking the filename PM.EXE in the PM directory. (Chapter 1 explains how to click, double-click, drag, and perform other mouse moves.)

Before you produce a publication, you should know the type of printer (laser, dot-matrix, typesetter, and so on) that will be used for the final version of the publication, so that you can resize graphics and select fonts and know that those graphics and fonts will print properly. When you select a printer, the selection remains in effect until you change it. One of the benefits of using PageMaker is that you can change the printer at another time in the production process. When you change the printer, the publication is automatically recomposed to compensate for the fact that different printers use different fonts and options.

For example, you might choose an HP LaserJet at 150 dpi resolution, print the publication, and then change the printer selection to an Apple

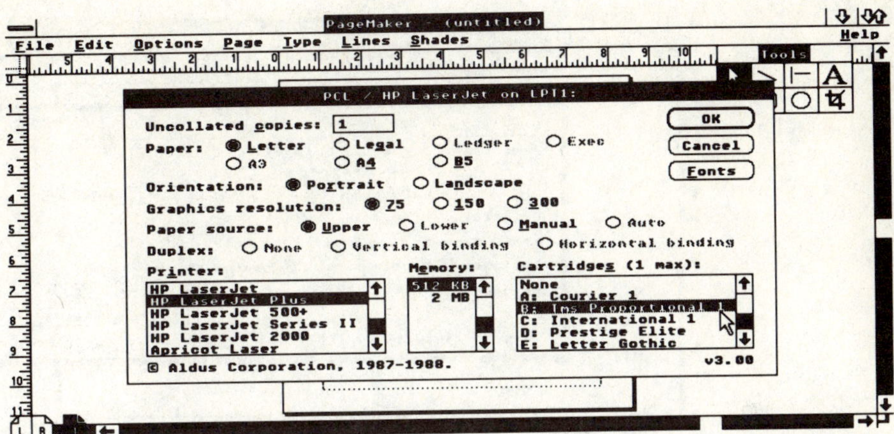

Figure 2-3. The Setup dialog box for the Hewlett-Packard LaserJet Plus.

LaserWriter (300 dpi). The publication's line lengths change because the character widths of the fonts are different. Different printers use different fonts, and if the same size font is not available, PageMaker reformats the text in order to use the size closest to (but smaller than) the font you chose. Line weights are also affected by a change in resolution.

It makes sense to select a printer that is already connected to your system, so that your initial production effort will pay off with a finished publication that looks good. To select the printer, drag down the File menu to the Printer setup command (Figure 2-2). Select the printer from the list shown in the dialog box.

If a printer is not connected to your system, you should still pick a printer in order to determine which fonts are available for your publication. (Many desktop publishing service bureaus and copy shops permit you to rent time on a self-service laser printer and PC system that you can use to print the final publication—so select a printer that is offered at your local service bureau or copy shop.)

Click the Setup button, and PageMaker displays another dialog box that contains specifications for the printer that you selected. For example, if you choose the HP LaserJet Plus, PageMaker displays a dialog box with a choice of font cartridges, resolutions, paper sizes, and page orientation (Figure 2-3).

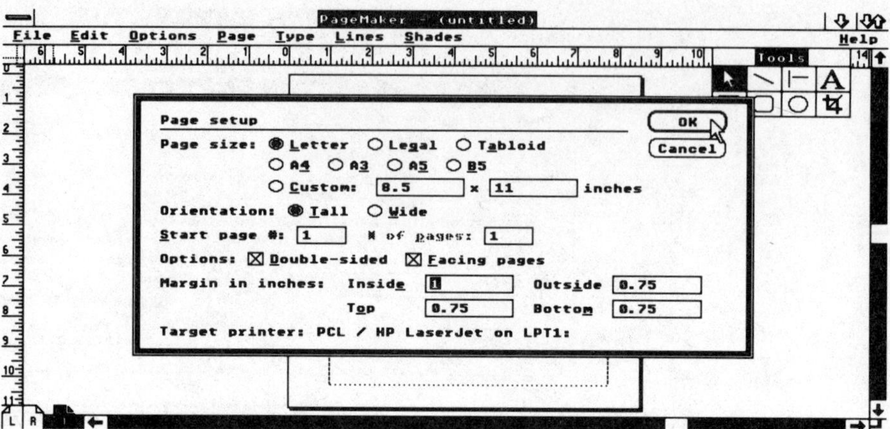

Figure 2-4. The dialog box for page setup to define the page margins, size, and orientation.

When you start a new publication, you need to either define the margins of the page or else accept the default settings. (In this example, the newsletter uses the default settings.) You can bypass this decision entirely by choosing a template and loading it into PageMaker, using the Open command in the File menu. A *template* is a predesigned publication file that is empty of text and graphics, but is ready for use in page makeup.

This chapter assumes that you want to design something completely new so that you can learn how to use all of PageMaker's tools. Start by selecting New from the File menu. When PageMaker displays the dialog box shown in Figure 2-4, click the OK button and accept PageMaker's default settings for the page.

Designing the Layout

Every page of the newsletter example has two columns. Set the two-column format on the master pages (which will be explained shortly), so that new pages start with a two-column format. You aren't locked into this format—on each page, you can either change the columns or keep the

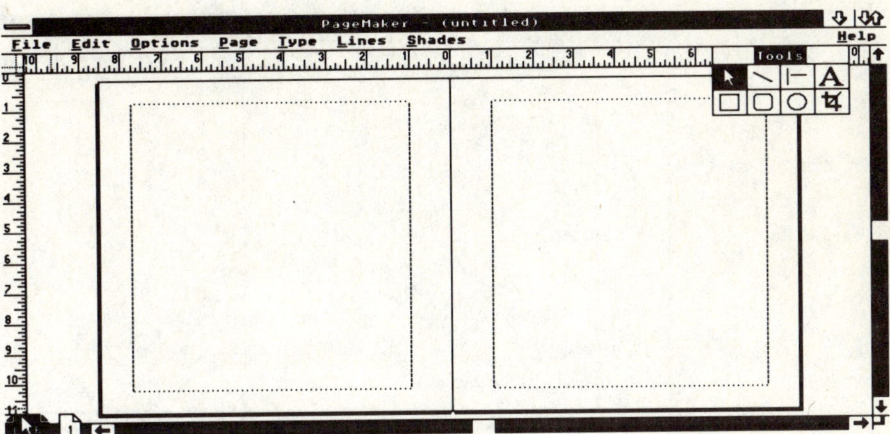

Figure 2-5. Select and display the master pages.

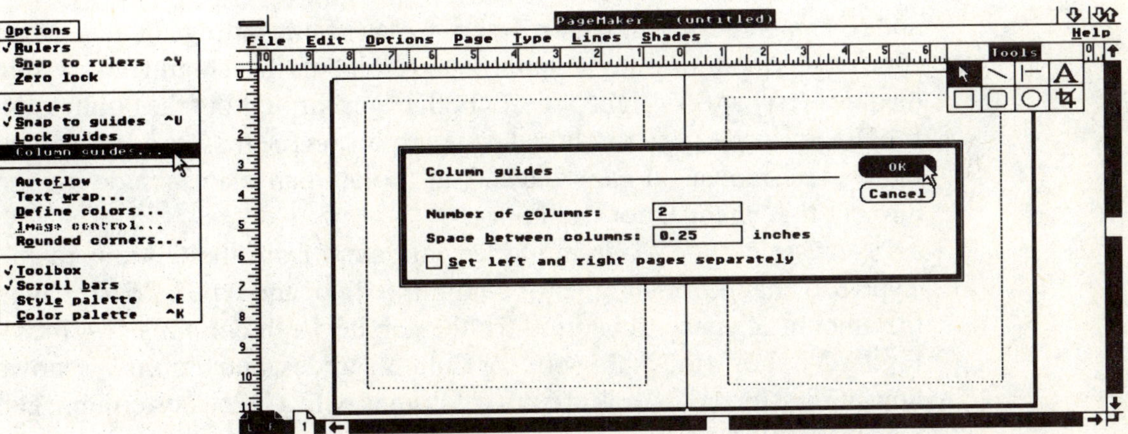

Figure 2-6. Select the dialog box for Column guides, and change the number of columns and the width of the space between columns.

format that was set in the master page. The Column guides dialog box always shows the number of columns on the current page.

First, select the master pages by clicking the page icons labeled "L" and "R" at the bottom left corner of the window. Figure 2-5 shows the left

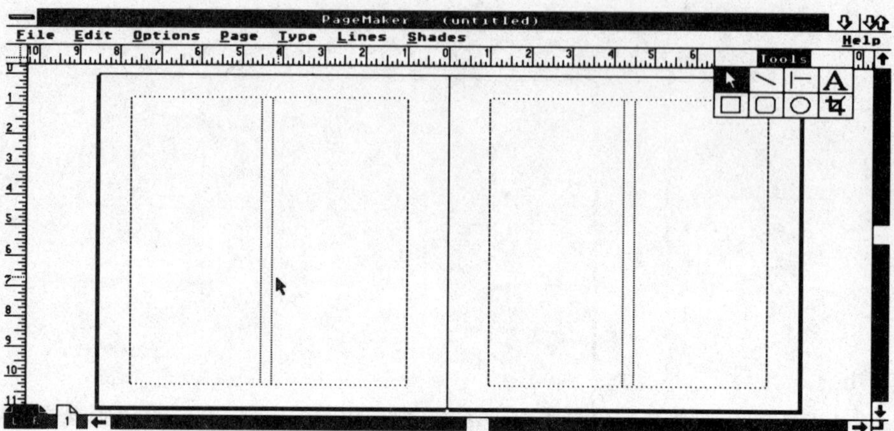

Figure 2-7. The Master pages of the publication, after the column guides are set.

and right *master pages*, which describe the default settings of all left and right pages, including any graphic or text elements that should be repeated on every left page, or right page, or both pages throughout the publication file. For example, you might put page footers on the master pages so that the footers repeat on each page. The footers can also include a page number that changes for each page.

Next, select the Column guides command from the Options menu. Type **2** to change the number of columns to two, and type **0.25** to change the amount of space to be used for the gap between columns (1/4 inch). Figure 2-6 shows the dialog box for Column guides, and Figure 2-7 shows how the master pages look after two columns with a 0.25-inch column gap have been set.

When the page setup menu was displayed (Figure 2-4), you could have selected a single-page orientation by clicking the marked box next to Double-sided in order to delete the "X" in the box. (When the "X" is deleted, the option is turned off.)

The Double-sided option, which is usually on, sets up left and right master pages with margins that are properly offset from the spine where pages will be bound. Clicking this option off sets up only one master page, and assumes that the publication does not have double-sided pages. Most publications use double-sided page styles, starting with a title page as a

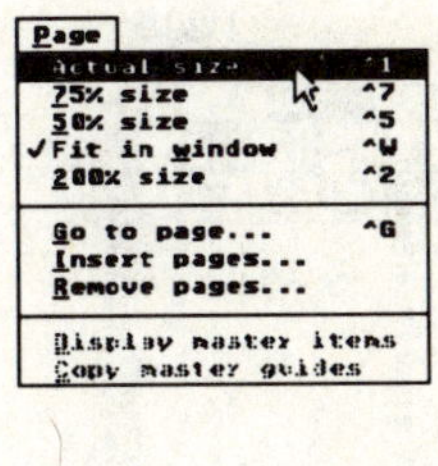

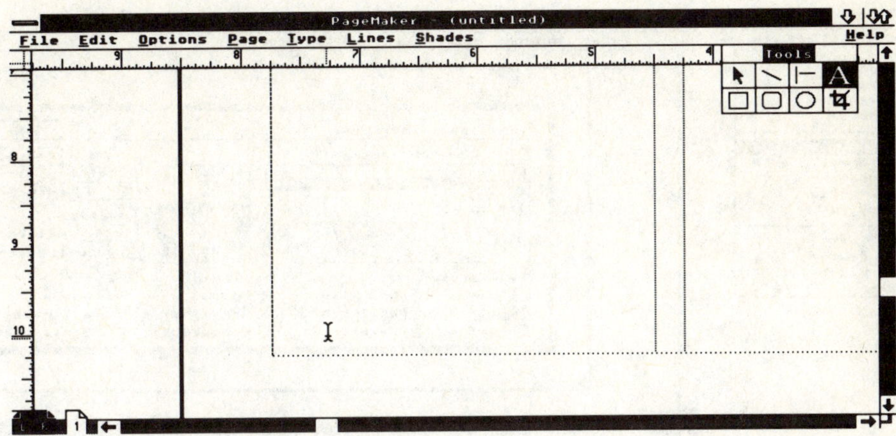

Figure 2-8. To zoom into a detailed view of the left master page, select Actual size from the Page menu.

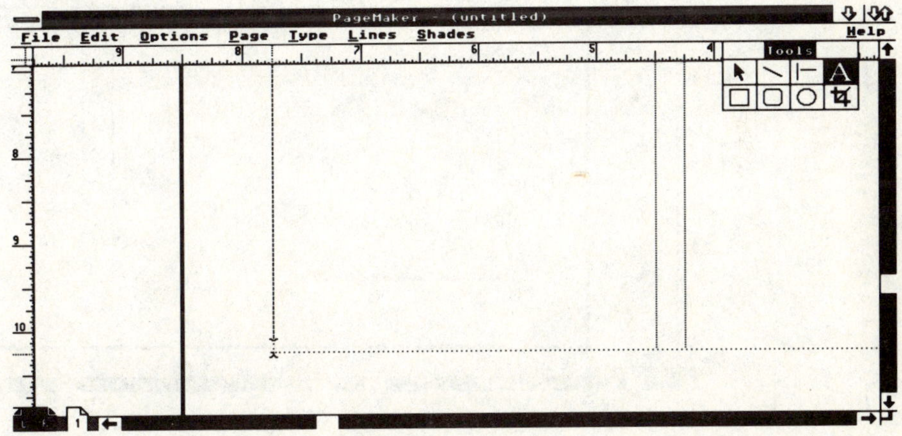

Figure 2-9. Click the text pointer in the left corner of the left master page (so that the pointer nearly disappears behind the guide lines).

right-hand page, followed by two-page spreads.

You can zoom into a more detailed view in order to type text for footers that can appear on each page. Each footer can hold a marker for the page number. First, choose Actual size from the Page menu (Figure

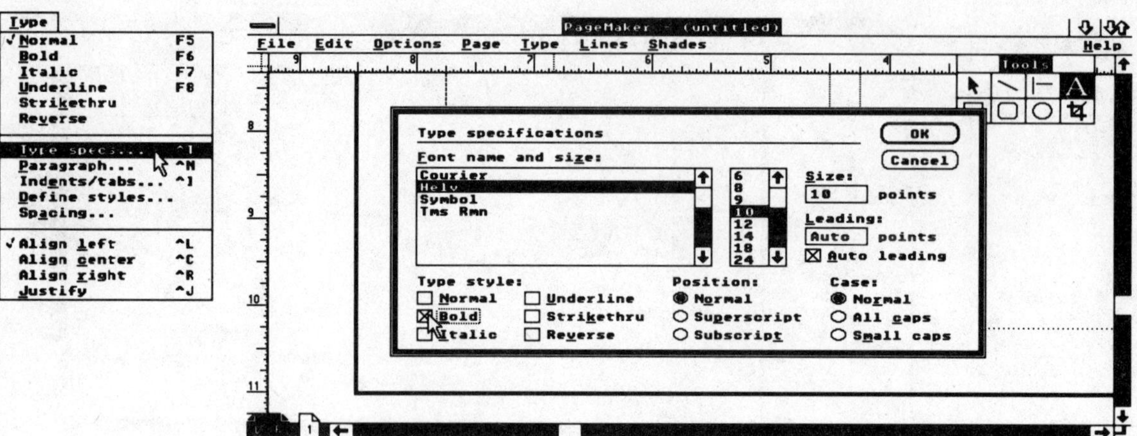

Figure 2-10. The Type specifications menu with specifications for the footer text.

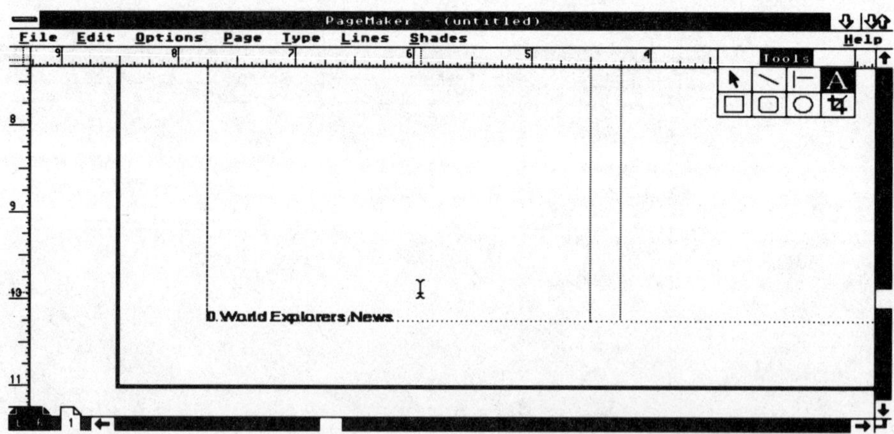

Figure 2-11. Type the page number marker and footer text for the left master page.

2-8). Click once in the right scroll bar below the scroll box, and click once to the left of the bottom scroll box, so that the bottom left corner of the left master page is in view. Then choose the text tool, click an insertion point at the left margin (Figure 2-9), and choose the Type specs option from the Type menu (Figure 2-10). Select Helvetica as the font, select 10 points as the type size, click the box next to Bold, and then click the OK button. You

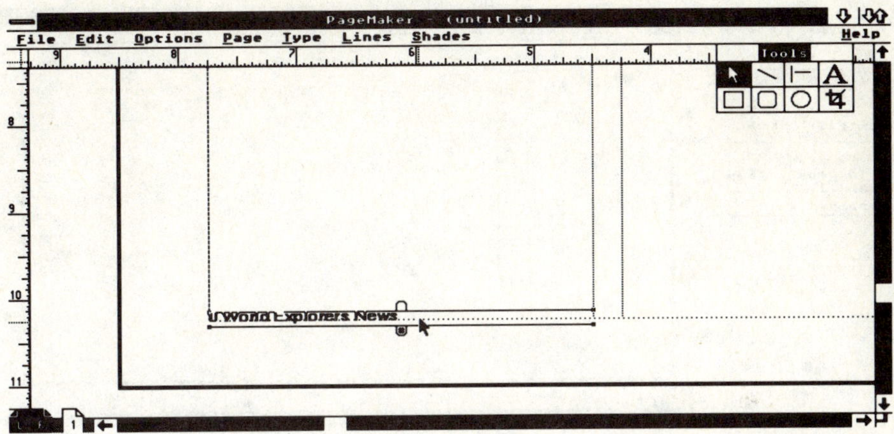

Figure 2-12. Select the footer text for copying.

can now type the text of the footer. (If you are not using the text tool, switch back to it before you type the text.)

Begin the footer with the automatic page number marker. To set the marker, hold down the Control (Ctrl) key, the Shift key, and the numerical 3 key (in that order, and hold all keys down together). PageMaker displays **0** to mark the place of a page number. You can then add a space or two and add the text of the footer, as shown in Figure 2-11. After you type the footer, choose the pointer tool, and click anywhere in the middle of the footer's text. Two parallel lines appear above and below the footer (Figure 2-12).

Now choose Copy from the Edit menu in order to copy the footer to the Clipboard. Click to the right of the bottom scroll box to view the right master page (Figure 2-13), and choose Paste from the Edit menu. A copy of the footer appears (Figure 2-14), and you can drag it into position on the bottom right corner of the right master page (Figure 2-15). Because the footer is left-justified, change to the text (A) tool, drag the text pointer across the footer text, and choose the Align right command from the Type menu (Figure 2-16).

To finish the job, click a text insertion point just to the right of the page number marker in the footer. Drag to select just the marker and spaces (but not the footer text), and choose Cut from the Edit menu in order to cut the

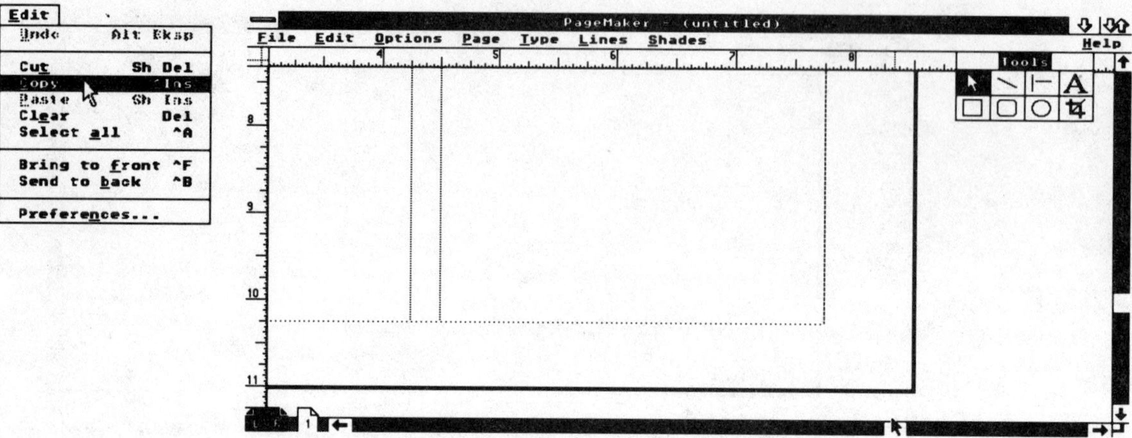

Figure 2-13. Scroll (using the bottom scroll bar) to the right bottom side of the right master page, after copying and before using Paste.

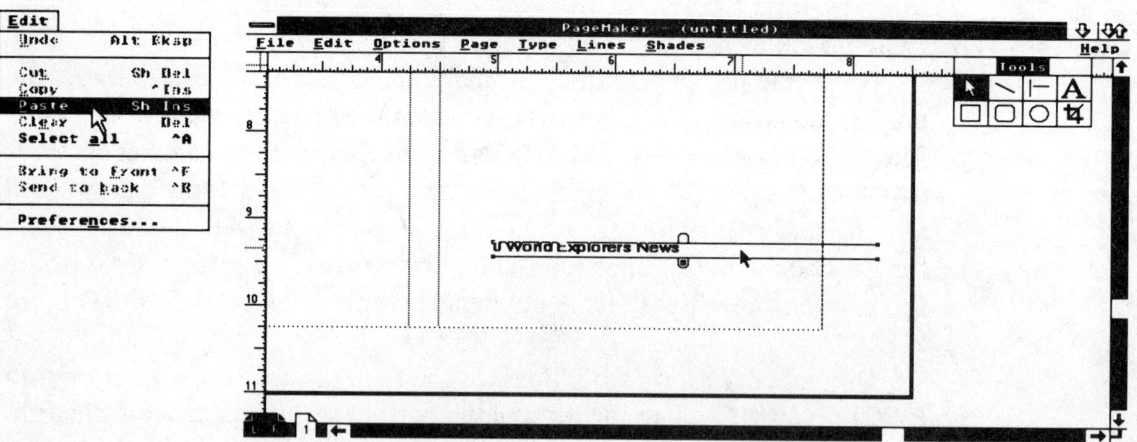

Figure 2-14. The copied text element appears on the page after Paste is used.

page number marker (Figure 2-17). Click another insertion point at the end of the footer against the right margin, type a space or two (just as you did for the left footer), and then choose Paste from the Edit menu (Figure 2-18). Delete the extra space or two that follow the right page number

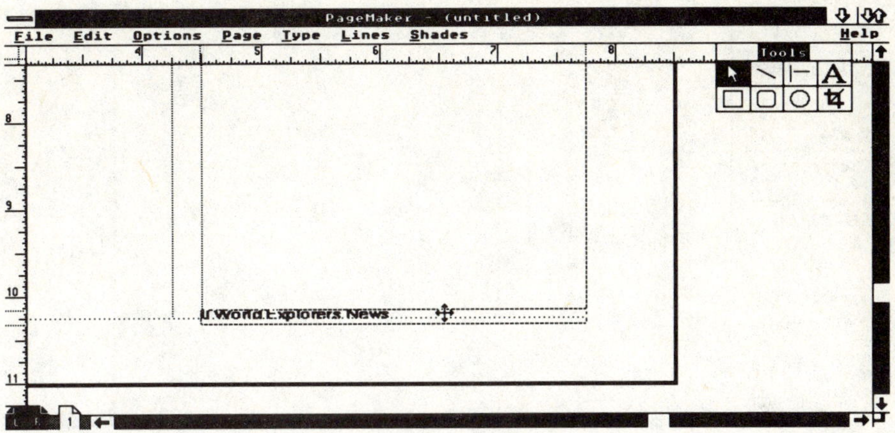

Figure 2-15. Moving the copied text element into position in order to make a footer for the right master page.

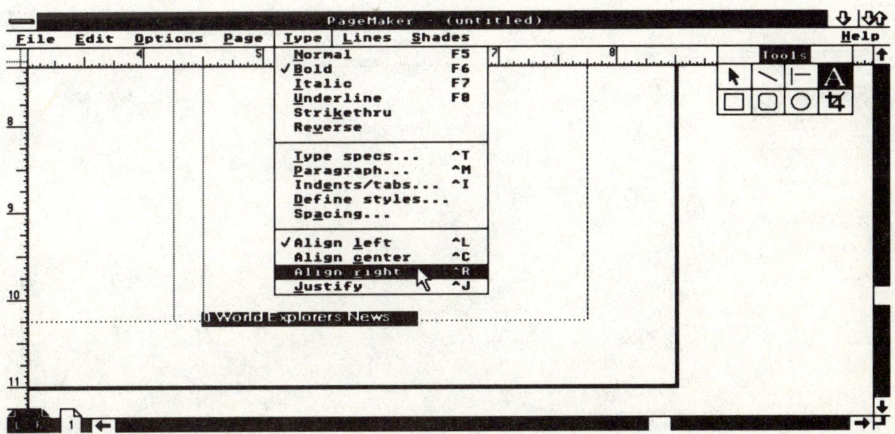

Figure 2-16. The Align right command changes the alignment of the selected text in the text element. (Before using this command, first select the A tool, and then select the text by dragging the text pointer over the text).

marker by selecting and cutting the spaces.

Now, save your publication file (you should save the file often). Since you started from scratch with the New command, choose the Save

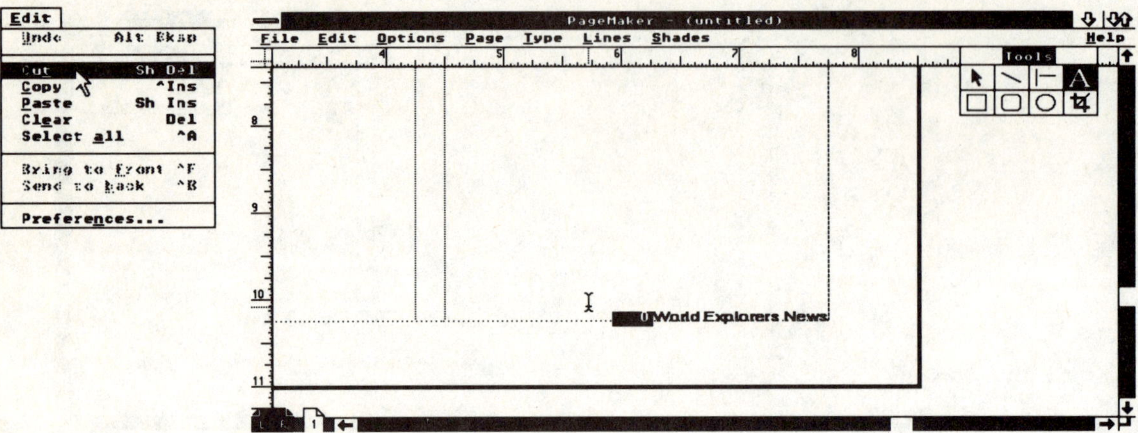

Figure 2-17. Cut the page marker from the left side of the text element, after first selecting the text with the A tool.

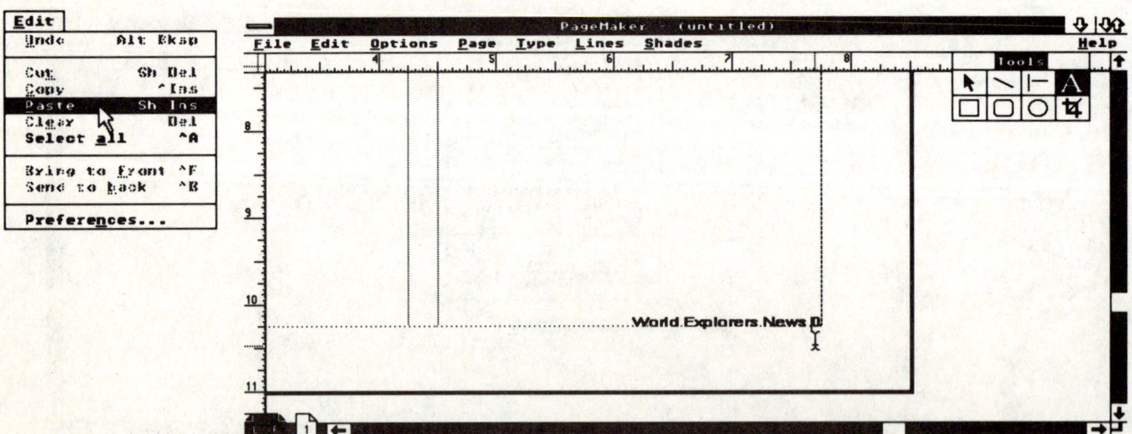

Figure 2-18. Move the text cursor to the right side of the text (at the end). Type a space and use Paste to paste the page number marker back into the text element, so that the page number appears at the end of the text.

command from the File menu (Figure 2-19) so that you can use the same design for new publications without having to redefine the master page. Name the publication file **NEWSTEMP** and press Enter or click OK. The

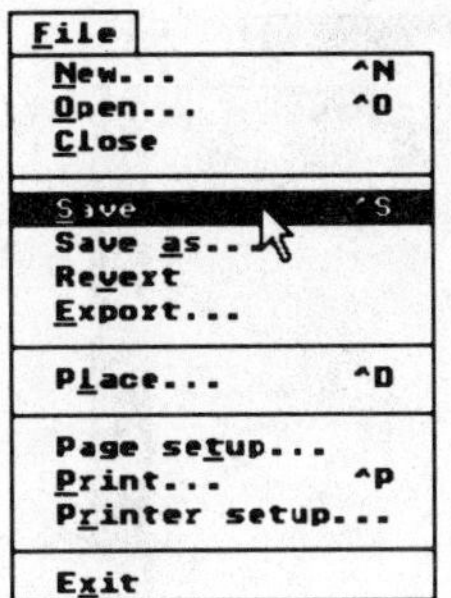

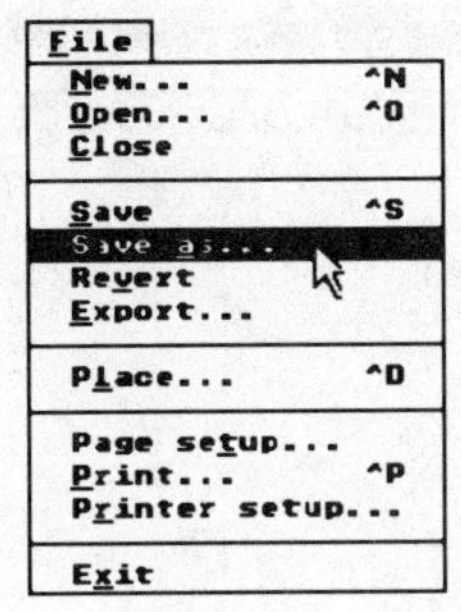

Figure 2-19. The Save (and Save As) dialog box lets you type a name for the newly created publication file. It automatically appends the ".PM3" extension to the name in order to make a complete filename.

next time you start page makeup of a newsletter, you can simply click on this file in order to start PageMaker with these settings for the master pages.

Designing the Title Page

The style of a newsletter is characterized by its title page, which can say more about your publication than a carefully worded statement can convey. A very simple design was chosen for this example in order to move quickly through PageMaker's features. To move to page 1 of the newsletter, click the page 1 icon in the lower left corner of the screen.

It may help your design task to display a ruler. To do so, select Rulers from the Options menu. The ruler automatically uses inches as the unit of measurement, but you can change the unit of measurement to centimeters or to picas with points by selecting Preferences from the Edit menu. In the newsletter example, the ruler is measured in inches.

You may also want to use guides on the page, because you can attach text and graphics blocks to the guides without needing to position a mouse exactly. The Snap to guides command in the Options menu controls this feature. The Snap to guides feature is active until you turn it off by selecting it; to turn it back on, select it again. Ruler guides can be positioned anywhere on the page, locked into position, unlocked, moved, and deleted. When the Snap to guides feature is on, the placement of elements is easier and the alignment of the elements is guaranteed. Ruler

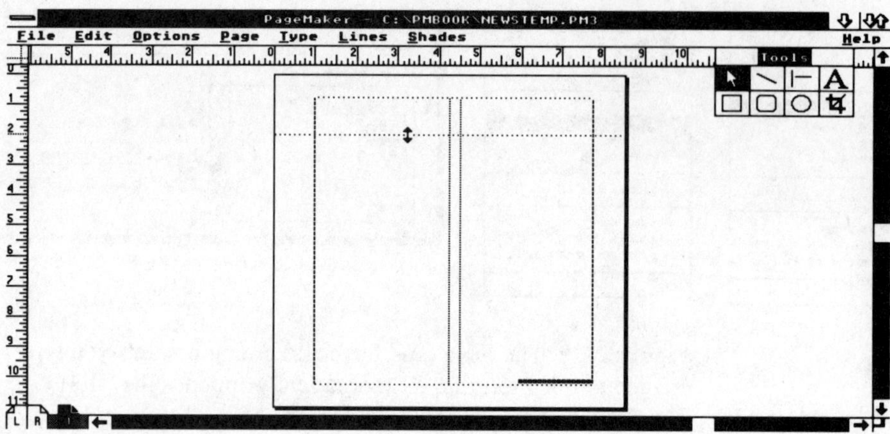

Figure 2-20. Add a ruler guide to help place text and graphic elements accurately.

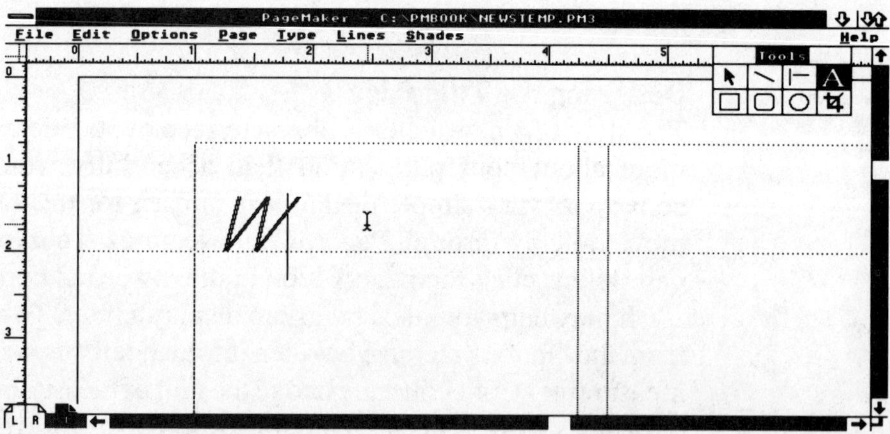

Figure 2-21. Type the newsletter's title with the text tool.

guides (calibrated to within 1/1,440 of an inch) should be used whenever you want to align anything. To be sure that elements are aligned properly, select the 200% size page view from the page menu (which is the most accurate view for lining up items on a page) and ruler guides.

To position a ruler guide, click anywhere in the ruler. Drag the ruler guide to the desired position on the page, using the dotted lines in both the

Figure 2-22. Change the column width of the newsletter's title by dragging the bottom right corner with the pointer tool.

horizontal and vertical rulers to measure the position. Figure 2-20 shows a guide placed two inches below the top of the page (exactly on the 2-inch mark) to show where the first line of the newsletter title should be typed.

Some designers begin with the finished newsletter logo and title, and other designers start with imaginary text blocks and a blank space for a graphic logo and title. You can choose any starting method with PageMaker. If you are in a hurry, start with a simple title and graphic as shown in the next example, or just use the box tool to draw a box as a place holder for such a title, and then place all of the articles first. You can go back later and adjust the title or add graphics.

To add a simple title, first select the type style and font using the Type specs command in the Type menu. The Helvetica font at 60 points with automatic leading, and both the Bold and Italic styles, were selected for the newsletter example. Click the text tool and type the title, as shown in Figure 2-21. Type **WORLD**, select the Type specs command again, and then change the point size to 36 points. Click OK, press Enter to start a new line, and type the rest of the title as **Explorers News**. Notice that the text wraps around within the column width. You can change the text block's width by switching to the pointer tool and dragging the bottom right corner of the block of text that is to be wider, as shown in Figure 2-22.

Figure 2-23. Move the text element into position by holding down the mouse button until the pointer turns into four arrows, and then dragging the element.

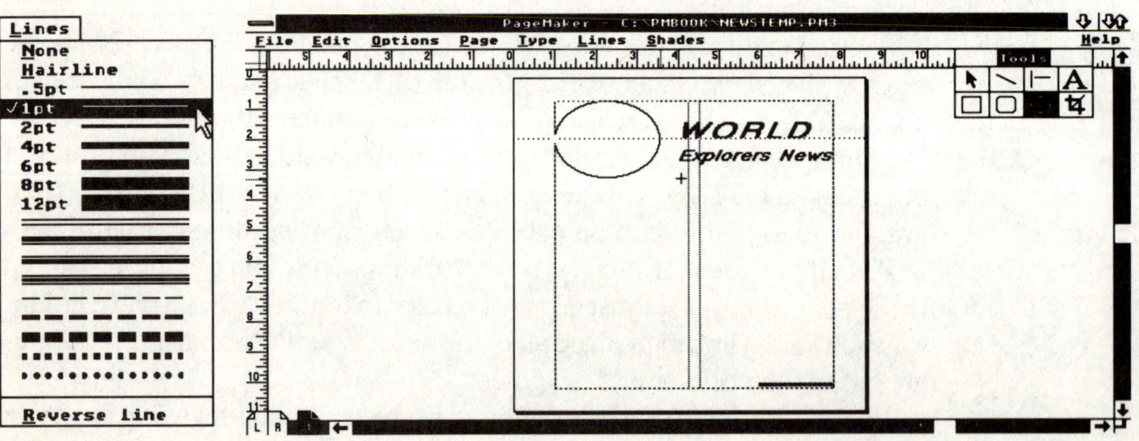

Figure 2-24. To draw a perfect circle with the circle drawing tool, hold down the Shift key while drawing.

For easier viewing of the title, select the Fit in window display option in the Page menu. To go to the Fit in Window view from any page view, hold down the Control (Ctrl) key and type **W**.

PageMaker has many such shortcuts. Use the pull-down menus until

Figure 2-25. The newsletter title, the circle graphic, and the horizontal rule on the title page.

you learn the keyboard shortcuts, which are displayed in the menus. You can even pull down the menu to see the keyboard equivalent for a command, such as Copy (in the Edit menu) or Type specs (in the Type menu), and then drag your mouse to the top of the menu to put the menu away without selecting anything. As you learn PageMaker, you'll begin to remember the shortcuts for the commands that you most often use, and you won't need to use their menus.

To move the title into position by using the pointer tool, press and hold down the mouse button over the title until the four-arrows symbol appears (Figure 2-23). Continue to hold the mouse button down and drag the title into the proper position on the right side of the page so that the word "WORLD" rests on the guide line. You now have space to draw a circle to represent the globe graphic. Select the circle drawing tool from the toolbox. Move the crosshairs cursor to the top right corner of the page. Next, hold down the Shift key, and drag downward and to the right in order to create a perfect circle, as shown in Figure 2-24. (If you don't hold down the Shift key, the shape will be an oval.)

Figure 2-25 shows the newsletter title together with a horizontal rule at the 3 1/2-inch mark, which was drawn using the perpendicular-line tool from the toolbox. Press down on the main mouse button to create an

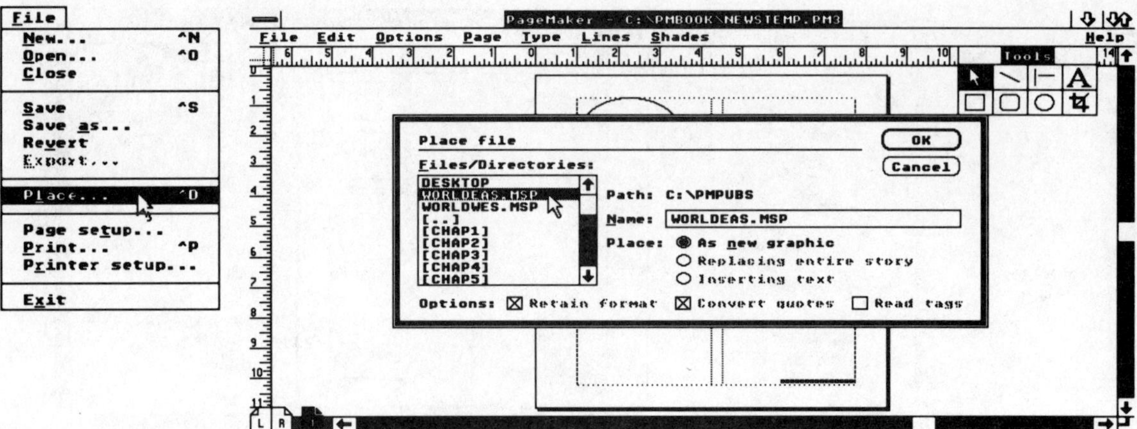

Figure 2-26. The Place command's dialog box.

insertion point under the title at the left margin, and then drag to the right margin. You can pick the line width and style in the Lines menu.

Placing a Graphic

When you are designing the title page and using a graphic in the title, place the graphic (or a rough version of the graphic, if it is not finished) onto the page so that you can see the entire layout with the image. The graphic should be in a file format acceptable to PageMaker, as described in Chapter 1. If the graphic can be copied to the Windows Clipboard, you can use the Paste command to place the graphic on the page. For the best results, use PageMaker's Place command to place the graphic directly from the file onto the page. If your graphic is not yet available, use PageMaker's toolbox to create a simple representation of the graphic's outline.

Choose the Place command from the File menu. The Place dialog box appears (Figure 2-26). To scroll the list of file names, move the elevator box in the scroll bar or click the arrows. The elevator box in Figure 2-26 is located at the top of the scroll bar, and names of subdirectories appear within brackets (as in [CHAP1]). The subdirectories can be clicked open in order to list the files inside them. To move back out, click the double dots (..). The newsletter example uses a Microsoft Paint (.MSP) file that

Figure 2-27. Placing the graphics file.

Figure 2-28. To scale the image in equal proportions, hold down the Shift key while dragging a handle on any corner.

contains a graphic of a world globe. You can place any file that contains a graphic image, such as the supplied .MSP or .PIC files from Aldus or Microsoft.

Select the graphics file and click the Place button (or double-click the file name). Because the graphics file contains a paint-type graphic, the pointer turns into the paintbrush icon. Move the icon to the upper left corner of the right-hand (second) column, and click in order to place the image (Figure 2-27). Use the same method to place a draw document (an object-oriented graphic, which is represented by a pencil icon), a scanned photo in a TIF format (an X inscribed in a square icon), a paint document (a paintbrush icon), a graphic saved in EPS format (a PS icon), or a chart or graph document (usually a pencil icon). PageMaker's pointer icons tell you what type of file you are placing.

To scale the graphic down in size so that it fits next to the title, hold down the Shift key and drag the bottom right corner of the image up and to the left (Figure 2-28). Hold down the Control (Ctrl) key along with the Shift key in order to scale the image in proportions that are optimal for your printer.

Placing the Lead Article

The first article's heading should be in a size that is not so large that it can be confused with the newsletter title, but not so small that it appears insignificant next to the text. The heading must also be located close enough to the graphic image or the photo that accompanies the article so that when the readers see the graphic image or the photo, the heading is the next item that draws their attention.

The best page designs contain elements that are balanced so that the page does not appear to be overly designed. A good page design should catch the reader's attention and direct the eye movement across and down the page.

Another decision to make is where to put a graphic image or a photo that accompanies the article. You should leave space on the first page for the image or photo, but you have the classic problem of not knowing how long the text will be when it is in typeset form. You can solve this problem with PageMaker by drawing a simple box to represent the graphic or photo, placing the text of the article, and then changing the size of the image area for the graphic or photo in order to accommodate the text. You can also add another text or graphic element to balance the page and avoid excessive white space. Figure 2-29 shows a box (drawn with the box tool)

Figure 2-29. Draw a box to act as placeholder for a graphic or photo, using a 1-point line.

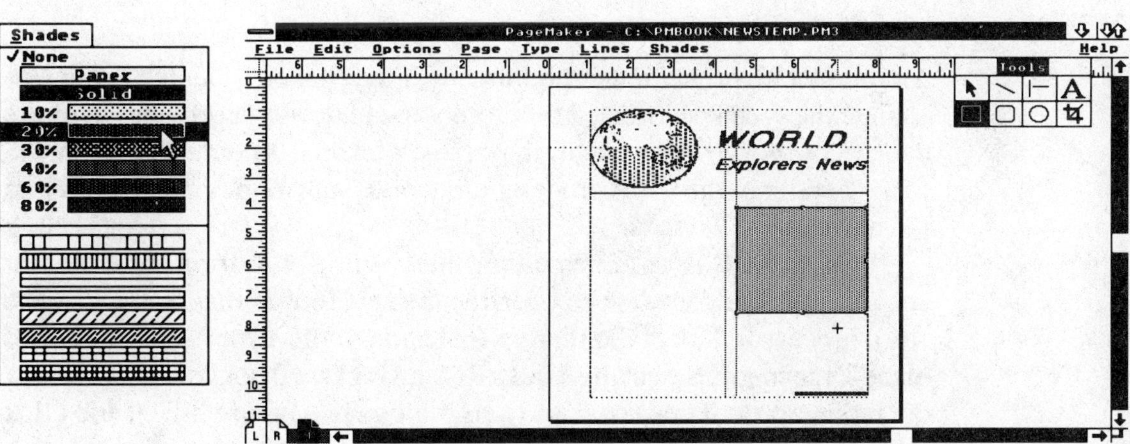

Figure 2-30. Set a 20-percent shade for the placeholder.

that acts as a placeholder for a graphic or photo. Next, select a 1-point line from the Lines menu, and select a 20-percent gray shade from the Shades menu (Figure 2-30).

You are now ready to place the text of the article. Although your text file may be properly formatted for printing with Microsoft Word or

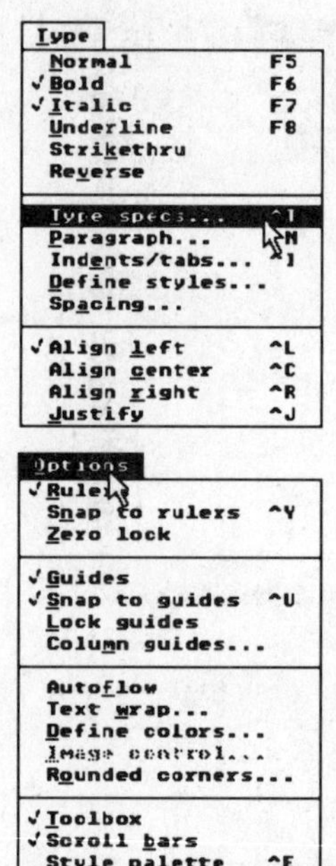

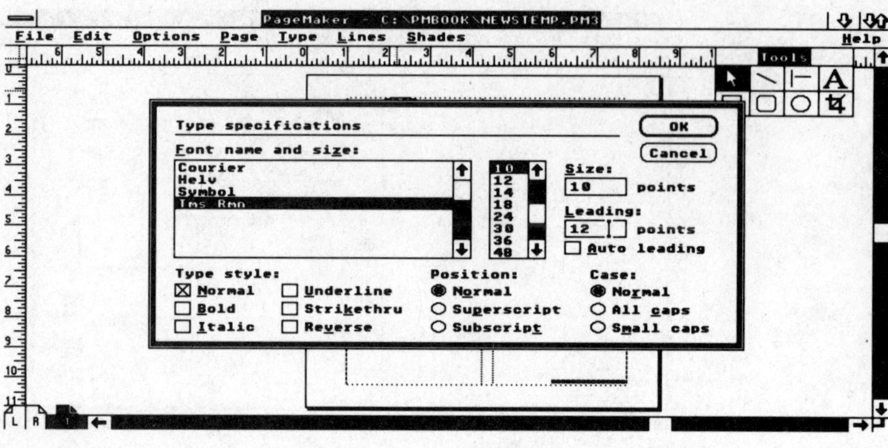

Figure 2-31. These type specifications for the text body were set before placing the text file, so that they control the format of the text and override any format selected in the word processor.

another word processor supported by PageMaker, you may want to change the type specifications before you create a typeset version of the document. For example, you may have picked 10-point type with 11-point leading in the word processor, but you want 12 points of leading in the newsletter.

This discussion assumes either that you did not format the text in advance, or that you wish to override the text format that was set by the word processor. Select the pointer tool and use the Type specs command in the Type menu. Select the Times Roman font at 10 points with 12 points of leading in the Type specifications dialog box (Figure 2-31), and click OK. Because you will be pouring text slowly, one column at a time, you need to be sure that the Autoflow option is turned off. You also want to be sure that the Snap to guides option is turned on, so that you can attach elements easily to guides on the page. Check the Options menu to see if the Snap to guides option is on, and if the Autoflow option is off. (A check mark should appear next to the Snap to guides option, and no check mark should appear next to Autoflow.)

To place the text, choose the Place command from the File menu. Select a text file and click the box next to the Retain format option off (the

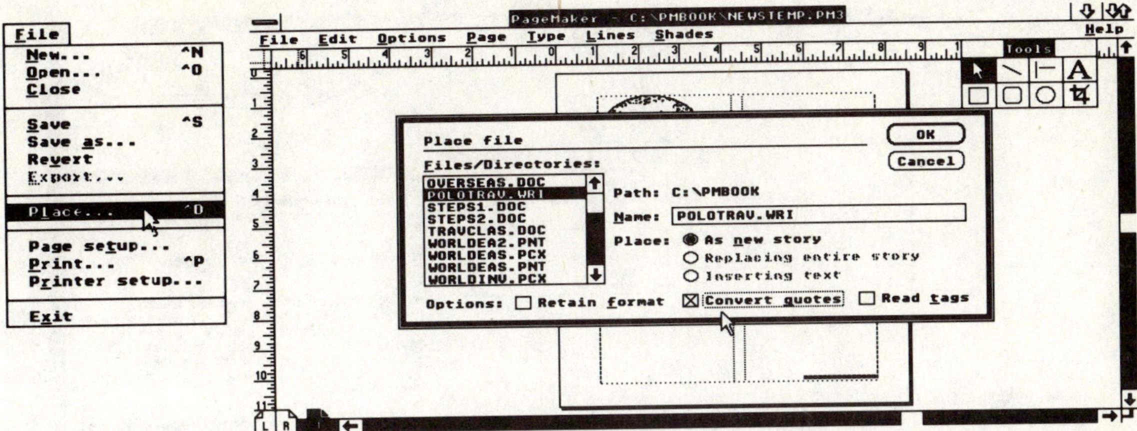

Figure 2-32. Use the Place command to place the text of the lead article, with the Retain format and Read tags options off and the Convert quotes option on.

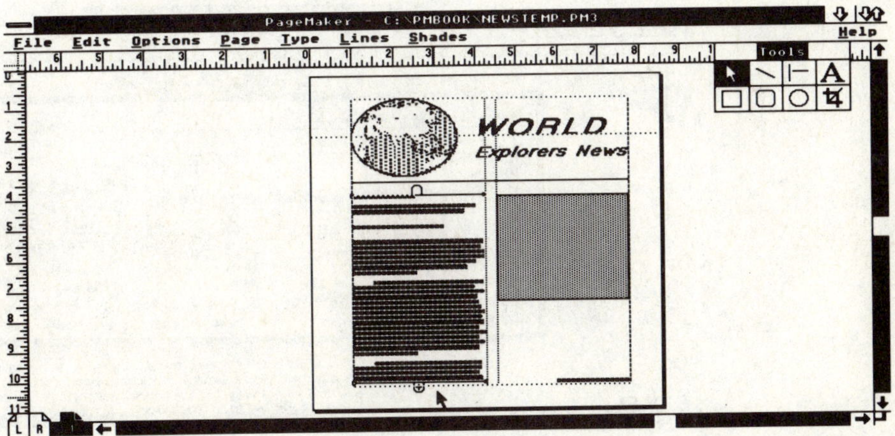

Figure 2-33. Text flows down the left column, and stops when Autoflow is off.

"X" should disappear), so that the Place command does not retain the formatting settings from the word processor and PageMaker's type specifications are used instead. Click the Convert quotes option on (Figure 2-32), and click the Read tags option off. Finally, click Place (or press Enter).

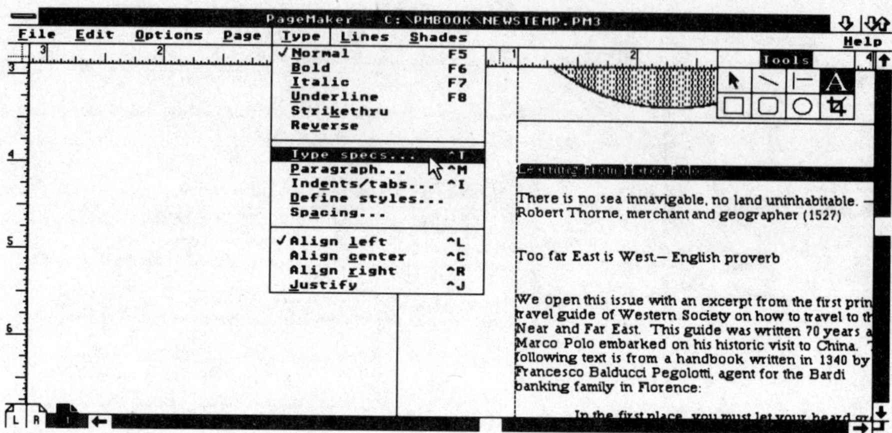

Figure 2-34. Choose Type specifications after you select the lead article's headline with the text tool.

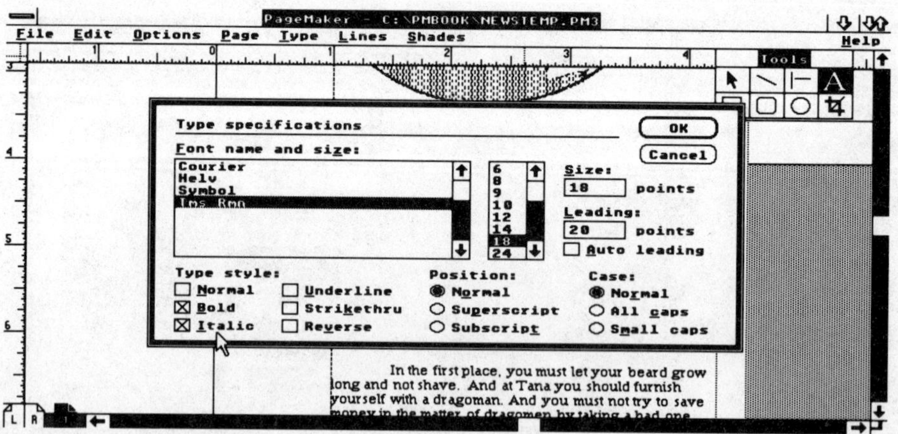

Figure 2-35. Change the headline text to Times Roman at 18 points in size with 20 points of leading, and bold italic.

The pointer changes into the manual text flow icon. Place the icon appropriately in the left column, and click the mouse. Text now flows all the way down to the bottom of the page, and two handles on the text block (top and bottom) appear (Figure 2-33).

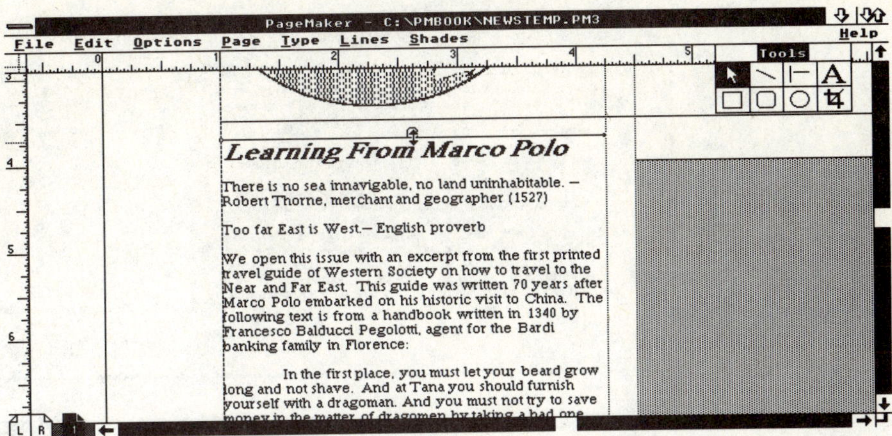

Figure 2-36. Drag the text element's handle up in order to move the text higher on the page while retaining its column margins.

The article's heading must be changed. To display an actual- size view of the page, hold down the Control (Ctrl) and Alt keys and click the mouse while you point to a specific spot on the page. (To return to the full-page view, perform these steps again; the command toggles the displays.) Select the headline text by clicking the text tool and then dragging over the text in order to highlight it.

Choose the Type specs command from the Type menu (Figures 2-34 and 2-35) in order to change the font of the headline to Bold Italic at 18 points in size with 20 points of leading, and click OK. Then drag the text element's handle up in order to move the text higher on the page (Figure 2-36).

The left column is too long—the bottom of the column lines up with the page number footer. It helps to place a guide at the bottom of the page that runs across the text measure, so that the right column's text can be aligned with the left column. Click the horizontal ruler at the top of the page and drag down a guide. Release the mouse button when the guide is located at the 9 5/8-inch ruler mark (Figure 2-37).

Use the pointer tool to select the text element again. The bottom handle of the left column displays a + symbol, which signifies that the text file contains more text to be placed. To shorten the column, click the +

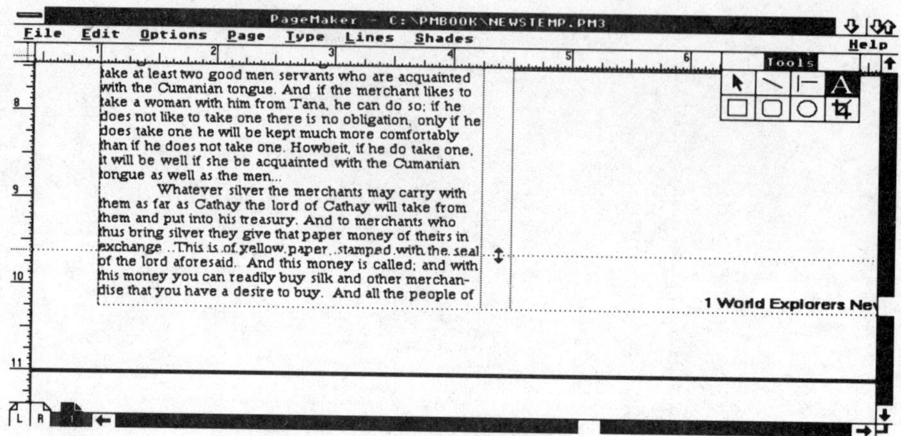

Figure 2-37. Set a guide at the bottom of the page to help align text blocks.

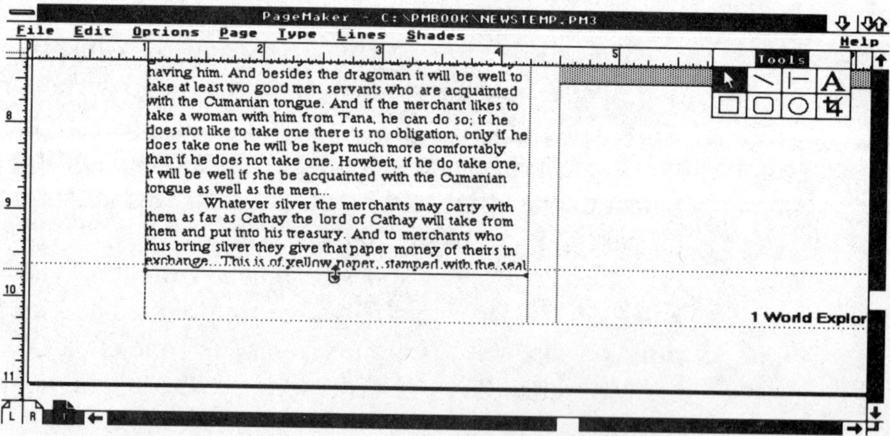

Figure 2-38. Shorten the text block in the left column.

symbol and drag the bottom handle up as if you were pushing up a window shade. The text block is shortened as you move the bottom handle. Align the text with the guide, then release the mouse button (Figure 2-38).

Change the display to a full-page view by pressing the Control (Ctrl) and **W** keys (or by picking the Fit in Window option from the Page menu).

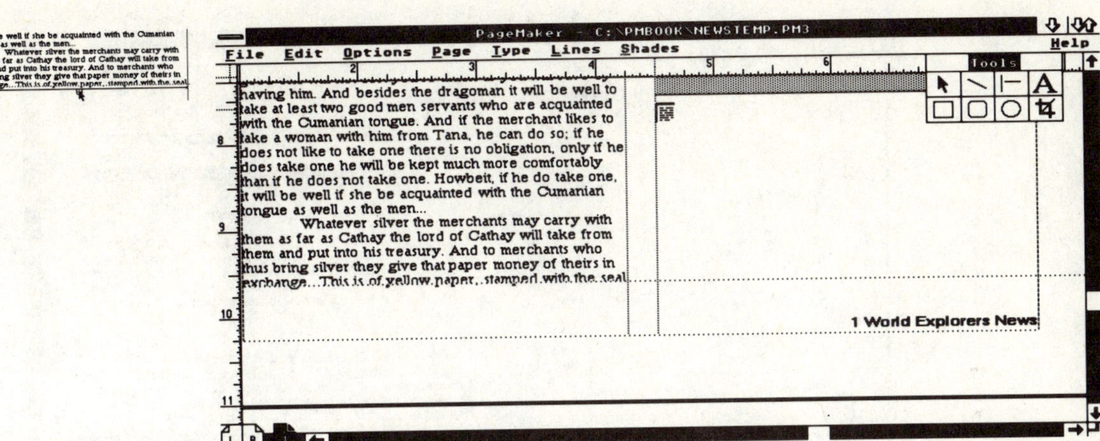

Figure 2-39. Place the rest of the article in the right column.

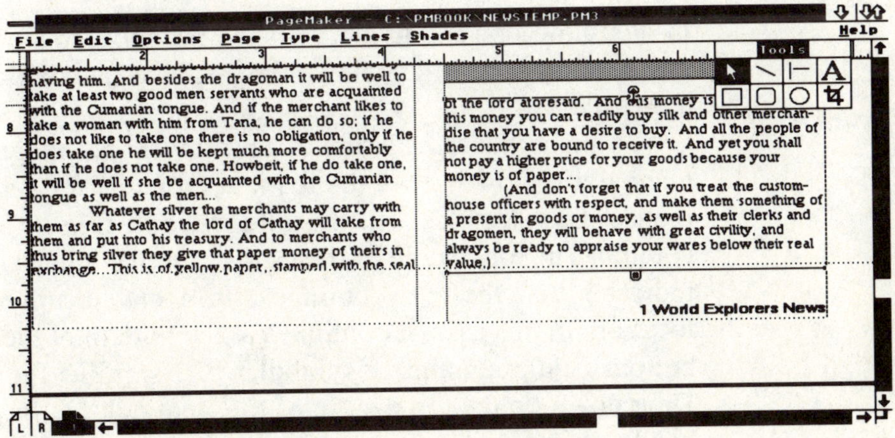

Figure 2-40. Line up text in two columns using a guide.

To continue the text to the next column under the image block, point to the bottom handle of the first text block and click it. The program changes your pointer to the manual text flow icon.

You can still move around the page using the scroll bar, and you can select options from menus, change pages, and also insert new pages while

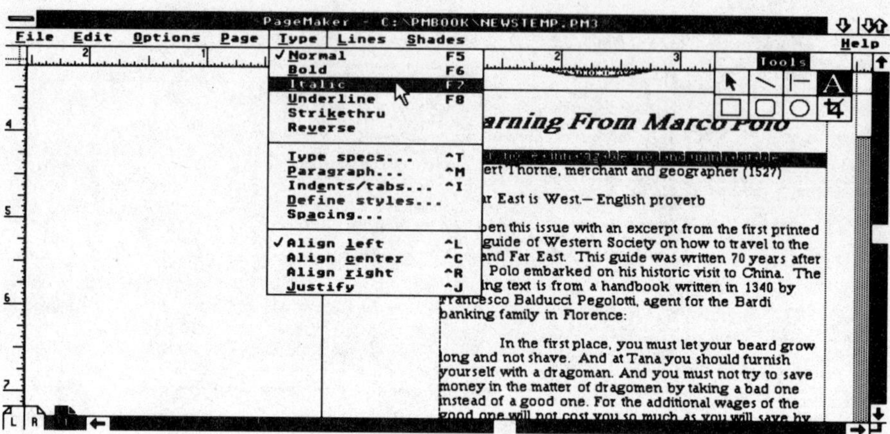

Figure 2-41. Change selected text to Italic.

the text flow icon is activated. But if you change to the arrow pointer tool, the text flow icon will no longer be displayed and will not be loaded with a text file.

To place the next block of text under the image block, move the manual text flow icon to the mark at around 7 5/8 inches, and click the mouse. This step places the rest of the article (Figure 2-39) in the second column. The top handle of the right column contains a + symbol, which indicates that the text continues from that location back to another location (in this case, it continues to the bottom of the left column). The bottom handle contains a # symbol, which signifies the end of the text file. Drag down on the top handle of the right column or pull up on the top handle to line up the text, as shown in Figure 2-40.

Selecting and Changing Text

To change the type style of the quoted text in the article, switch to the text tool. Click at the beginning of the text, and drag across the text to the endpoint before releasing the mouse button. Select Italic type from the Type menu (Figure 2-41) or press function key F7.

To change the entire excerpted text in the article to italic, select the text by clicking a starting point and dragging the shortest distance across both

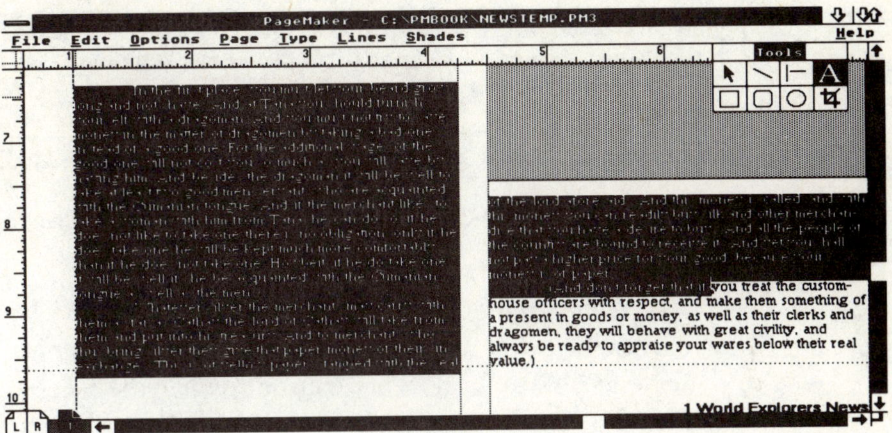

Figure 2-42. Select an area of text that spans two columns by dragging across the columns from starting point to endpoint.

columns to the endpoint. The entire text in both blocks between those points is highlighted (Figure 2-42). Press function key F7 or choose Italics in the Type menu to change the selected text to italics.

You can also use the keyboard cursor movement and editing keys to move an insertion point in the text, after you have first selected an insertion point by using the text tool and clicking the mouse. Depending upon your keyboard, the cursor movement and editing keys may be the numeric keypad keys (with a NumLock key for switching between numbers and editing keys) or they may be separate keys.

The left/right cursor movement keys move the insertion point by a single character or space. The up/down cursor movement keys move the point by a single line. To move the insertion point to the beginning of the next word or the previous word, hold down the Control (Ctrl) key and press a left or right key. When you hold down the Control (Ctrl) key and press an up or down key, the point is moved to the beginning of the next paragraph or the previous paragraph.

The Home or End key moves the insertion point to the beginning or the end of the current line (or the next line, if the point is already at that position). When the Control (Ctrl) key is pressed, the Home or End key

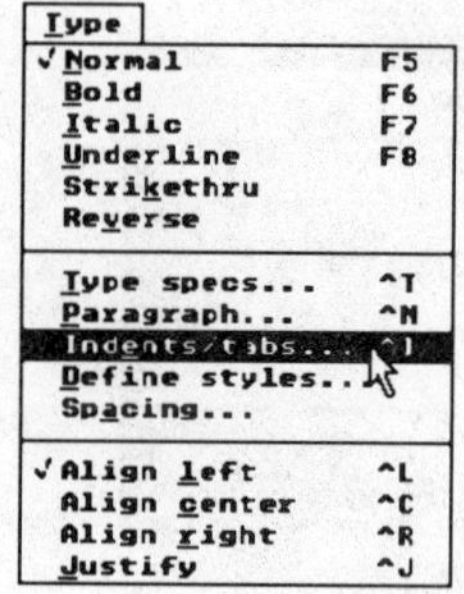

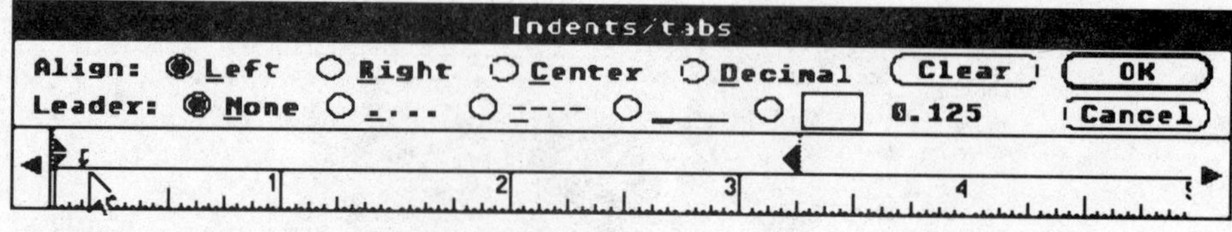

Figure 2-43. The Indents/tabs dialog box allows you to change paragraph indents and tab settings.

moves the point to the beginning of the next sentence or of the previous sentence. You can also move up or down in the text block quickly with the PageUp (PgUp) or PageDown (PgDn) keys. When the Control key is pressed, the PageUp or PageDown key moves the insertion point to the beginning or to the end of the text that has been placed.

There are several different ways to select text. To select a single word, double-click the word. You can then drag in any direction in order to select a group of words. To select a single paragraph, triple-click anywhere in the middle of that paragraph.

To extend a selection from an existing selection, hold down the Shift key and click a new ending point. (You can also use the cursor movement keys, rather than the mouse.) Another way to select a large area of text is to click a starting point at one end, then Shift-click the ending point at the other end. The easiest way to select all of the text is to click anywhere in the text once, and then choose the Select all command from the Edit menu (or press the Control (Ctrl) key and type **A**).

While the text is still highlighted (selected), change the tab spaces at the beginning of each paragraph. You can change the tab settings so that the tab space at the beginning of each paragraph is much smaller.

You may want to switch to Actual size or even to 200% size (in the Page menu) in order to increase the detail in the ruler. Then select the Indents/tabs option from the Type menu, and move the first tab marker on the ruler in the Indents/tabs dialog box (Figure 2-43) to exactly 1/8 inch. The dialog box displays a fractional number that changes as you move the tab marker. When that number is 0.125, release the mouse button and click OK. The paragraph tabs change in the selected text.

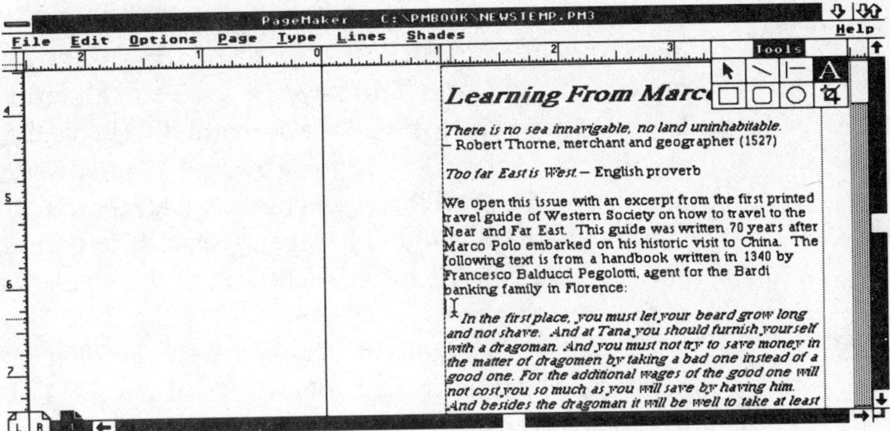

Figure 2-44. Click an insertion point with the text tool, then press backspace to delete a blank line, or press Enter to add a blank line.

Adjusting Columns and Editing for Space

The lead article is one line too long, but one line of space is present near the beginning of the article. The easiest adjustment is to delete that blank line.

You may want to change the display to Actual size (the Page menu). A quick way to do this is to hold down the Control (Ctrl) and Alt keys and click the mouse with the pointer tool. Point to the area that you want to see in actual size, hold down the Control (Ctrl) and Alt keys, and then click the mouse. Try this combination again, and note that the program changes the display to reduced size so that the entire page is displayed. You can switch back and forth from actual size to reduced size with this key-click combination. If you use a two-button mouse, another way to switch is to the use the right button of the mouse.

Switch to Actual size to make most text adjustments. For the most accurate view of the page as it will look when printed, check the alignment by going to 200% size (Command **2**). Make any final adjustments in the 200% view. You probably don't want to be slowed down by working at the 200% size all of the time because more scrolling is necessary with this view.

The fastest and most precise way to move the window is with the *grabber hand* (press the Alt key and then drag). The grabber hand can also be constrained by the Shift key to move vertically (press the Alt and Shift keys and drag up or down), or horizontally (press the Alt and Shift keys and drag left or right). When you move the window with the grabber hand or by using the scroll bars, you have to wait for the screen to redisplay. If you use a full-page display screen, you will find the 200% size easier to use, because you can increase the size of the window and see more more of the page at once.

To delete the blank line, choose the text tool and click at an insertion point at the beginning of the blank line (Figure 2-44). Press the backspace key to delete the blank line. The entire text block is reformatted, and the bottom lines of both columns should now line up.

What if you wanted to keep that blank line on the page? In addition to adding or subtracting a blank line, you can align columns in a number of other ways:

1. You can edit the text to add more words, and thereby extend one more line in the right column;

2. You can stretch the size of the image block to be longer, so that the text in the right column is pushed down one line; or

3. You can change the word spacing that PageMaker uses to determine line endings.

If you chose the first method, select the text tool and add enough words somewhere in the text to create a new line. Usually you can break a long paragraph into two paragraphs, and use the break to create a new line.

If you chose the second method, select the image block with the pointer tool. Click the bottom handle of the block, and drag it down 1/6 inch. Then select the column text and push the top handle of the text down by one line. The two columns should then be lined up.

The third method is perhaps the easiest. To change the word spacing, first use the text tool and click an insertion point in the article or select an area of text. Choose the Spacing option in the Type menu (Figure 2-45).

The Spacing dialog box shows the Minimum percentage, the Desired percentage, and the Maximum percentage of the font's standard space amount, which are used to make spaces between words and letters. These settings, and any changes made to them, control the spacing for the entire

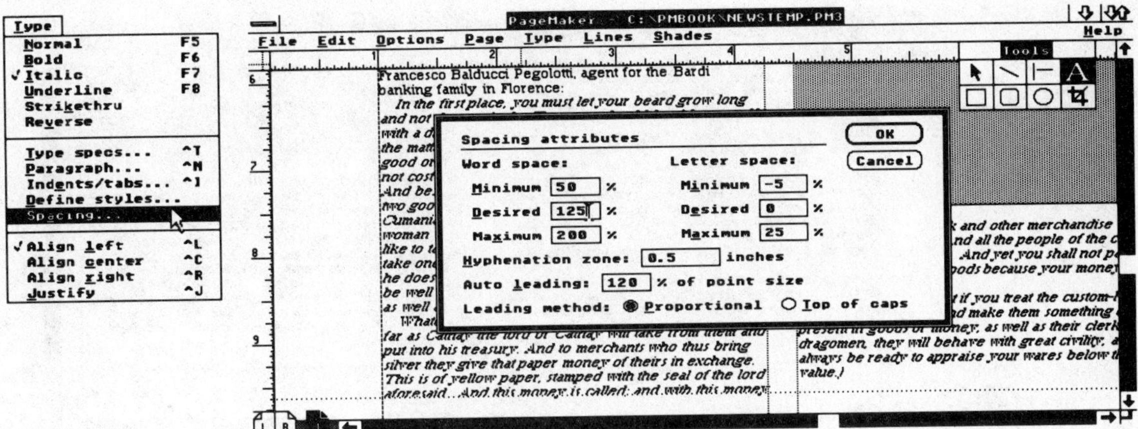

Figure 2-45. Choose the Spacing option from the Type menu and increase the desired word spacing in order to make ragged-right columns of text use more space.

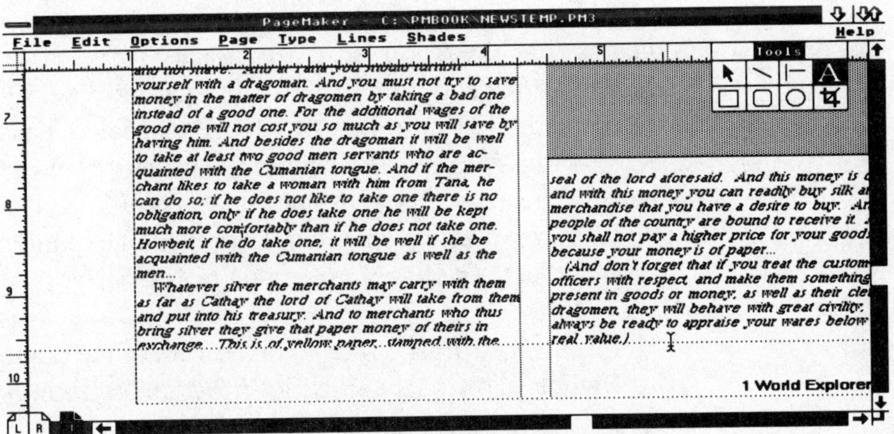

Figure 2-46. After the Desired word spacing is expanded, the right column extends a line in order to line up with the left column.

text of the placed article, not just for the selected area of text or the column where you just clicked the insertion point. The entire article's spacing changes but the newsletter title and other text that was typed or placed separately from this article are not affected.

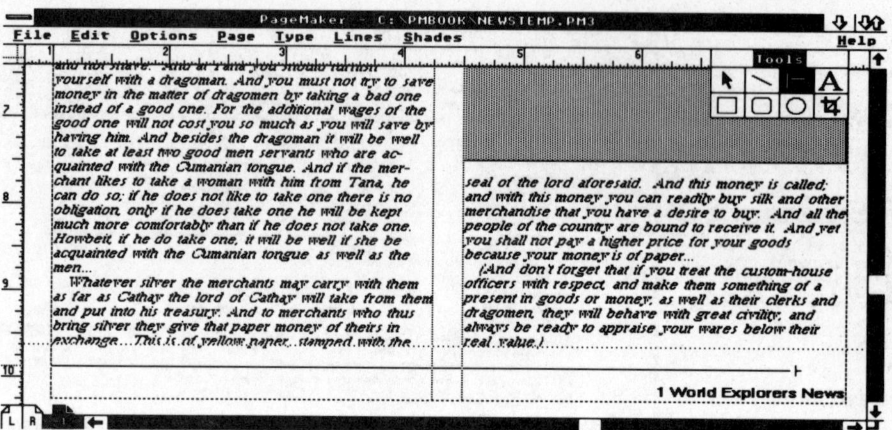

Figure 2-47. Draw a line across both columns at the bottom of the page, using the perpendicular-line drawing tool.

Don't change the letter spacing (zero is the correct value, which indicates that there are no extra spaces between letters). Change the Desired word spacing to 125% (this spacing is set by default to 100%). With ragged-right columns of text, PageMaker uses only the Desired spacing value for all word spacing. The program uses the other values when it spaces words for justified columns (you'll experiment with justified text in the next chapter). The result of expanding the desired word spacing is that the right column now lines up perfectly with the left column (Figure 2-46).

You can now draw a line at the bottom of the page to provide an even look. Switch to the perpendicular line drawing tool. Align the crosshairs cursor (+) to the left margin of the left column at the 10-inch ruler mark, and drag across the column to the right margin of the right column. The program draws a straight horizontal line (Figure 2-47).

Now would be a good time to save the publication, if you haven't done so already. Choose the Save as command from the File menu. Type a new name for the publication (such as **ISSUE1.PUB**), thereby keeping the original version as a startup publication file or a template. This approach allows you to preserve the original file and also to have a custom version of the file. The process of starting with a template, saving the revised template as a new file for further customization and the addition of new elements, and leaving behind an empty template for future use, should soon become second nature to you. To make the new template an official PageMaker template, open the empty template and use the Save as command with the Template option. The use of templates is described in more detail in Chapter 3.

Placing Formatted Text

Rather than placing a text-only file, this time you can place a file that has been prepared and preformatted on a word processor. As described in Chapter 1, word processors can be used to preformat text for PageMaker, depending upon how many formatting options are available in the word processor. This discussion assumes that you have used a word processor such as Microsoft Word or Windows Write, both of which have options for italic and bold type styles, as well as for font selection. In this example, a Times Roman 10-point font with 12 points of leading was selected, with some text to be bold and some text in italic. PageMaker can read this information with the text and then place it using these already-defined formatting options.

If you don't start by using a template file or by opening an existing publication file, PageMaker (by default) displays one page that is ready for placing text and graphics. (You can change this default setting from one page to several pages in the Page setup dialog box.) You can add pages very easily by choosing the Insert pages command from the Page menu. The Insert pages dialog box (Figure 2-48) automatically adds two pages if you click OK, and you can change that number in order to add more or fewer pages. PageMaker automatically uses the column settings plus any graphic or text elements that are stored on the master pages, as long as both the Display master items and the Copy master guides options in the Page menu are marked with check marks.

Normally, the Display master items and Copy master guides options are marked with check marks. When the Display master items option is not checked, the text and graphic items defined on the master pages are hidden so that they don't print. When the Copy master guides option is not

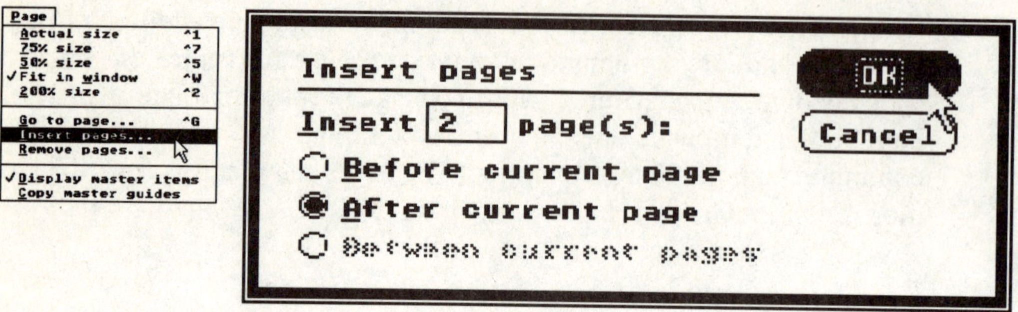

Figure 2-48. Use the Insert pages dialog box to add two pages.

checked, the column and ruler guides in the master pages are hidden. By selecting an option, you either turn on the check mark or turn it off. Keep these options turned on unless you need to remove master items or guides from a page.

To begin the second article on the second page, click the icon for page two, which is located at the lower left corner of the screen. PageMaker displays two facing pages (two and three) in the Fit in window view. To center the display window at Actual size on page two, point to the left-hand page and click the mouse while you hold down the Control (Ctrl) and Alt keys.

Because the article that you want to place is already formatted, and you want to retain and use the word processor formatting settings when the text is placed, simply use the Place command, with the Retain format option turned on (Figure 2-49). Point and click at the spot on the page where the second article should begin.

Next, select the heading and subheading of the second article with the text tool. Use the Cut command to cut the heading and subheading to the clipboard (Figure 2-50). Next, click the text pointer to a place above the article, and use the Paste command to paste the text in that location. PageMaker creates a new text element that is separate from the body of the article. Now, select the heading and use the Type specs command (Figure 2-51) to set the type at 30-point Times Roman bold with 36 points of leading. Select the subheading and change it to 18-point Times Roman bold italic with 20 points of leading. To move the new text element, click

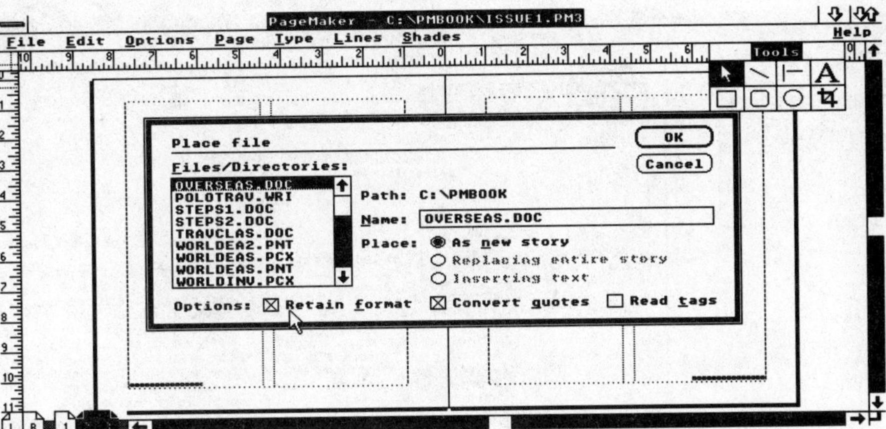

Figure 2-49. The Place dialog box, with the Retain format option and the Convert quotes option turned on.

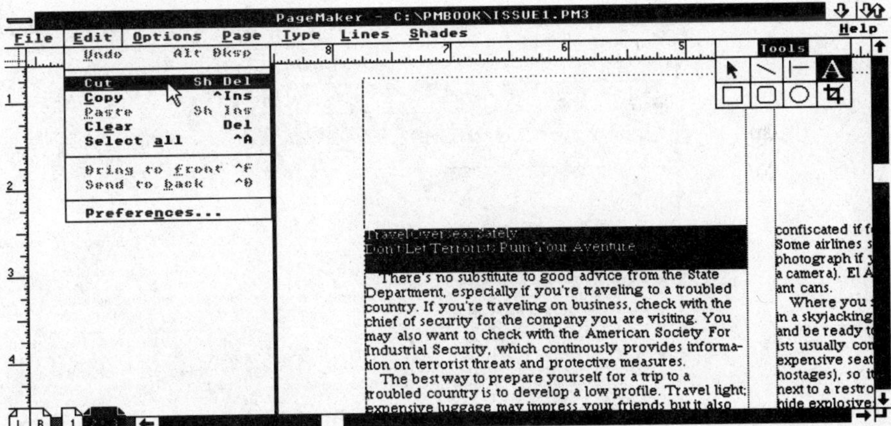

Figure 2-50. After selecting the heading and subheading text, use Cut to cut the text out of the text element and place it temporarily in the clipboard for the next use of the Paste command.

the middle of the headline and drag it into place. Next, drag the bottom left corner out toward the right margin to stretch the headline block so that the headline fits on one line (Figure 2-52).

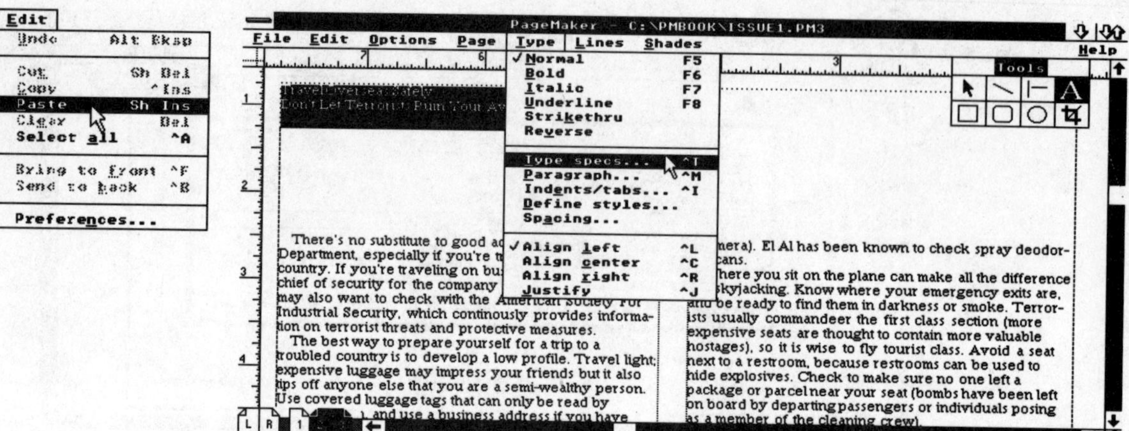

Figure 2-51. After pasting the text into place, choose Type specs to change the text's size and leading.

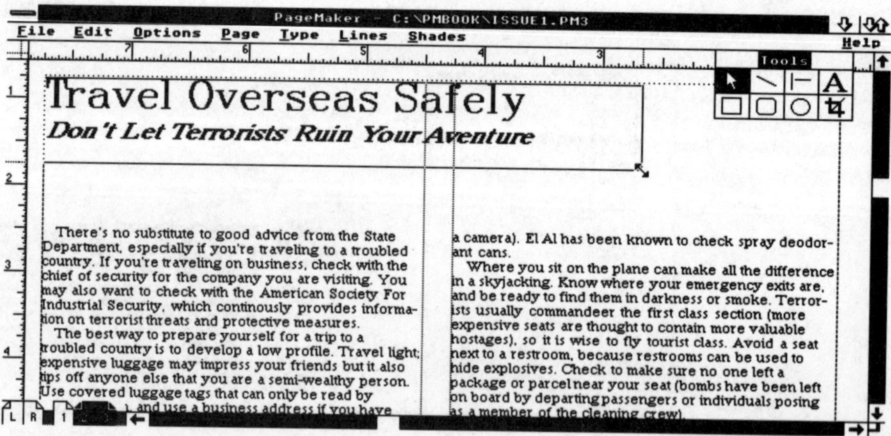

Figure 2-52. Stretch the headline (which is now a separate text element) so that the heading and subheading each fit on one line.

To continue the article in the next column, click the bottom handle of the text block (the pointer becomes a manual text flow icon as long as the Autoflow option is off) and click at the top of the next column. The text flows down to the bottom of the page. To extend the article to the next

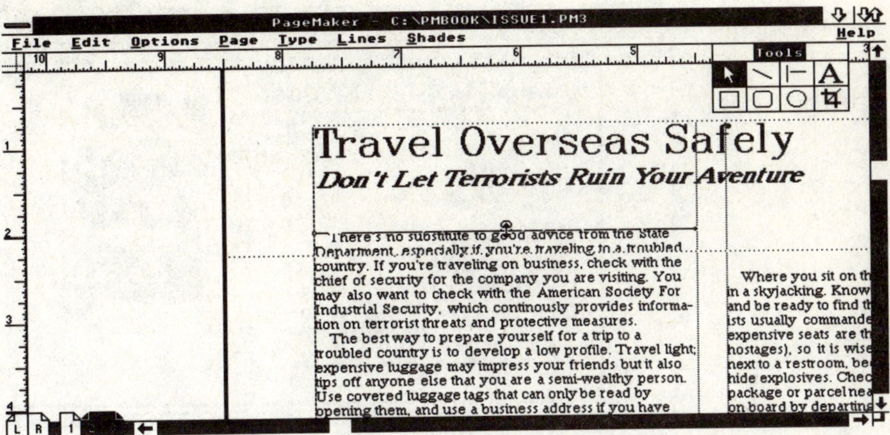

Figure 2-53. Adjust the top of the text block using a ruler guide.

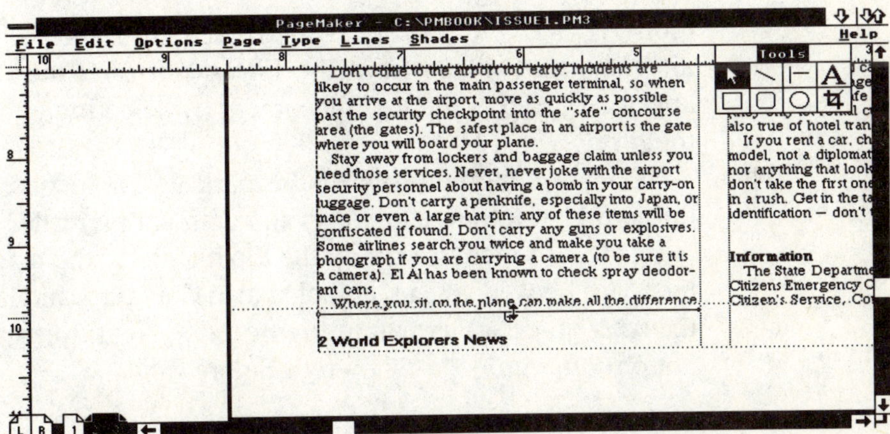

Figure 2-54. Adjust the bottom of the text block using a ruler guide.

page, click the bottom handle of the text block to get the text flow icon, and then click at the top of the column on page three. If you had a very long text file, you could continue to place text in columns on pages by clicking the bottom handle to get the text flow icon, and then switching pages by clicking the page marker icon. (You can switch pages or select options from some menus while using the text flow icon, but you can't switch

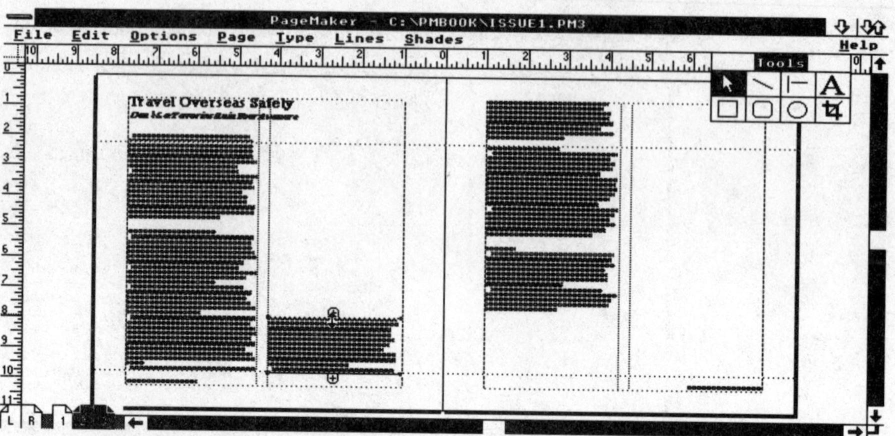

Figure 2-55. Move the text block out of the way to fit the special text.

tools.) If you have not yet begun to place a file, and you change your mind after choosing Place from the File menu (and the text flow icon has appeared), cancel the text placement by selecting another tool from the toolbox.

Drag a ruler guide down to the mark at 9 3/4 inches, then move up (use the scroll bar to move quickly) and drag another ruler guide down to the mark at 2 1/4 inches. Pull up the top handle of the text block to close up the space between the text block and the heading, and line up the text with the ruler guide, as shown in Figure 2-53. Next, line up the text with the bottom ruler guide, as shown in Figure 2-54.

Changing the Layout

PageMaker is versatile—you can try one layout, then change to another layout very quickly, without losing the first try. If you have enough space on disk, use the Save as command in the File menu to save the publication file under another name as a second version before you change the layout. In this way, you can go back later to the first version.

You may want to change the layout of the second and third pages. Assume that the second article does not fill up the entire two pages, and that you want to include a special section (a sidebar). You can move the

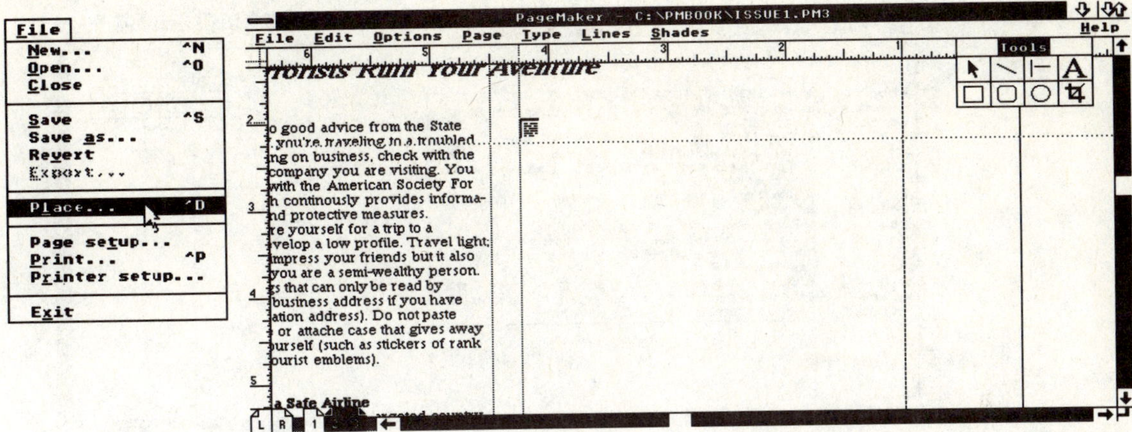

Figure 2-56. Use the Place command to place the sidebar text in the right column.

text block in the left column of page two (Figure 2-55) and the text block in the right column of page three out of the way, so that you can use those areas for the sidebar. Place the sidebar text file, and click the manual text flow icon at the top of the right column (Figure 2-56).

The sidebar consists of two lists, each with seven numbered items. The lists can be lined up side by side at the tops of the two columns, each boxed and shaded separately. Click the bottom of the text block at the seventh item (Figure 2-57), and continue placing the rest of the block in the left column of page three (Figure 2-58).

In order to put a box around a text block in a column, make the text block thinner than the column, and draw the box so that it aligns with the column margins. To make the text block thinner, select the text box with the pointer tool and drag the bottom left corner inward (Figure 2-59). It will be easier to move the text block if you turn off the Snap to guides option in the Options menu. (To turn this option off, select it in order to remove the check mark.) When the block is not attached to guides, it can be moved freely and placed very close to guides without becoming attached to them.

Position the text block so that it is centered in the column. Select the box tool and draw a box around the text by clicking a starting point above the top right corner of the text, and dragging across the text to a point

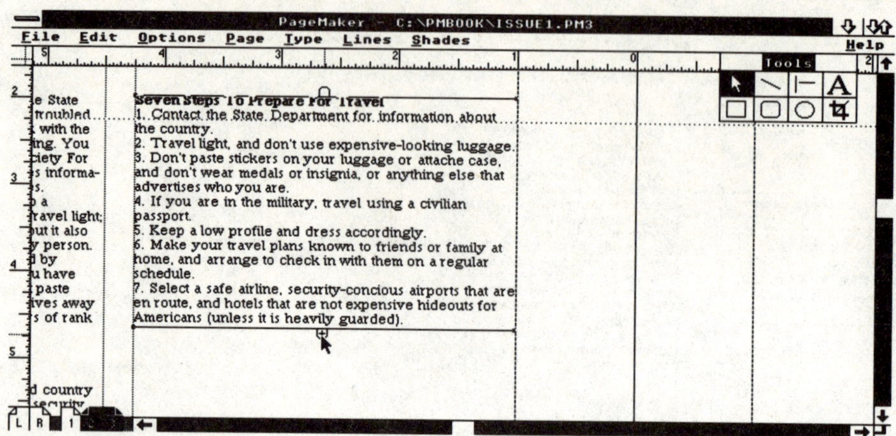

Figure 2-57. Click the bottom of the text block that holds the first seven items of the list.

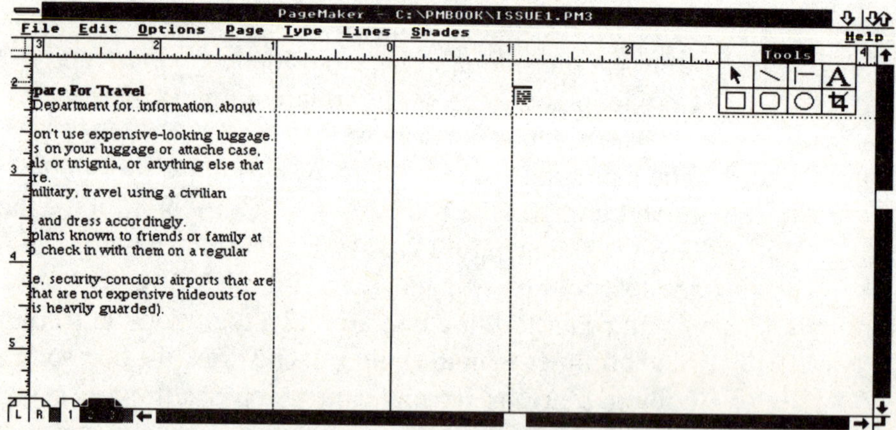

Figure 2-58. Place the second half of the text block on the next page in the left column.

below the bottom left corner, as shown in Figure 2-60. Line up the outer edges of the box with the column margins and leave the same amount of space at the top and bottom to separate the box from the inside text. When you release the mouse button, the program completes the box. If you don't

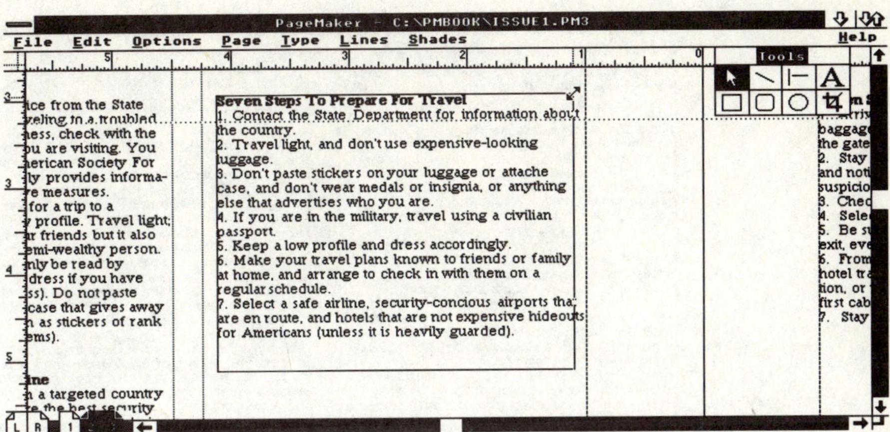

Figure 2-59. Change the text block's width to accommodate a box around the text.

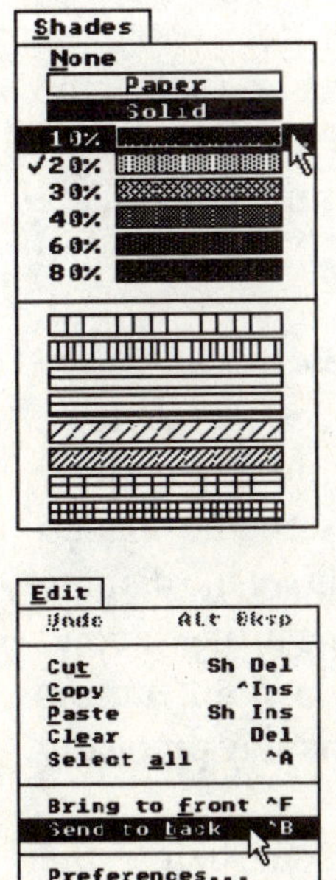

Figure 2-60. Draw a box around the text.

like the box, select the Undo command from the Edit menu, or simply press the Backspace key because the box is already selected (it has handles) in order to delete the box. You can also resize a selected box by dragging on one of its handles with the arrow pointer tool.

While the box is still selected (that is, displaying its handles), pick a line width from the Lines menu (such as a 1-point line), and a percentage

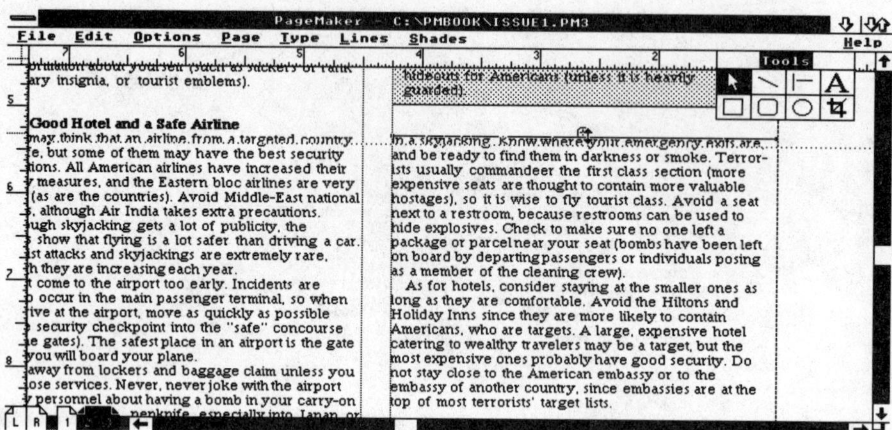

Figure 2-61. Drag the article up to fill the space, using a ruler guide to line up the text in all of the columns.

of gray shading from the Shades menu (such as 10%). After you select the shading, the box will look empty because the shading hides the text. To bring the text back into view, choose the Send to back command from the Edit menu. This command sends the selected shaded box into the background, behind the text.

Now you are finished with the first section of the newsletter. Move over to page three and apply the same treatment to the second section. Make the section of text thinner, center the text in the column, and draw a box around the text. Set the line width and shade, and send the shaded box into the background. While you are drawing the box, move the display window so that you can see the first box on page two and line up the second box on the same ruler mark. If you hold down the Alt key, the pointer turns into a "grabber hand." Use the grabber hand to move the display precisely and easily.

Drag the top handles of the article up to fill the space below the sidebars in both columns. Use a ruler guide to line up the text with the first column and the other columns (Figure 2-61). Drag the bottom handles down to the bottom ruler guide.

The article does not completely fill up the space, but you can push down the text in the left column of page three (Figure 2-62) and place a

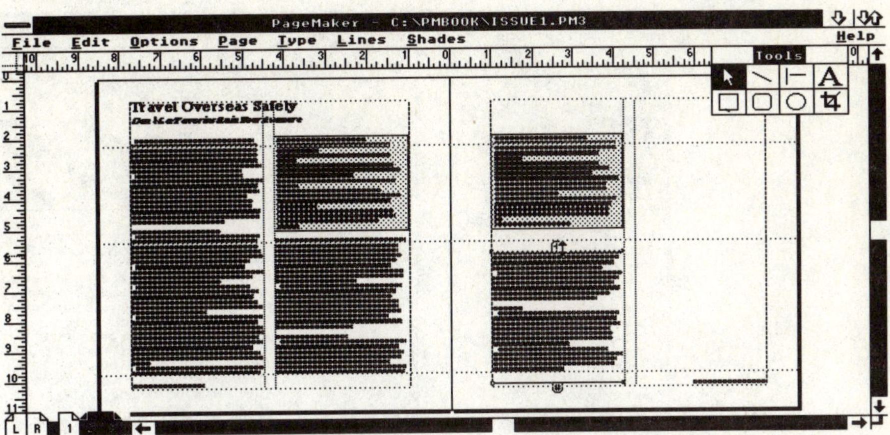

Figure 2-62. Move the text down to fill the space with a pull quote.

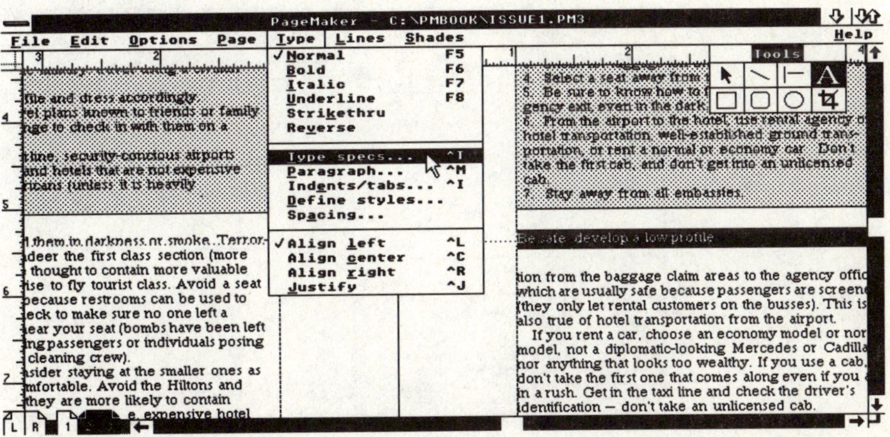

Figure 2-63. After typing a pull quote, select it with the text tool and change its type style and size.

pull quote, which is an excerpt set in a larger font and used to attract the reader's attention. Simply type the pull quote, or else use the Copy and Paste commands to copy text from the article. Select the text with the text tool. Change the text's font to Helvetica Italic at 18 points in size with 20 points of leading (Figure 2-63).

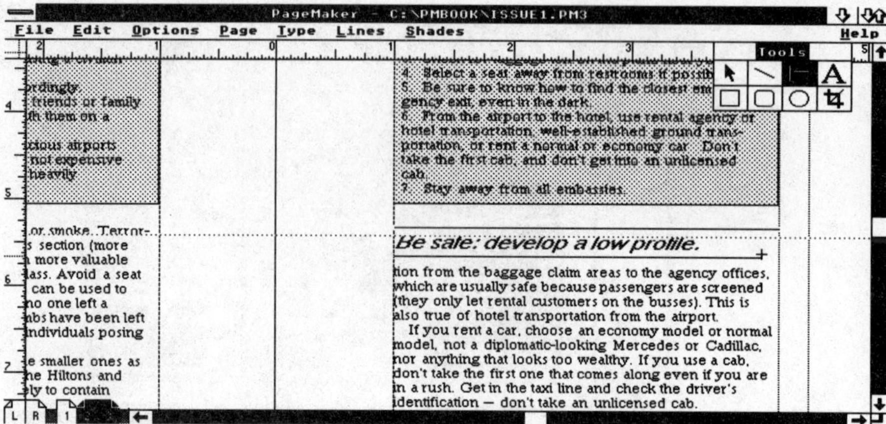

Figure 2-64. Move the pull quote into the column and draw lines above and below it.

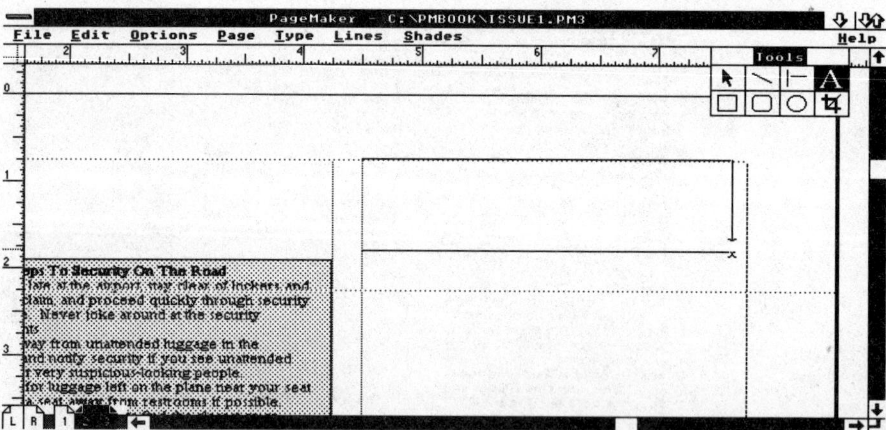

Figure 2-65. Drag the text editing pointer to define a new text block that will be used for typing text directly onto the page.

Drag a ruler guide down and align it with the text on page two (at the 5 3/8 inch mark). Use the pointer tool to select the text block under the pull quote. Drag the top handle up to a point below the pull quote, and then drag the bottom handle down to the bottom of the column. Push down on the top handle until the text is aligned properly with the text on the second

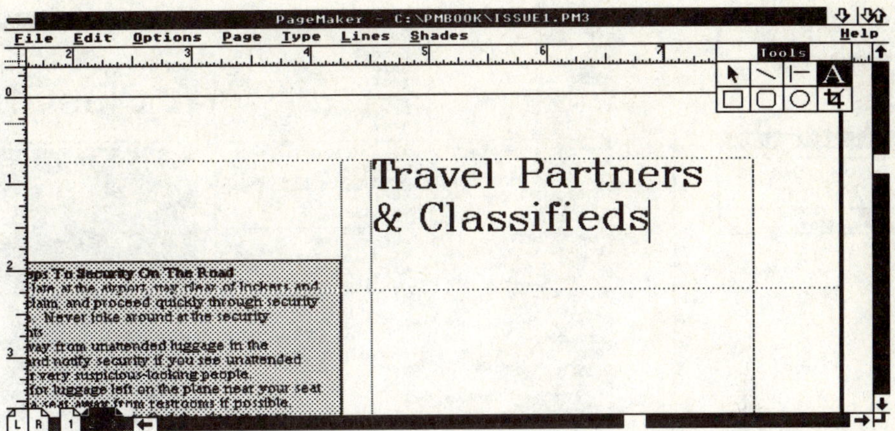

Figure 2-66. Type directly into the new text block after setting the Type specifications.

page and with the bottom ruler guide. Select the perpendicular-line drawing tool, and draw a 1-point line above and below the pull quote, as shown in Figure 2-64.

Placing More Articles

You now have a full first page, a full second page, and a half-full third page. You can place a third article (this example uses classified ad text) to fill the space on page three, and place another article (this example uses a questionnaire) for the fourth page.

Before placing the article, drag the text tool pointer across the top of the column in order to estimate the size of the text block (Figure 2-65). Then set the Type specifications to Times Roman 30-point bold text with 36-point leading. Finally, type the headline for the article (**Travel Partners & Classifieds**), as shown in Figure 2-66.

Choose Place from the File menu, and turn on the option to retain the formatting settings and to convert quotes. Place the article so that it starts near the top of the right column on page three. When the article is placed, go back up to the top and use the ruler guide to align the text.

The text is already formatted as 10-point Times Roman with 12 points of leading, but the tabs at the beginnings of paragraphs are not the same.

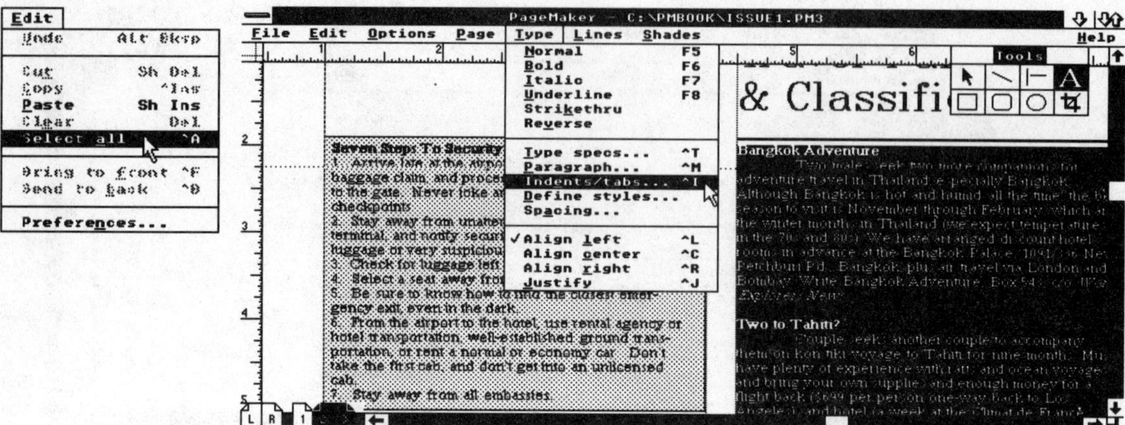

Figure 2-67. Select the entire text of the article, and change the tab setting.

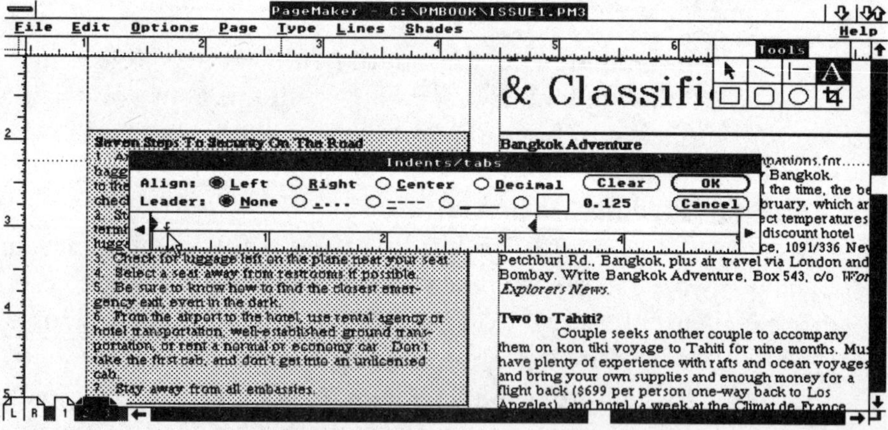

Figure 2-68. The Indents/tabs ruler shows more detail when the window is displaying at Actual size or 200% size (this is Actual size). The tiny down-pointing arrow above the ruler represents a tab stop.

To select the entire article text, click anywhere in the text with the text tool, and choose the Select all command from the Edit menu. The entire article is highlighted, and you can now change the type specifications or other settings (Figure 2-67). Change the tab setting with the Indents/tabs

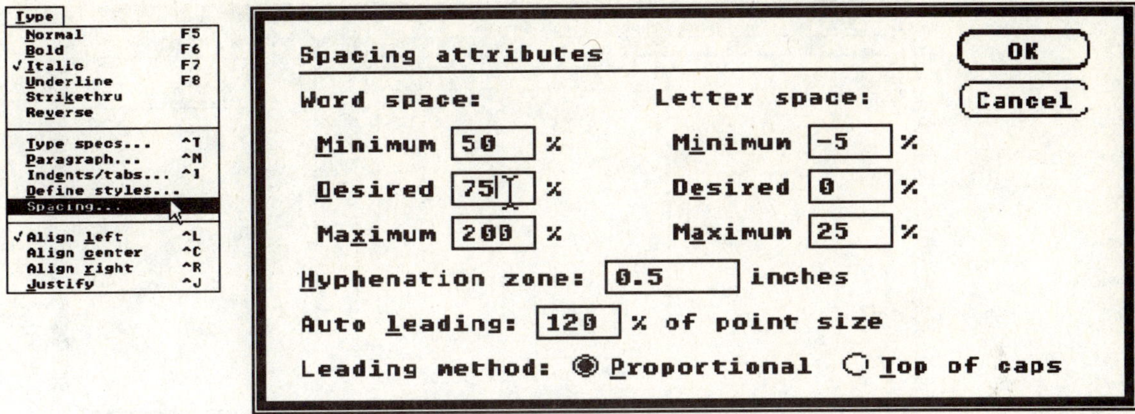

Figure 2-69. Reduce the desired word spacing (used for ragged right columns) to 75% of a regular space in order to fit the text in the column.

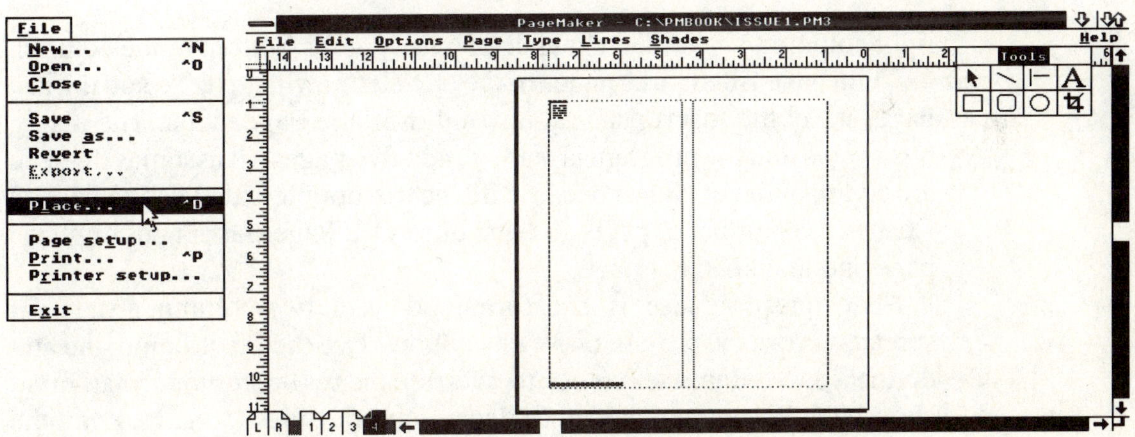

Figure 2-70. This icon appears after the text file to be placed is chosen, but before the manual text flow icon is clicked.

option in the Type menu (Figure 2-68).

Also, because the article is about one line too long, use the Spacing command in the Type menu (Figure 2-69) to reduce the Desired word spacing to 75%. (The Desired word spacing is the setting used for ragged-

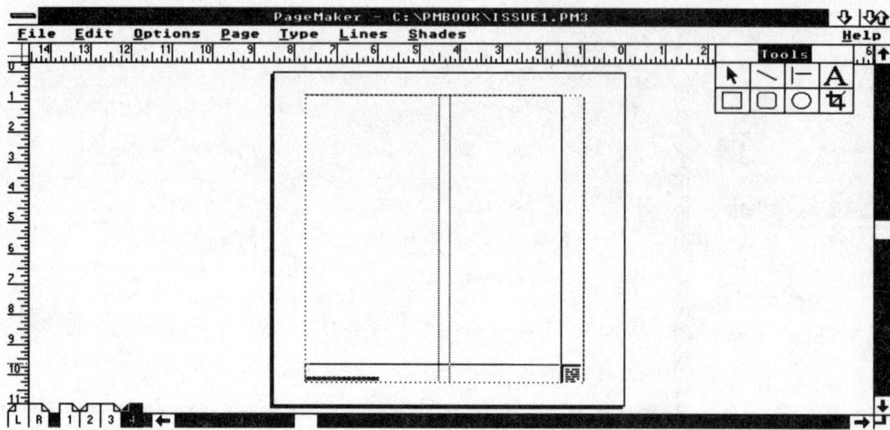

Figure 2-71. Drag the Place icon across the entire page to define a single-column text block and override the two-column format.

right columns.) Now the text ends precisely at the bottom of the column.

You have filled three pages of the newsletter with text. To add the last page, select the Insert pages command from the Page menu. The dialog box shows that the program is ready to add two pages. (It assumes that you are adding pairs of pages, because it is set for double-sided facing pages.) Change the number of pages to **1** and click OK. PageMaker adds only one page and displays that page.

The questionnaire is not formatted as a two-column article—it spreads across the page in one wide column. Use the Place command and define a one-column text block to override the two-column format. First, choose the Place command and filename for the questionnaire. Point the manual text flow icon at the top left corner of the page without clicking (Figure 2-70). Next, hold down the mouse button and drag the icon across the entire width and length of the page (Figure 2-71). When you release the mouse button, the questionnaire text fills the page in a single column.

Figure 2-72 shows the printed version of the page, printed with an AST TurboLaser/PS (a PostScript printer). If you don't use a PostScript printer, you can't use Zapf Dingbats (unless a version of this font is supplied for your laser printer). You can, however, use PageMaker's box tool to draw a small box and specify no shading or white shading, and a

WORLD EXPLORER PROFILE

NAME: ______________________________
ADDRESS: ______________________________
CITY/ST/ZIP: ______________________________
TELEPHONE: ______________________________

1. Would you use World Explorers specialty travel brokerage services prior to one of your next trips?
- ❑ For expert advice on destinations?
- ❑ For expert advice on skill development?
- ❑ For participation in tax deductible or scientific expeditions?
- ❑ For family or teenagers summer travel?
- ❑ For rapid identification of travel bargains, membership discounts and low airfares?
- ❑ Other (please specify): ______________________

2. What seasons do you prefer to travel?
❑ Winter ❑ Spring ❑ Summer ❑ Fall

3. Which of the following places would you like to visit in the next two years? (Put a 1 in the box of your first choice, a 2 in the box of your second choice; and fill any particular countries of interest)
- ❑ Continental US / Alaska / Canada
- ❑ Mexico & Central America
- ❑ South America
- ❑ Australia / New Zealand
- ❑ Hawaii & Pacific Islands
- ❑ South America
- ❑ Orient: China & Japan
- ❑ Indian Subcontinent / Himalayas
- ❑ South East Asia
- ❑ Africa & Middle East
- ❑ Islands: Caribbean & Mediterranean
- ❑ Europe (incl. Russia & UK)

Please indicate countries or states of interest:
Year 1: 1)____________ 2)____________ 3)____________
Year 2: 1)____________ 2)____________ 3)____________

4. If you are seeking travel services, what are they for?
- ❑ Family vacations
- ❑ Active Baby Boomers
- ❑ Trips open to all ages
- ❑ Summer adventures for teenagers

5. When travelling on a personal basis, what type of accommodations do you seek?
- ❑ Deluxe
- ❑ First Class
- ❑ Basic
- ❑ Bargain

6. Which type of trip are you interested in?
- ❑ Soft Adventures (exotic trips with deluxe / first class accommodations).
- ❑ Moderate Adventures (active tours for anyone in good physical health, may involve camping).
- ❑ Ultimate Adventures (very rugged and strenuous trips, high altitude treks and backpacking).
- ❑ Discovery Tours (informative travel; hone your photo skills, join and assist scientific expeditions).
- ❑ Leisure & Popular Tours (winter sun or powder skiing).

7. What are your interests when traveling?
- ❑ Wildlife
- ❑ Nature Tours
- ❑ Religions
- ❑ Scenery
- ❑ Birdwatching
- ❑ Tribes & Costumes
- ❑ Archeology
- ❑ Historical Sites
- ❑ Marine Life
- ❑ Local Festivals
- ❑ Music Festivals
- ❑ Spas, Health & Fitness

Other 1)____________ 2)____________ 3)____________

Date:____________ Signature:______________________

4 World Explorers News

Figure 2-72. The printed version of Page 4 (from a PostScript printer that prints the questionnaire's Zapf Dingbats symbols).

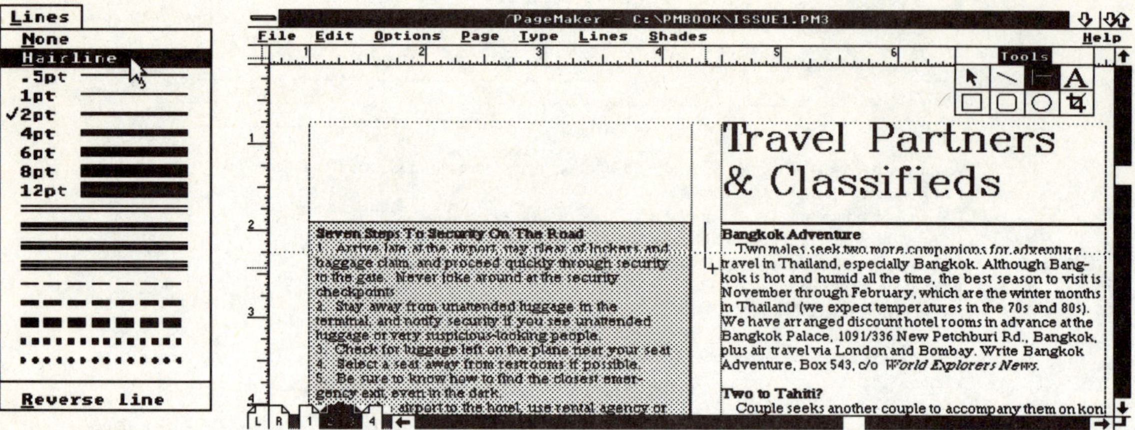

Figure 2-73. The starting point of the hairline column rule.

hairline or a half-point line. Then use the Copy and Paste commands to copy the box for every multiple-choice answer.

Adding Final Touches

You can add more graphic elements to the pages, such as vertical lines, called *column rules*, between the columns on each page. If you use an HP LaserJet or compatible printer driven by the Printer Control Language with the PCL driver supplied with Windows, allow extra time to print pages that have vertical lines (or else don't use vertical lines in your publication). Many designers prefer to see white space, rather than rules, between columns. The goal is to balance all of the elements on the page without crowding them. White space is considered to be as much of an element as are text, line art, rules, color, and halftones.

To draw a column rule, select the perpendicular-line drawing tool and choose a hairline from the Lines menu. Click the starting point for the rule at the top of the column where the body text starts (Figure 2-73). The pointer turns into a crossbar (+) so that you can line up the hairline to the ruler guides. Drag downward to draw the hairline to the bottom of the column (Figure 2-74), and then release the mouse button. With the

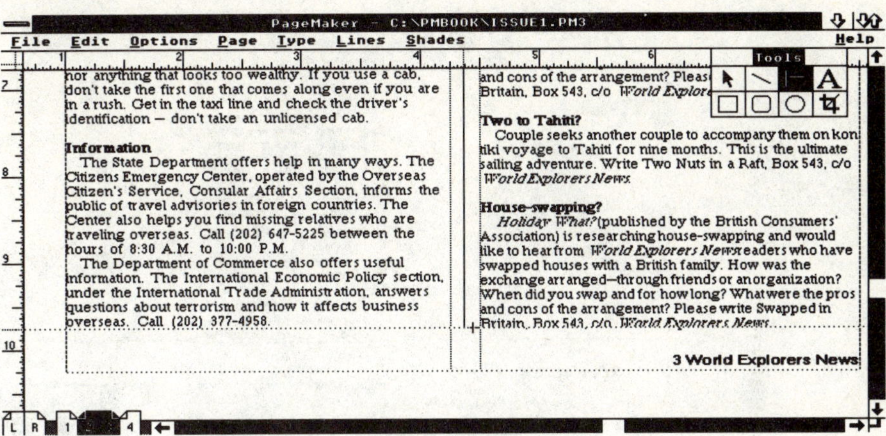

Figure 2-74. Drawing a perpendicular hairline column rule.

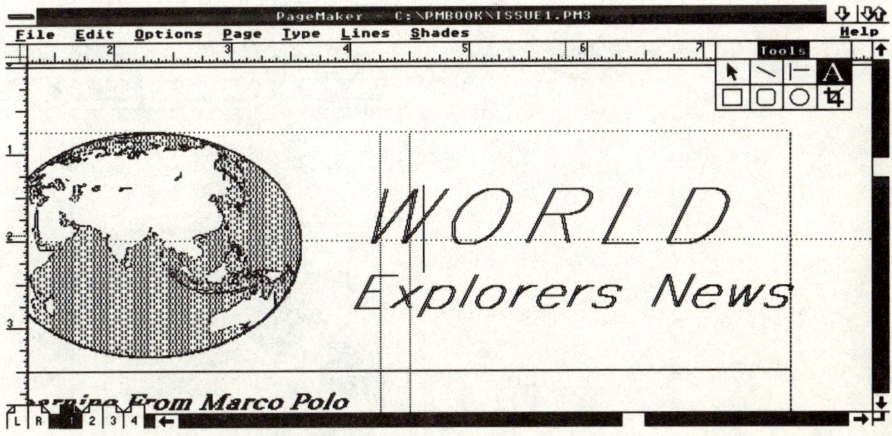

Figure 2-75. Manually kerning letters in the newsletter title.

perpendicular-line drawing tool still selected, turn to page two and add a hairline column rule to separate the two articles from the top to the bottom of the columns.

You can tinker with the newsletter title to make it more attractive. You can try a different font, or manually *kern* some of the letters (bring them closer together), especially at large type sizes. To kern a letter so that it is

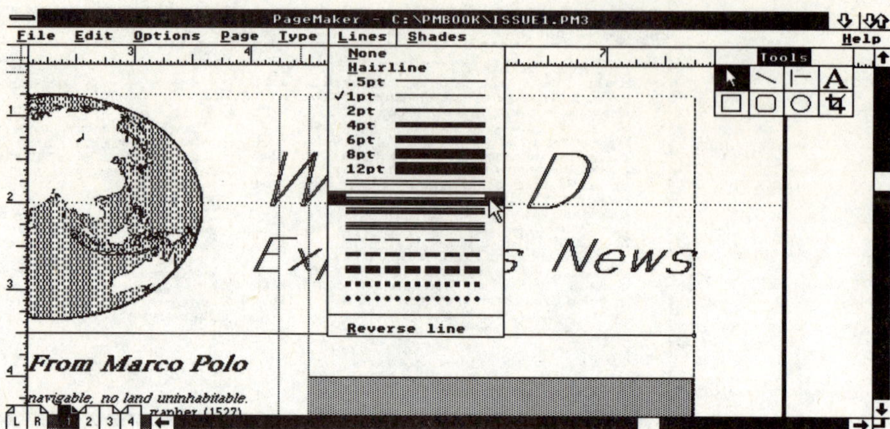

Figure 2-76. Change the line style of the line that separates the title from the body of the newsletter.

Figure 2-77. The finished front page, with a shaded box that represents a graphic image.

closer to the previous letter, click with the text tool just before the letter. Hold down the Control (Ctrl) key and press the backspace (or delete) key once for each increment of space to be deleted between the letters (Figure 2-75).

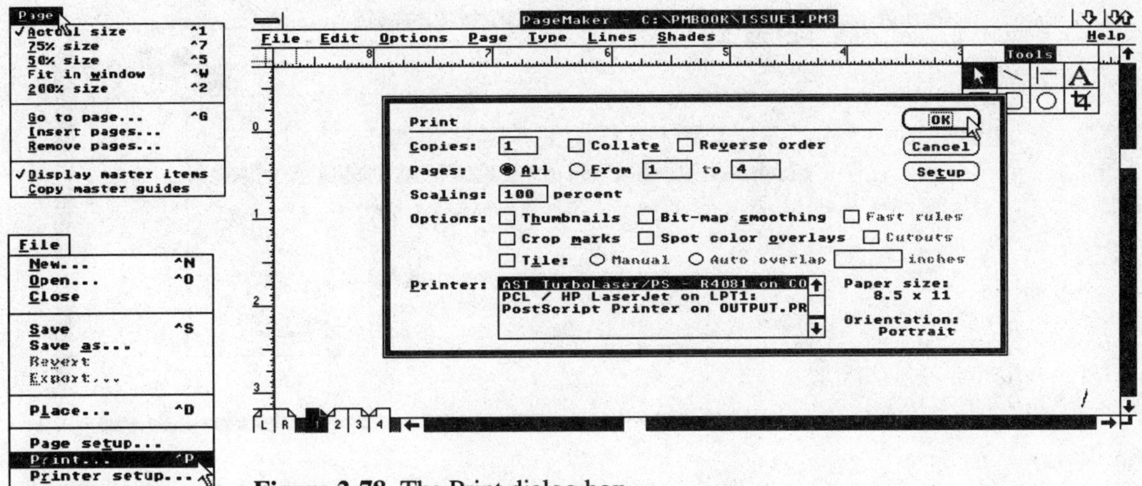

Figure 2-78. The Print dialog box.

Another enhancement that can be made to the newsletter title is to change the line style of the line underneath the title. Select the line with the arrow pointer tool and choose a line style from the Lines menu (Figure 2-76). The newsletter's front page now contains every element except the graphic image (Figure 2-77).

Save your file when you have finished making changes. PageMaker performs a mini-save operation whenever you turn the page, so even if the system crashes, you will not lose much of your work. You can revert back to the layout of the publication file at the time of the last full save operation. You can also revert back to the last mini-save operation by holding down the Shift key when you select Revert.

Printing the Publication

Before you print the publication, return to the title page (page one) and select the Display master items option from the Page menu. This option (which is usually turned on and marked with a check mark) means that PageMaker copies text and graphic items (such as footers) from the master pages to the selected page for displaying and printing. The only master item in this example is a page number footer, which is usually left

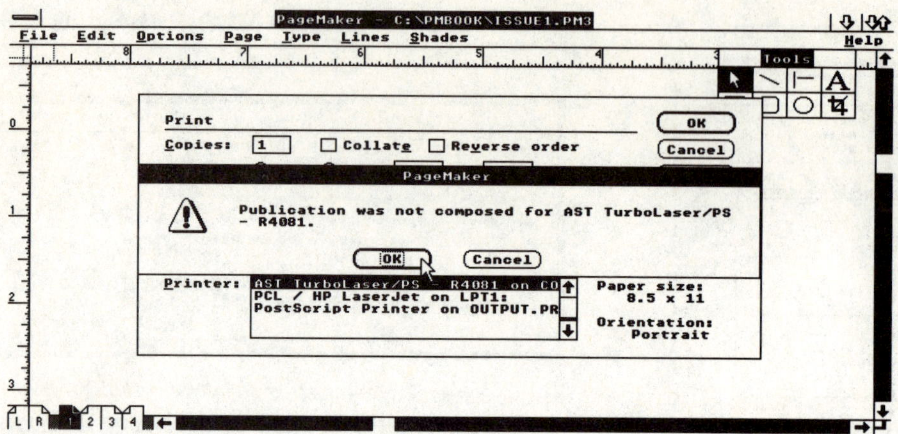

Figure 2-79. If you select a different printer from the one already assigned, this message appears, to ask for confirmation. PageMaker automatically recomposes a publication for a different printer, but this operation may change line endings of text.

off of the title page. Turn off the display (and printing) of master items for page one by selecting the option again (the check mark disappears). The option remains on for the other pages.

You are now ready to print the pages that you have assembled. Select the Print command from the File menu to display the dialog box shown in Figure 2-78.

Depending upon your printer, you can select several print options. Click OK to accept the default settings (one complete copy at 100 percent scaling factor printed in the usual order of pages for your printer) or the last settings that you chose for printing. You can select any number of copies, and/or specify a range of pages to be printed. Other options include *thumbnails* (mini-pages that are useful in design and production planning), collated copies, printing in reverse order, crop marks, and printing pages larger or smaller than the original page size. You can even print with tiling settings for oversized pages. (*Tiling* is the process of printing a large image on several pages so that edges of the image can be overlapped and pasted together.)

You specified the margins for the page in the Page setup dialog box when you first created the publication file. The default settings are usually fine for all printers. If you change those settings, refer to your printer manual to be sure that your design does not extend beyond the maximum print area of the printer. You can choose Page setup from the File menu to change the margin settings, but that method will affect your layout and will make changes that you may not want. To print the complete pages without changing the layout, select the Print dialog box from the File menu at print time, and scale the publication to less than 100 percent (if your printer supports scaling).

If you select a different printer than the printer you had assigned before, PageMaker displays a confirmation message that warns you that the publication was composed for a different printer (Figure 2-79). You can cancel the new printer assignment, or retain it by clicking OK. If you retain the new printer assignment, PageMaker may recompose the entire publication for the new printer because PageMaker must use the new printer's font information to perform proper kerning, justification, and spacing. For this reason, you may want to open a file as a copy, rather than opening the original file (both methods are options in the Open dialog box), before you print to a different printer, so that the original file remains intact.

The recompose operation should take no longer than a few minutes (or a few seconds for a short publication). It may change the line lengths of some lines of text, so look over your publication carefully. For this reason, you should always have the appropriate printer in mind at the outset.

Summary

If you follow the steps presented in this chapter, you can successfully complete four pages of a newsletter and print them with excellent results. A summary of the desktop publishing steps discussed in this chapter appears below.

Starting PageMaker

First, choose a printer. Next, open a template file (such as the templates included in *Aldus Portfolio: Designs for Newsletters*), or else choose New from the File menu. Use or modify the default page setup so that you have double-sided, facing 8 1/2- by 11-inch pages, with a 1-inch inside margin, and 3/4-inch outside, top, and bottom margins.

Designing Master Pages
Choose Column guides from the Options menu in order to specify the number of columns for setting up a layout grid, which can be changed later. Use the toolbox to create left- and right-hand footers, to place automatic page numbering markers, and to position all other elements on the left and right master pages that you want to repeat on all left- or right-hand pages.

Saving Your Publication File
Choose Save from the File menu, and give your new publication file a name. If you want to preserve the original file, choose Save as from the File menu and give your new publication file a new name. Save your file as often as necessary to prevent lost work.

Designing Title Page
The Option menu offers Rulers with a selectable unit of measurement. You can use default rulers, which measure in inches, or else select Preferences from the Edit menu in order to display centimeters or picas. The Option menu also offers Snap to guides (which are on by default). Snap to guides are used to create an attraction between the elements that you place and any column guides that you have set, so that elements automatically attach to the column guides they are closest to, creating automatic precision alignment of elements to columns.

Typing Text
Select Type specs from the Type menu and choose a font, style, size, and leading, then click the text tool. Move the I-beam text editing pointer into position. Click the left mouse button to establish an insertion point (if Snap to guides are on, the insertion point will snap to the nearest guide), and start typing. Text automatically wraps (and hyphenates, if hyphenation is set to automatic) to the next line if the text extends past the right margin setting.

Changing Width of a Text Block
Select the pointer tool from the toolbox (the I-beam icon changes back into an arrow pointer) and drag the bottom right corner of the text block to the desired width.

To move the title into position on the page, position the pointer tool over the title and press down — but don't release — the mouse button. The four-arrows icon appears to indicate that you can move the selected text or graphics element to a new position on the page. After the element is repositioned, release the mouse button to fix the element at the new position (if Snap to guides are on, they will affect the placement).

Drawing Circles and Horizontal Rules
To draw a circle, select the oval drawing tool. To size the circle, move the crossbar icon into position on the page and hold down the Shift key while dragging to the right and down (not holding the Shift key draws an oval.)

To draw a horizontal rule, select the perpendicular-line tool. Move the crossbar pointer to the starting position, click the mouse to start drawing the line, and drag the line until you reach the end position for the line.

Placing Graphics
Use the pointer tool and select Place from the File menu. Select from a list of suitable graphics files (paintings, drawings, scanned images, charts, or graphs in formats that PageMaker recognizes). Click the place button, or double-click the file name. Move the icon into position on the page and click to place the file. After placement, you can scale graphics by dragging a corner handle of the selected image. You can also select an image at any time and scale it. To scale in proportion without distortion, hold down the Shift key while dragging a corner handle of the image. For paint-type graphics, use built-in sizes for the target printer by holding down the Control (Ctrl) key while dragging. Use both the Control and Shift keys to resize a paint-type graphic in proportion and to get the best results on the target printer.

You can also place a graphic by using the Copy (or Cut) command from the Edit menu to copy the graphic from a Windows application. Then use Paste to place the image on the PageMaker page.

Placing Formatted Text

After selecting the Place command and a text file that contains text formatted by a word processing program, you can place the formatted text with the Retain format option on. If this option is turned off, you can place the text and ignore its formatting settings. If you are not retaining the text's format, first change any of PageMaker's default type specifications that you need to change, before you place the file.

Autoflow (in the Options menu) must be turned off if you want to manually flow text from column to column. Move the text flow icon to the desired position on the page and click once to place the first column (if Snap to guides are on, the column flows within the preset columns). After selecting the article's headline with the text tool, change the Type specs (from the Type menu) to be bigger and bolder. Push up or drag down on the bottom handle of the text block to position the end of the column. Click on the bottom handle in order to continue placing text in the next column.

After placing the text, you can select text and then change type specs, tab settings, word spacing and letterspacing for the entire article, the amount of text on the page, and the page size view. You can insert pages, change settings that affect the page (such as Display master items and Copy master guides), turn the page, and place more text (with new Type specification settings if needed). To change the type specifications and the position of headings and subheadings, select them with the text tool.

Changing the Layout

Change the layout to include sidebars of boxed text. Adjust column widths to be narrower so that they fit within a box. Set the box line style, width, and shading. Create and place a pull quote and change its type specifications, and resize the column width of the separate block.

Placing More Articles

Adjust the headline of an article to be wider, and reposition the headline on the page. Pull the first column text block to a better starting position by pulling up on its top handle. You can place preformatted text (retaining its formatting settings) and still apply new settings for tabs and word spacing or even change the Column guide settings in order to place a file that was formatted to be one column wide onto a two-column page, with the same line endings. Add special symbols and characters by using defined Control (Ctrl) key sequences.

Final Touches

Add column hairline rules, and kern headline type (if necessary) to bring letters closer together. If desired, draw vertical rules as column separators. If you have a PCL-type printer (such as the HP LaserJet or LaserJet Plus), the rules may take an extremely long time to print, so you may want to avoid using them.

Printing the Publication

Select the Print command from the File menu. Specify print options (if your printer supports them) such as thumbnails, whether to print all pages or a specified range of pages, the number of copies of each page to be printed, collated or not, printed in reverse order or not, printed with or without crop marks, scaled in size to print smaller or larger than the original or to print at 100 percent size, and whether to use tiling (which controls options for printing oversize publications across several pieces of paper). If you select a different printer than the printer you had previously assigned, PageMaker displays a confirmation message to let you either cancel or continue the new printer assignment. If you continue with the new printer assignment, PageMaker may recompose the publication for the new printer. You may want to open a file as a copy, rather than opening the original file (in the Open dialog box) before printing to a different printer, so that the original file remains intact.

3 Business Reports and Manuals

This chapter describes how to design and produce mid-sized to large publications, such as an annual business report or a full-size instruction manual. One characteristic that these publications have in common is that they should be designed with a consistent format, in order to present a unified image of the company or product and to make the publications more readable.

Because the readers of such documents usually do not read them by choice, use a simple design with consistent treatment of titles, headings, subheadings, charts, figures, and so on in order to present the information more clearly. Your company logo together with a unified design scheme can be effectively used for all of your documents—business cards, letterhead and envelopes, product packaging, documentation, annual reports, and advertising—to present an image that will be remembered.

You can enforce a uniform style for a publication by creating master pages and then saving the publication as a blank template publication file. Graphics from one publication can be easily copied into another by using the Copy and Paste commands in the Edit menu.

You can also start with a template for one type of publication, modify the template for use with another type of publication, and then use the Save as command to save the modified publication as a new template without changing the first template.

PageMaker is a good program to use for the production of an annual report or manual because it can accept charts, graphs, and illustrations from different programs or even from different types of computers. The report or manual can be printed on a laser printer for final proofing, updated very quickly, and then transferred to a typesetter for a very professional look. (The typesetter prints with a much higher resolution of 1270 or 2540 dpi, compared to the typical laser printer resolution of 300 dpi.)

PageMaker can handle any type of document that is up to 128 pages in size. Most instruction manuals and reference manuals are broken up into sections, and you can use PageMaker to produce each section separately. To do so, create a publication file for each section or chapter (each file can contain up to 128 pages). PageMaker provides automatic page numbering (up to page 9999), starting with any page number, and even produces page numbers such as "Page 4-2" (section 4, page 2).

Annual Business Report

Reports usually include charts, spreadsheets, and specialized graphics. (Chapter 1 describes all of the programs that can generate such elements for PageMaker pages—nearly every popular program for PCs is supported by PageMaker.) A report should also have the company logo (which can be placed on every page in the footer), a title page, and perhaps graphics or photos.

You can follow along with the example presented in this chapter by typing enough text to fill a few pages, or by borrowing text from a file that you already have. You can also create a company logo, such as the logo in the following example, by altering one of the supplied graphic files in the PageMaker tutorial. (To alter the graphics file, use Microsoft Windows Paint, which comes with Windows.) Charts and graphs can be produced by various programs, including Lotus 1-2-3 and Microsoft Chart. For this example, Micrografx Windows "Draw!" was used to enhance a set of Lotus 1-2-3 charts and graphs before placing them onto PageMaker pages.

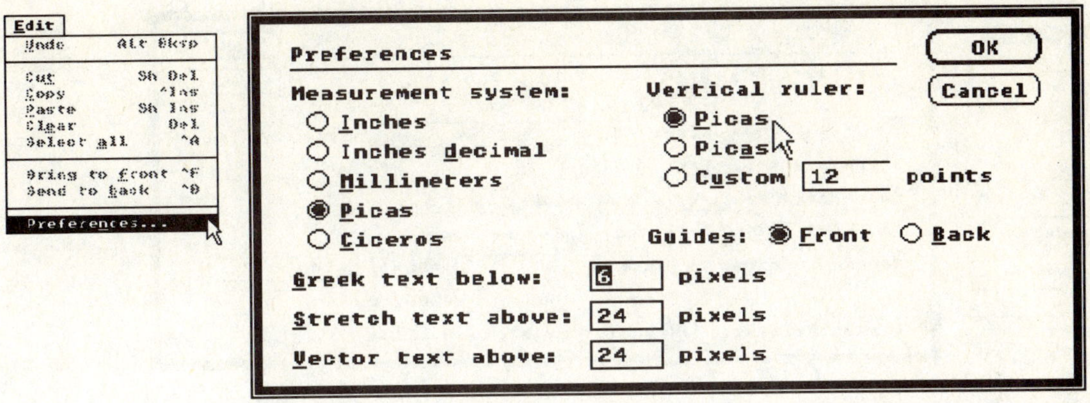

Figure 3-1. The Preferences dialog box allows you to set different ruler measurements. Both rulers are set to picas.

Setting up the Master Pages

An annual report should look sophisticated. Lay out the text with enough white space surrounding it so that the text appears very important. The design chosen for this example—one wide ragged-right margin, with headings, subheadings, and pull quotes in a thinner marginal column—helps preserve white space.

The process of laying out this design involves the use of a new measuring system that allows elements to be more precisely lined up on a page: picas and points. There are 12 points in every pica, and 72 points (6 picas) in an inch. You can change the rulers in PageMaker to display picas and points, or even to display picas and points on one ruler and inches on the other ruler. To change the ruler measurements, select the Preferences option from the Edit menu (Figure 3-1). For the examples in this chapter, set both rulers to picas and click OK. Changing the rulers does not change the placement of elements that have been previously positioned in the layout using a different measuring system. You can change the rulers at any time, whether a publication is open or not, so you always have the benefit of switching the unit of measurement on your rulers.

Begin the business report example by designing the master pages for a new publication file. Choose the standard tall orientation (Figure 3-2)

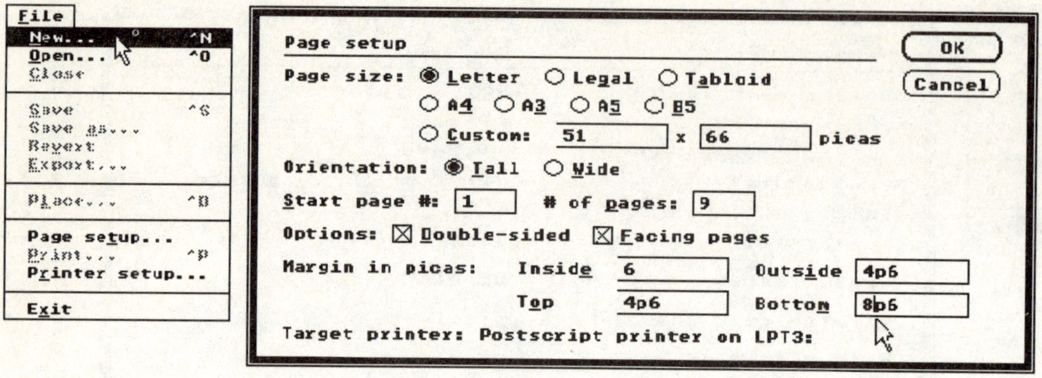

Figure 3-2. The page setup menu appears immediately after a New publication is selected from the File menu.

with the Double-sided and Facing pages options on. PageMaker creates two master pages—one for the right-facing page, and one for the left-facing page. Define the publication length as at least nine pages (you can add more pages or delete extra pages later). Change the default page margins so that the bottom margin is redefined as 8 picas and 6 points (8p6), rather than as 4p6. This step leaves enough space at the bottom of each page for both a footer and white space. (Always design pages with some thought to leaving enough white space for a more pleasing, less crowded look.)

Next, define the default column formatting for all pages of the report. (This default, of course, can be overridden on individual pages.) Switch to the left-right master pages, and unlock the guides if they are locked. The presence of a check mark next to the Lock guides option (above the Column guides option in the Options menu) indicates that the guides are locked. To unlock the guides, select the option until the check mark disappears. Then select Column guides, and change the number of columns to **2** (Figure 3-3). Change the space between columns to **1p6** (one pica, six points).

When the guides are unlocked, you can drag them in order to change the column widths. Drag the right-hand column guide on the left master page (Figure 3-4) over to the left side of the page, and line the guide up with the marker at 33p6. Scroll the screen over to the right master page,

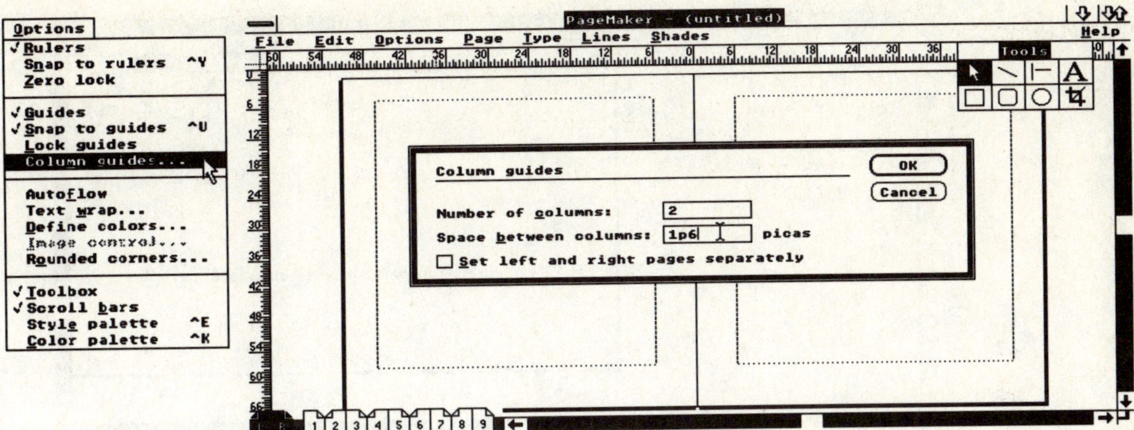

Figure 3-3. Change the number of columns to 2, and the space between columns to 1 pica and 6 points.

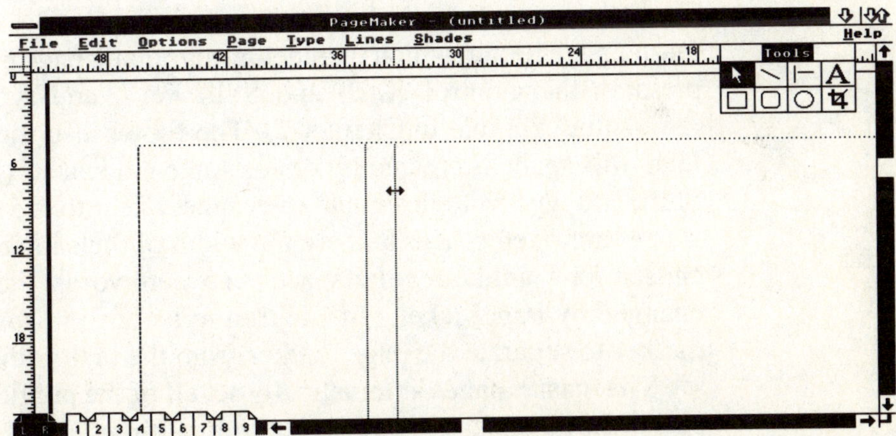

Figure 3-4. Move the unlocked column guide on the left master page to a custom position for all of the left-hand pages in the publication.

and line up its right-hand column guide on the 19-pica mark. Both pages should now have the same column layout.

Add page number footers to the master pages, as shown in Chapter 2. In the Type specs dialog box, set the footer text to be in Helvetica 10 point type with automatic leading. Figure 3-5 shows a closeup view of the left-

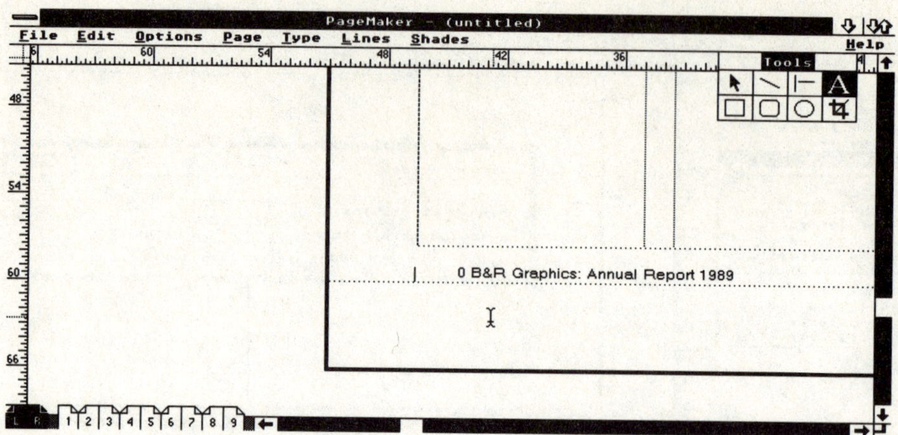

Figure 3-5. A different footer is set for left and right pages, with space to drop in a logo.

master page footer, which includes an automatic page number inserted by pressing the Control (Ctrl) and Shift keys, and typing 3 (as in the newsletter example in Chapter 2). The footer also includes space for a logo; this space is created by typing three em spaces (press Control and Shift, and type M to designate each space) next to the page marker. (*Em spaces* are fixed spaces that are the width of the capital letter "M" in the chosen font; unlike regular spaces between words, these spaces are not changed by PageMaker.) In addition, type one em space after the page marker to separate the page marker from the text of the footer.

The master pages automatically set all of the publication file's pages so that the pages start with these column settings and include footers. You can override these settings on each page and remove the footers, for example, or change the column layout.

Corporate Logo

If you place a company logo on the master pages, it appears in the report at the same location on every page. To create the logo, digitize a sketch or a previously designed logo on paper with a desktop scanner. The scanner creates a file that contains a bit map of the logo. You can edit and retouch the pixels on the screen by using a paint program (PC Paintbrush,

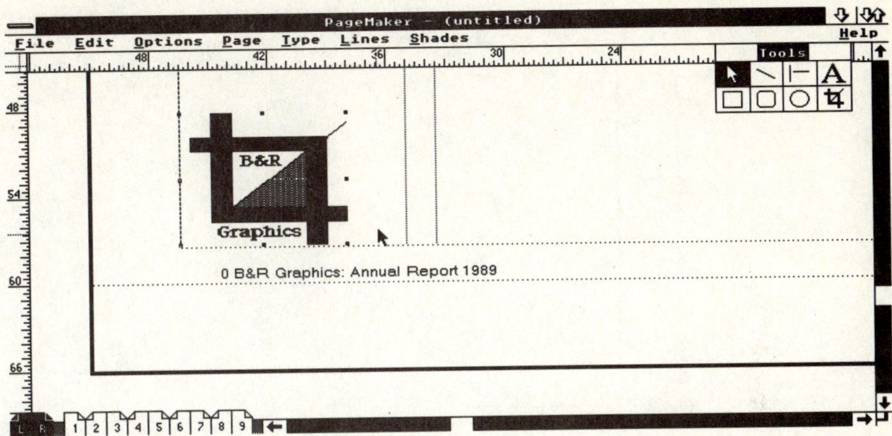

Figure 3-6. Place a logo on the left master page.

Microsoft Windows Paint, or others described in Chapter 1).

For this example, Microsoft Windows Paint was used to modify a version of the cropping tool image supplied on the PageMaker Tutorial disk (CROPTOOL.MSP in the PMTUTOR subdirectory), resulting in a simple logo. A triangle with a gray shade and a company name were added. If you prefer, you can use the sample cropping tool image supplied by Aldus, which is the same size and shape.

No matter which method you choose to use for creating a logo, you can manipulate the logo in PageMaker, as long as you use a graphics file format compatible with PageMaker. (Chapter 1 describes graphics file formats and graphics programs.) If you use a color graphics program, replace color selections with black-and-white patterns because the color selections in most programs do not correspond to standard color inks used by volume printers. You can supply a black-and-white version of the logo and then specify colors for volume printing.

To use the logo with PageMaker, switch to the Actual size view. Use the Place command from the File menu to place the logo's graphic file. Select the left master page and click the mouse to place the image (Figure 3-6). If the graphic is a line drawing (without patterns or many details), resize it by dragging a handle until the graphic is the right size for your layout. If the graphic has a pattern or contains fine detail, hold down the

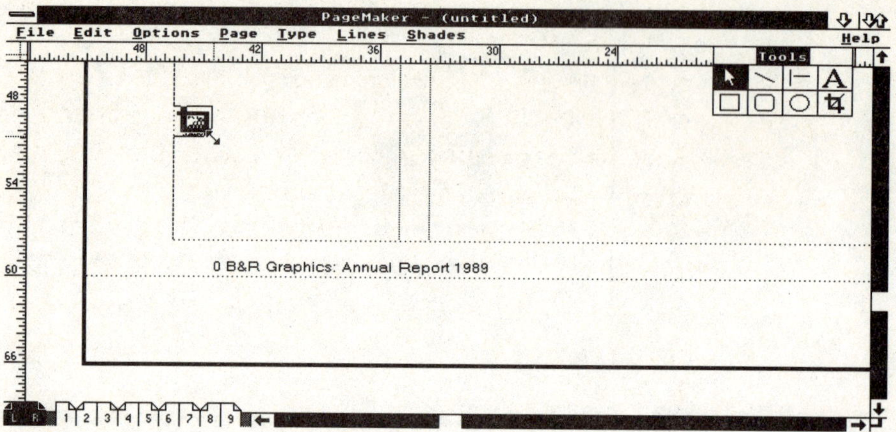

Figure 3-7. Scale the logo down in an equal ratio.

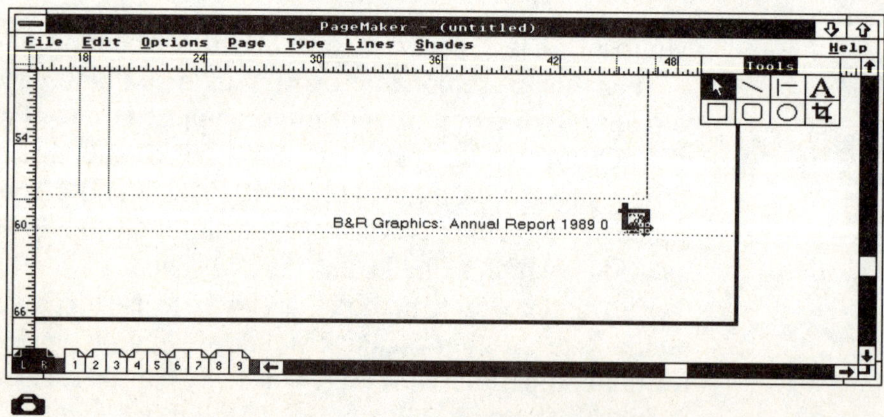

Figure 3-8. Place the logo on the master right page.

Control (Ctrl) key to automatically select the optimal sizes for your target printer. In addition, hold down the Shift key while resizing in order to keep the same proportions in the logo (and then release the mouse button before releasing the Control (Ctrl) and Shift keys). If you do not follow these steps, you can distort the image of the logo by stretching or compressing it from any side. In Figure 3-7, the logo is resized by holding down the Shift and Control (Ctrl) keys while dragging the lower right corner inward. This process scales the logo down in size and retains the logo's proportions.

After you scale the graphic to a size that fits in the space to the left on the footer, release the mouse button and then release the Control and Shift keys. While the graphic is still selected, choose Copy from the Edit menu to copy the logo into the Clipboard. Next, switch to the master right page and choose Paste from the Edit menu. Move the newly pasted graphic into position next to the footer on the master right page (Figure 3-8). The logos and footers will be repeated on every left and right page, unless you turn off the automatic Display of master items (in the Page menu) on any particular page.

Corporate Template

At this point, it makes sense to save a version of this publication as a blank template that other people in your company can use. The publication has a convenient footer with a logo on each page. To use this set of master pages for any other type of corporate report, all you have to do is change the text of the footer.

To save the publication as a template, choose the Save as command (or Save command because this is an untitled publication). Check the box marked Template, rather than accepting the default option (which is a standard publication). Supply an eight-character name without a file extension (such as **CORPORAT**). The Template option automatically appends the extension ".PT3" to the name (forming CORPORAT.PT3), so that you can launch PageMaker by double-clicking the template. This chapter describes how to use templates later.

Now, use the Save as command to save the template as a regular publication file under another name. Click the box next to Publication in the Save as dialog box, and type a new publication name (such as **ANNUAL89**). The Publication option automatically appends the extension ".PM3" to the name (forming ANNUAL89.PM3), so that you can launch PageMaker by double-clicking the name of this report.

The First Page

The text of the report can be preformatted, with the font, the type size, and the leading already set, and then brought into PageMaker using Place and

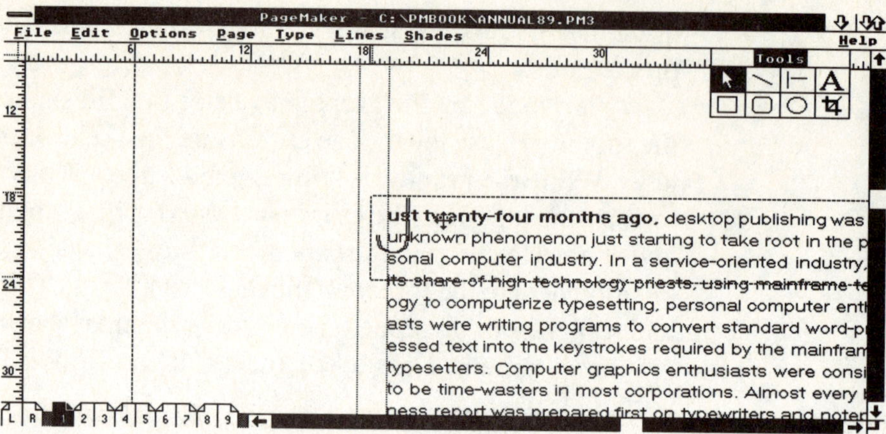

Figure 3-9. Move the large first character into position.

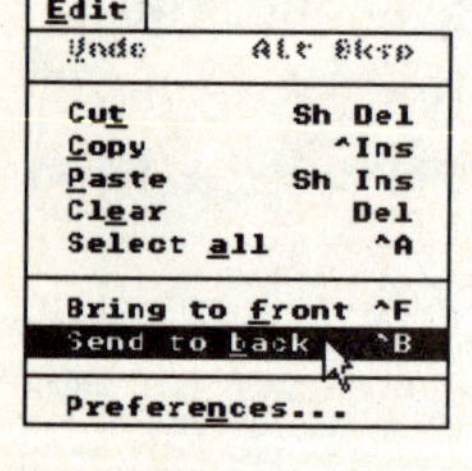

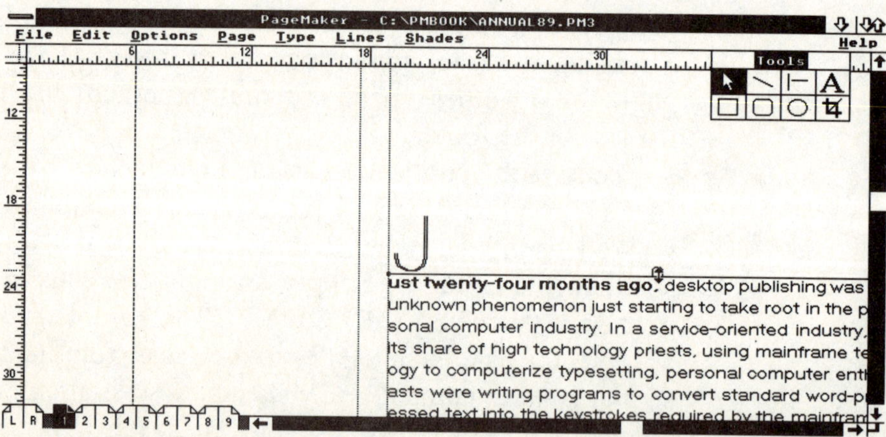

Figure 3-10. Push down the text from the top, and then click the handle to get the text flow icon.

the Retain format option. Alternatively, you can select the font, the type size, and the leading in the Type specs dialog box, and then bring the text into PageMaker using Place without the Retain format option. 12-point Helvetica and 16 points of leading are used for the body of the example report.

Place the text on the first page in the wide column at the 18-pica mark. The first phrase in the text file should be set in a bold style. After all of the

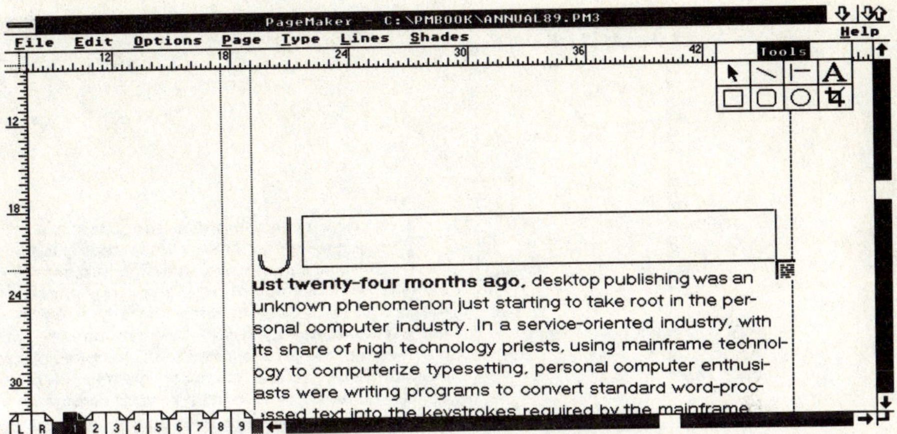

Figure 3-11. Drag the text flow icon across the column to define the new text element for the first three lines of text.

text has been placed, move back to the first page. To do so, click each previous page icon, one at a time; click the page icon scroll arrow; or press the Control (Ctrl), Shift, and Tab keys to move back one page at a time. Click the page 1 icon to move quickly to the first page. If you turned off the scroll bar display, use the Go to page command in the Page menu, and specify Page **1**.

To set the first letter as a large capital letter that extends below the baseline of the first line (this type of letter is sometimes called a large *dropped initial* or *dropped cap*), first highlight the letter by choosing the text tool and dragging across the letter. Cut the letter from the text and paste the letter back onto the pasteboard area or onto the page above the body text. Click an insertion point immediately after the large letter and press Enter in order to ensure that the line length of the large character is accurate. Choose the Type specs menu, and change the font size to 60 points with 70 points of leading.

Move the large letter back into the top part of the text, flush with the left margin of the wide column (Figure 3-9). Choose the Send to back command from the Edit menu, which lets you select the body text without selecting the large letter. Push the top handle of the body text block down below the large letter (Figure 3-10). Click the mouse on the top handle to activate the text flow icon, and drag the text flow icon across the area of

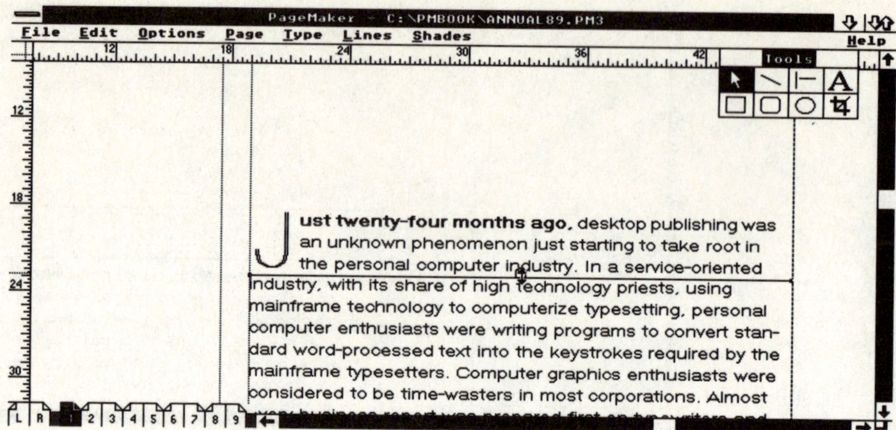

Figure 3-12. Push down on the lower text element's handle in order to correct the line spacing.

the column to be filled with text (Figure 3-11). When you release the mouse button, the first three lines should be in place next to the capital "J." You may need to adjust the text element below the first three lines in order to adjust the spacing correctly (Figure 3-12).

Due to the limited resolution of the PC screen, PageMaker can't accurately display the width of a letter in the Actual size page view. Use the 200% view (press the Control (Ctrl) key while typing 2, or choose the 200% size option in the Page menu) to view an accurate display when you adjust the column width. Alternatively, print the page, and then adjust the column width next to the letter if necessary.

To add a title to the report's first page, choose the text tool and click an insertion point at the left margin of the page, near the top of the page. Type the title with one space inserted between each letter, and one space inserted between each word. Highlight the title and change the font to Helvetica, bold italic, at 36 points in size with automatic (Auto) leading. Stretch the title block by dragging a corner handle out to the right margin (Figure 3-13).

Switch to the perpendicular line tool. Choose an 8-point line from the Lines menu, and drag a line at the 12-inch mark across the page under the title (Figure 3-14).

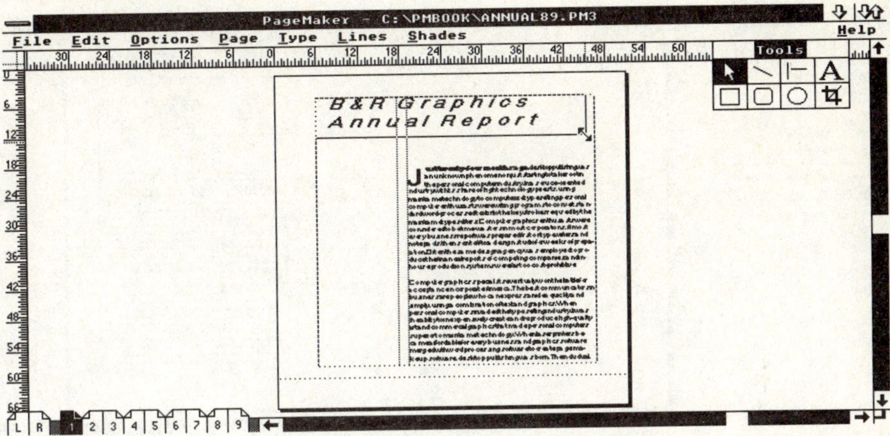

Figure 3-13. Stretch the title element to fit across the page.

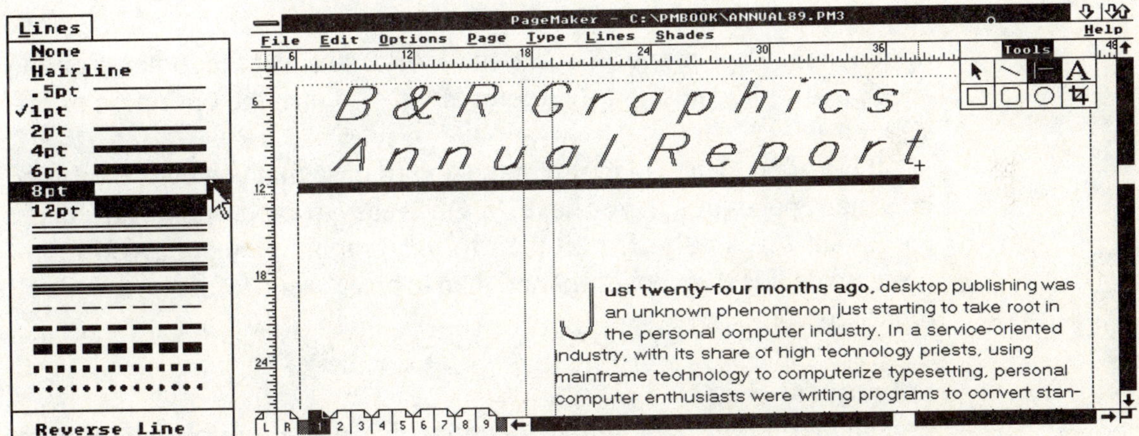

Figure 3-14. Draw an 8-point line under the title.

To complete the first page, move the logo into place by copying the logo from the master page and pasting the logo on Page 1). Resize the logo (Figure 3-15) by clicking the bottom right handle while holding down the Shift key. (You can also hold down the Control (Ctrl) key in order to choose PageMaker's built-in sizes for the printer you selected.) To be sure that the footer is turned off on Page 1, look at the Display master items

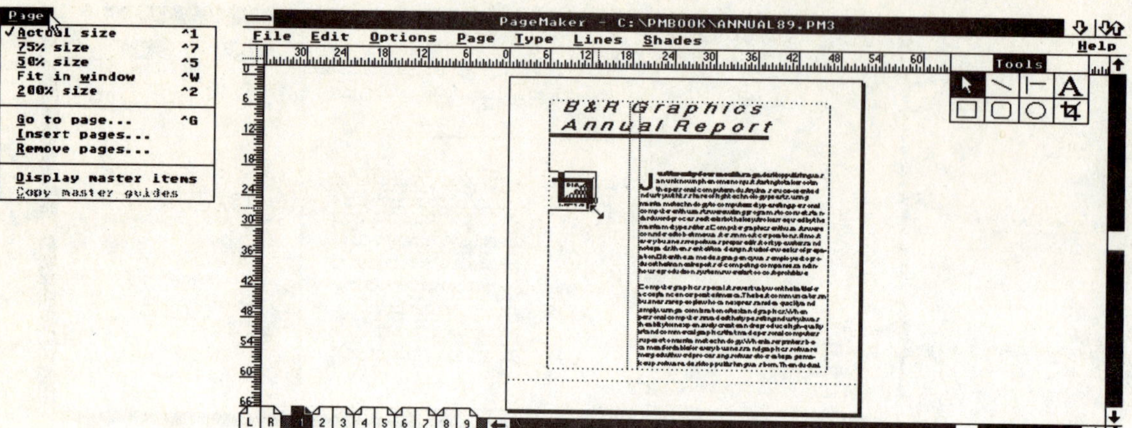

Figure 3-15. Resize the logo to fit in a prominent space on Page 1. The footers are turned off for Page 1.

option in the Page menu: A check mark indicates that the footer is on; no check mark indicates that the footer is off. (To turn the option on or off, select it.)

It is a good idea to place all of the text first, so that you can readily see how many pages of text you have. It is then easy to experiment and change the layout repeatedly. If you plan to use graphic elements, you might prefer to decide their positions and then to place them before you place all of the text.

Subsequent Pages

The annual report may contain sections that present information about market analysis, product information and life cycle, financial summaries, media campaigns, and anything else that describes the business. Each section should follow a consistent heading and subheading format.

To move a heading from the body text column to the narrow column, choose the text tool. Click and drag across the heading (Figure 3-16), including the blank line under the heading, and select Cut from the Edit menu. Click an insertion point at the left edge of the narrow column, and select Paste from the Edit menu. If the heading is not formatted, continue to use the text tool and drag across the heading again. Choose the Type

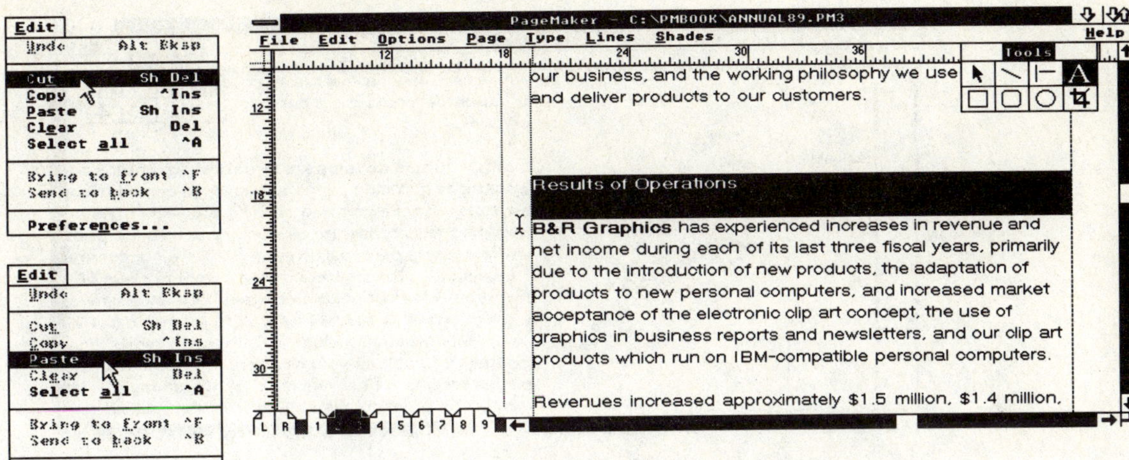

Figure 3-16. Select a section heading by using the text tool and Cut.

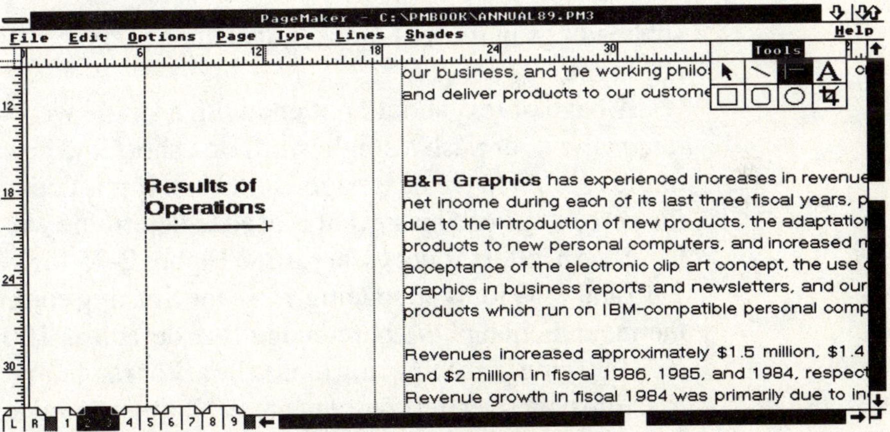

Figure 3-17. Draw a 2-point line under the heading.

specs menu, and change the font size to 14 points with 18 points of leading. Finally, draw a 2-point line under the heading (Figure 3-17).

Repeat these steps as necessary for each heading in the report. When you want a long headline to occupy two lines, select the text tool and insert an Enter (carriage return) at the place in the headline where you want the break to occur. (Note that headlines should not be hyphenated.) Leave

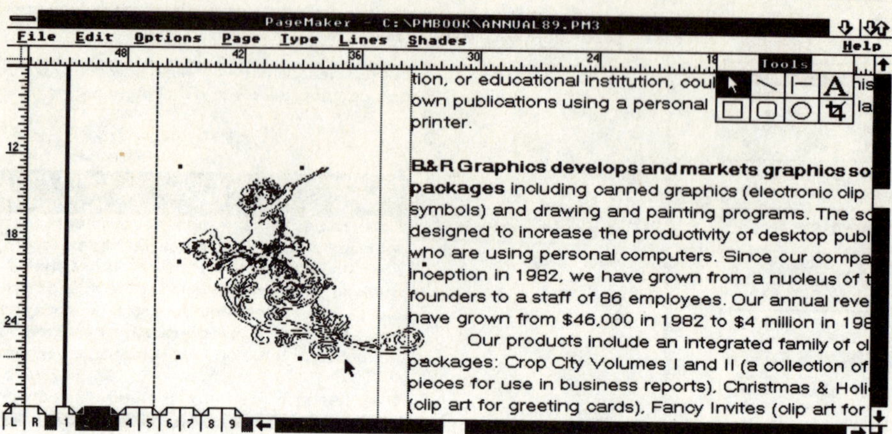

Figure 3-18. Place graphics in the narrow column.

subheadings in the text block, but change their specifications to 14-point bold type.

A page of text should not end with a single word or a very short line (an *orphan*), or push a single word or a short line less than half the width of the column to the next page (a *widow*). If this occurs, reduce or expand the percentage of a space that is used to determine word spacing, and then hand-kern letters if necessary. (See Figure 2-75 for kerning, and Figures 2-45 and 2-69 for type spacing.) Use the Spacing command from the Type menu, and change the percentage (the default is 100%) for the Desired word spacing in the Spacing dialog box. For ragged-right text, PageMaker uses only the Desired percentage. The other word spacing percentages (minimum and maximum) are used only for justified text.

The spacing settings are in effect for the entire text block, across all of the pages that contain that text file. Try a different percentage, and then check other pages to be sure that this percentage does not cause other widows or orphans to appear. You can undo the changed percentage immediately after you change it. (To do so, use the Undo command in the Edit menu.) You can also change the percentages back to their original values at any time, by retyping the original percentages in the Spacing dialog box.

To make room in a text block for spreadsheets, charts, graphs, or other elements, select the pointer tool, and then click anywhere inside the text block. Drag the bottom handle up to the top of the area to be reserved, and release the mouse button. To continue text below a reserved area, click the bottom handle and then click a starting point for the rest of the text.

Move a text block in the same way that you move a graphic—point in the middle of the block, hold down the mouse button until the four arrows appear, and drag the block into position. With Snap to guides on, you can attach a text block or a graphic to a column guide or a ruler guide. Use a ruler guide to help align text columns side by side.

Sizing and Cropping Graphics

The narrow column is useful for displaying images and graphics. Although it is unlikely that a business annual report would contain clip art graphics, a clip art library publisher is used in this example to point out that numerous libraries of electronic clip art are available for use in your publications.

Figure 3-18 shows a graphic image that was placed in the narrow column, resized to fit the column by using the Control (Ctrl), Shift, and drag sequence, and positioned to intrude slightly into the text. Place another graphic below this image in the same manner. Switch to the text tool, and type the caption in the narrow column. Resize the caption block to fit a vertical line for emphasis (Figure 3-19).

The cropping tool is useful for showing only part of a graphic image. (This tool does not change the original image—it just hides part of the image). Figure 3-20 shows how you can align the cropping tool over the handle, and Figure 3-21 shows the result of dragging the cropping tool icon and cropping the image. Add a caption just like the previous caption. Now, switch to the full-page display in order to see if the additional graphic elements are balanced on the two facing pages.

Text can be separated with a graphic or a photo in such a way that the element adds visual balance and makes the page more interesting. For example, you can add a photograph or scanned image to the page. (If you have used a scanner to scan your photograph, place the scanned version of the photograph so that your printer can use the scanned version as a

Figure 3-19. Add a caption and a vertical rule for emphasis.

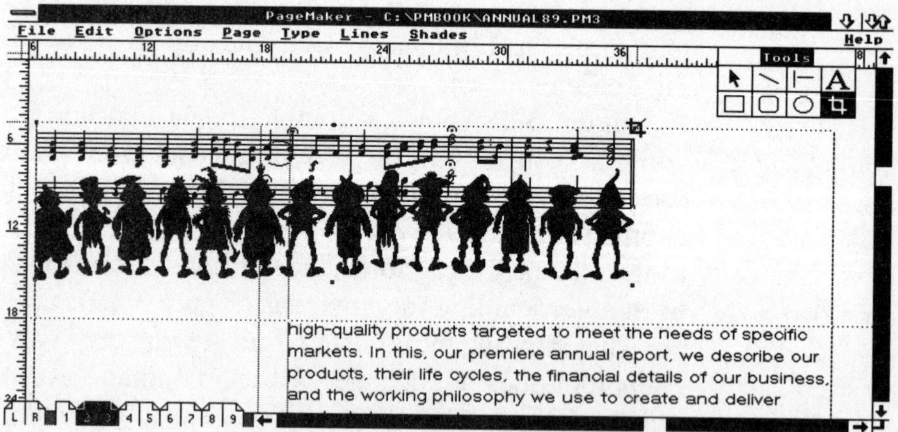

Figure 3-20. Select a resized graphic with the cropping tool.

guide to determine the position and cropping information for the original photograph.) If you do not intend to scan the photograph, and you do not have a scanned image to place, draw a placement box on the PageMaker page to represent the image. To draw the box, select a double-line style for the box edge from the Lines menu. Select the box tool, click a starting point at one corner of the box, and drag the mouse to draw the box (Figure 3-22). While the box is still selected, set its shading to 100% black by

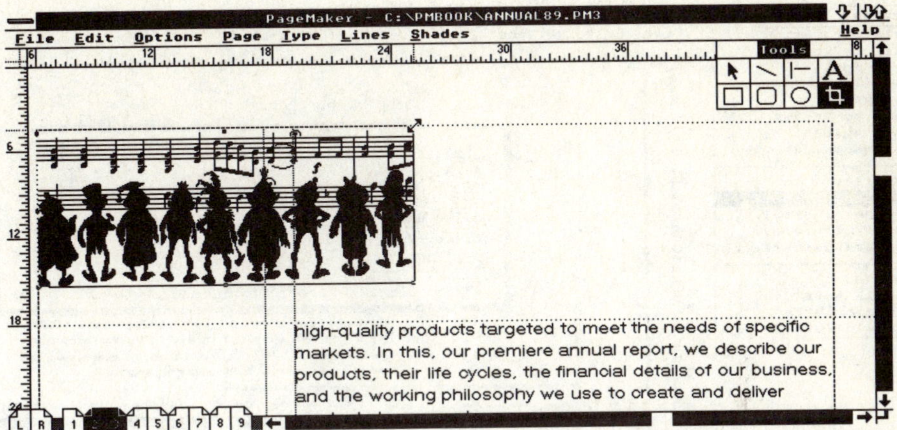

Figure 3-21. The result of dragging the cropping tool to crop the image.

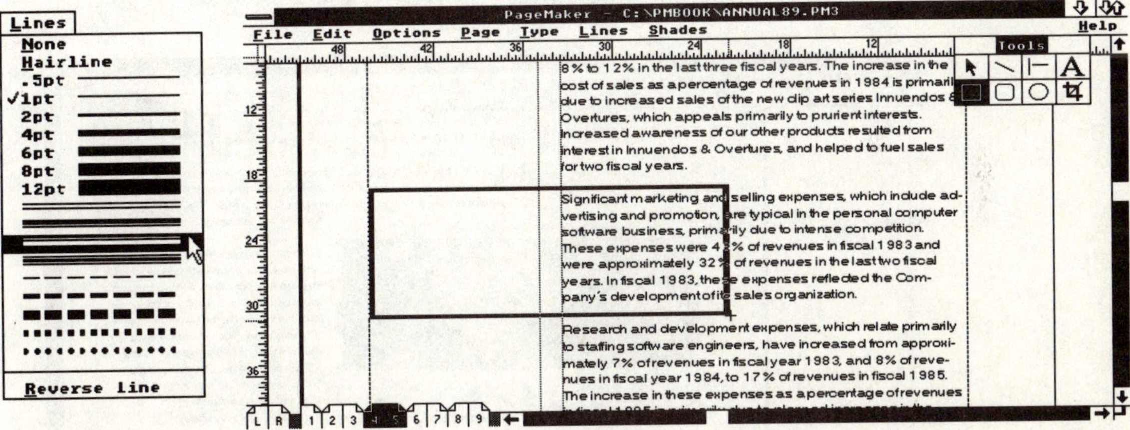

Figure 3-22. Draw a photo placeholder with a double-line style for a border.

choosing that option from the Shades menu.

With the box still selected, choose the Text wrap option from the Options menu. The Text wrap dialog box (Figure 3-23) lets you choose how to wrap text around graphics, and also lets you turn off text wrapping. Select the middle Wrap option and the right-hand Text flow option, so that text flows around the graphic image with a rectangular boundary. The result of this operation is shown in Figure 3-24. Chapter 4 shows how to

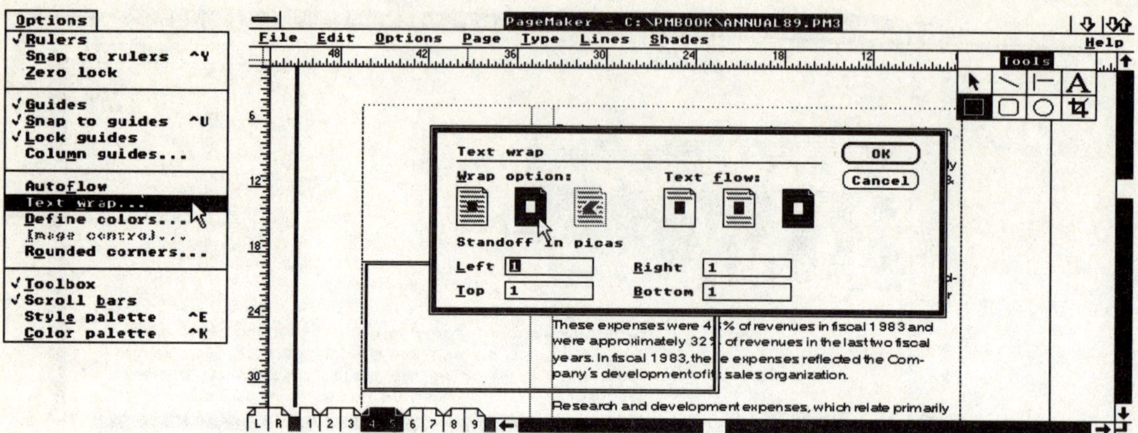

Figure 3-23. The Text wrap dialog box provides options for flowing text around graphics that intrude into text elements or are wholly contained by text elements. The middle wrap option is selected for a rectangular graphic boundary.

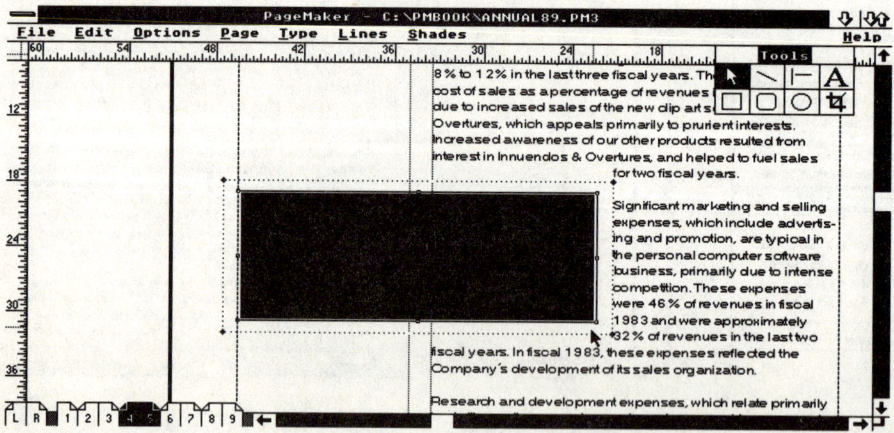

Figure 3-24. Wrap text around a placeholder with the default rectangular boundary.

adjust the boundary of an irregularly shaped graphic image.

Adding Spreadsheets

Reports usually contain financial data displayed in tables. These tables can be filled with data from spreadsheets. A *spreadsheet* is likely to

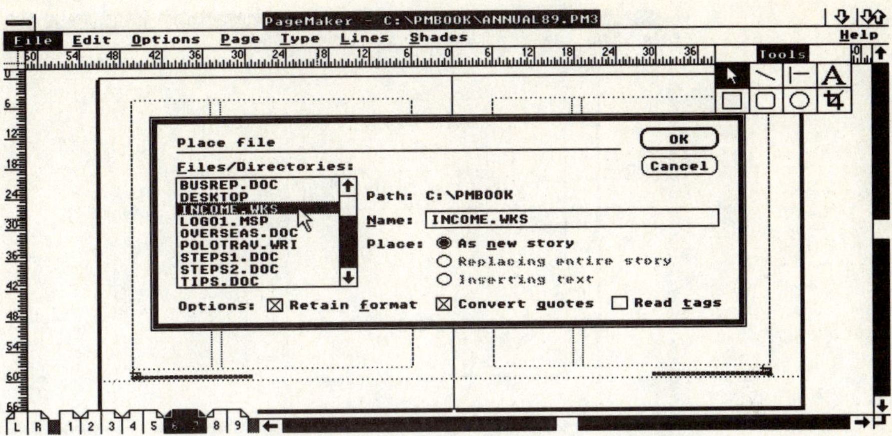

Figure 3-25. Select a .WKS spreadsheet file from Lotus 1-2-3.

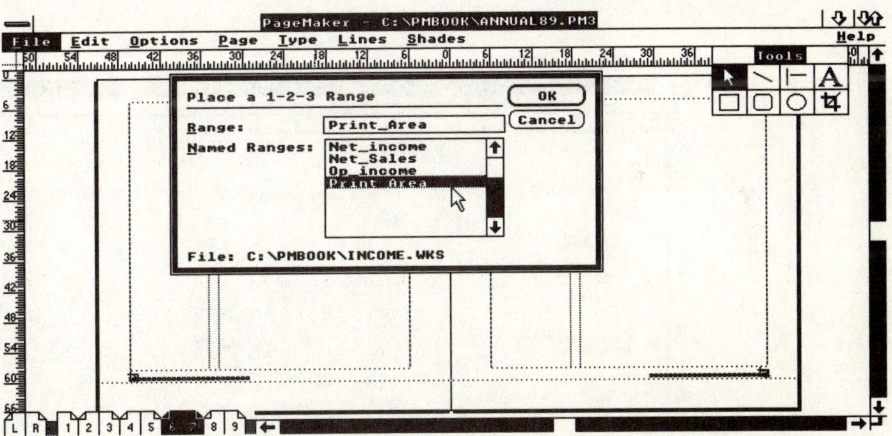

Figure 3-26. You can choose to place only a named cell range, or to place the entire defined Print Area of the spreadsheet.

consist of numerical information that is organized in rows and columns. Each number or text element in the spreadsheet is called a *cell*. Spreadsheets can have named cells, rows, and columns for easy reference.

If you can save the spreadsheet in a Lotus 1-2-3 format, such as a ".WKS" file, PageMaker can import the spreadsheet. If you installed PageMaker's Lotus 1-2-3 WKS filter and you use the Place command with a ".WKS" file (Figure 3-25), PageMaker displays a list of the named

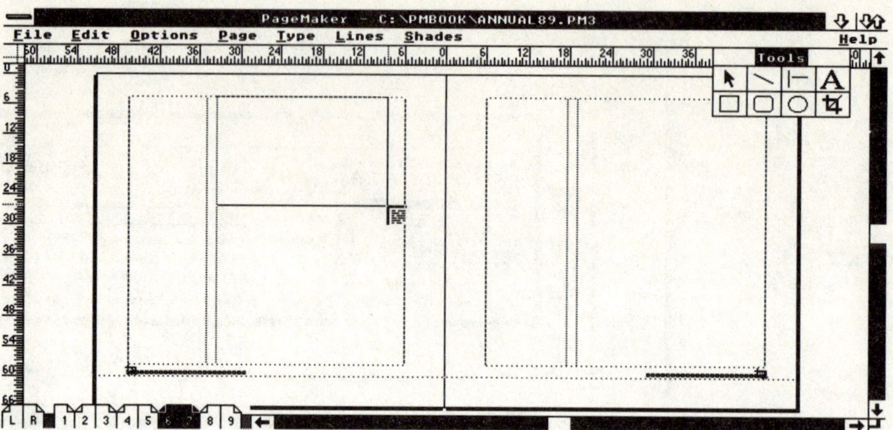

Figure 3-27. Drag the text flow icon across the page to define the text element for the spreadsheet.

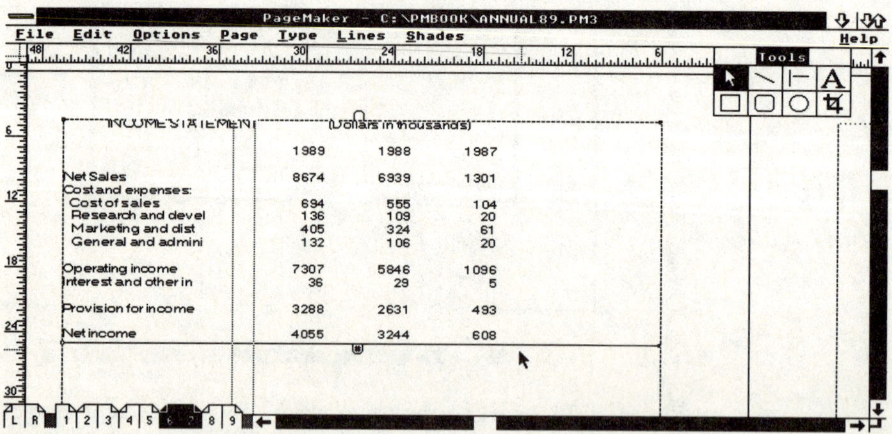

Figure 3-28. The result of placing the spreadsheet's defined print area. Note that formatting of tabs is not required.

cell ranges in the spreadsheet, including the Print Area defined in the spreadsheet (Figure 3-26). PageMaker recognizes the labels, numbers, and formulas, including all numerical, date, and time formats. PageMaker

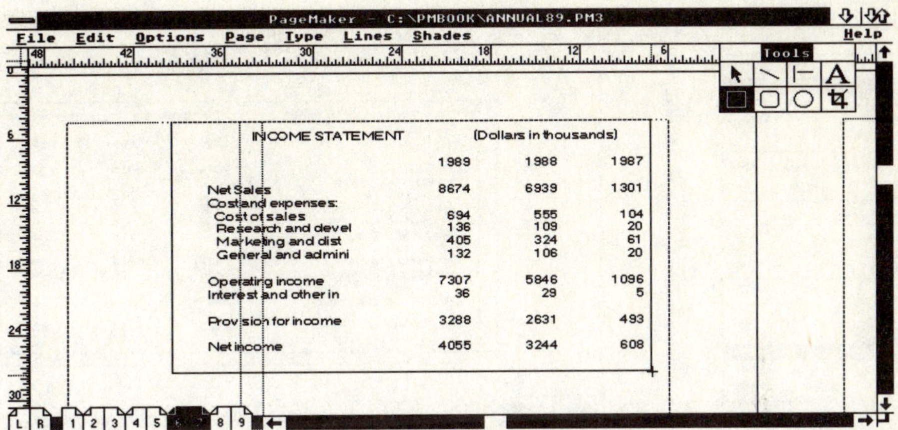

Figure 3-29. Draw a box frame around the spreadsheet.

also recognizes column alignment settings. You have the option to place a named cell range, or to place the Print Area, which loads the entire spreadsheet.

When the spreadsheet is loaded into the text flow icon, drag the icon across the page in order to define the text element (Figure 3-27). The result of this step is shown in Figure 3-28. The cells in the spreadsheet should line up properly. You do not need to set tabs in order to align text or numeric items, although you can adjust tabs that were defined by column widths.

If you can't place a spreadsheet directly, you can save it as a text-only ASCII file and then format the file with a word processor or PageMaker. It may be convenient to adjust the *delimiters* (commas, tabs, carriage returns, etc.) with the search and replace function of a word processor before you place the text into PageMaker. Use a word processor file format that PageMaker recognizes, or simply use a text-only file with no formatting options. Be sure to give your file a name that PageMaker can recognize. (The filename can usually be the same name as the default file name extension that your word processing program assigns when you save the file. See Appendixes A and B for suggested file name extensions.)

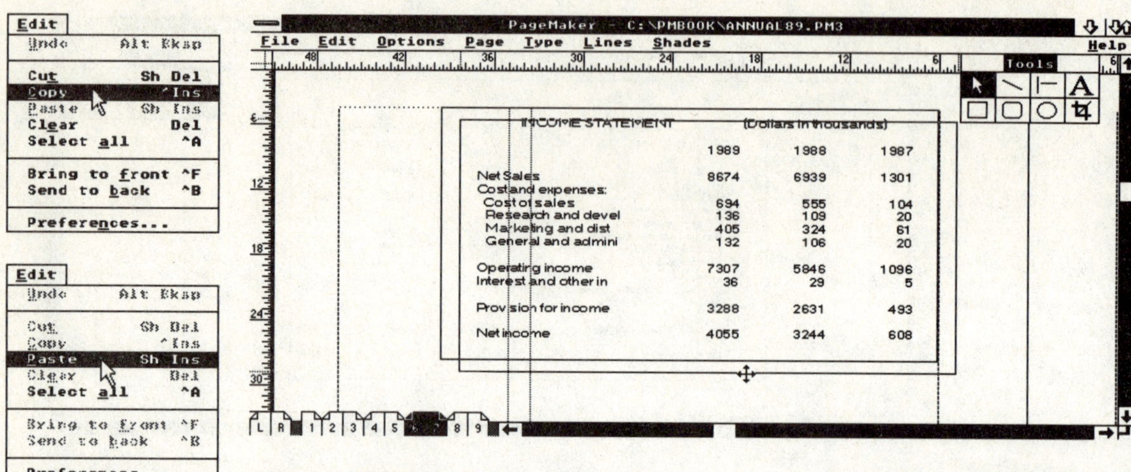

Figure 3-30. Move a copy of the first box into place as a drop shadow box.

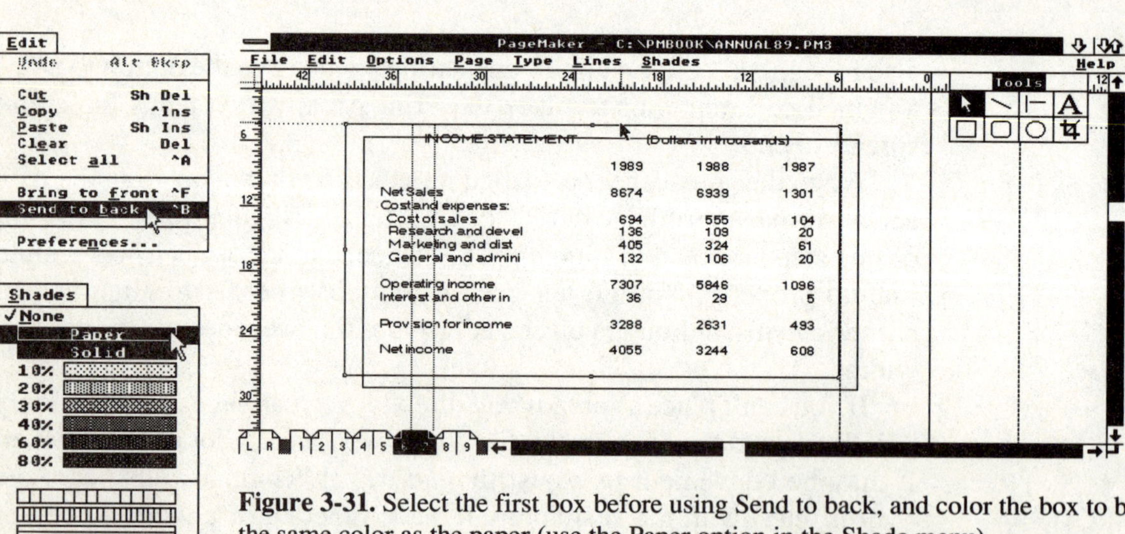

Figure 3-31. Select the first box before using Send to back, and color the box to be the same color as the paper (use the Paper option in the Shade menu).

Shadow Box

You can jazz up the spreadsheet by drawing a box as a frame and creating a drop shadow behind it.

Draw a box around the spreadsheet (Figure 3-29), and use the Copy and to Paste commands to copy the box and paste another version of the box onto the page. Move the second version into the position that a drop

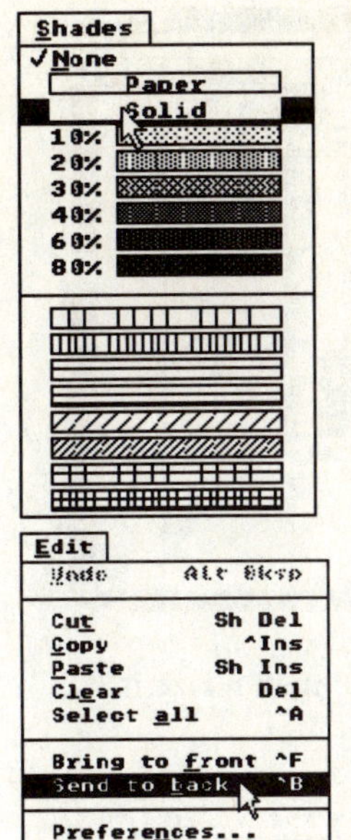

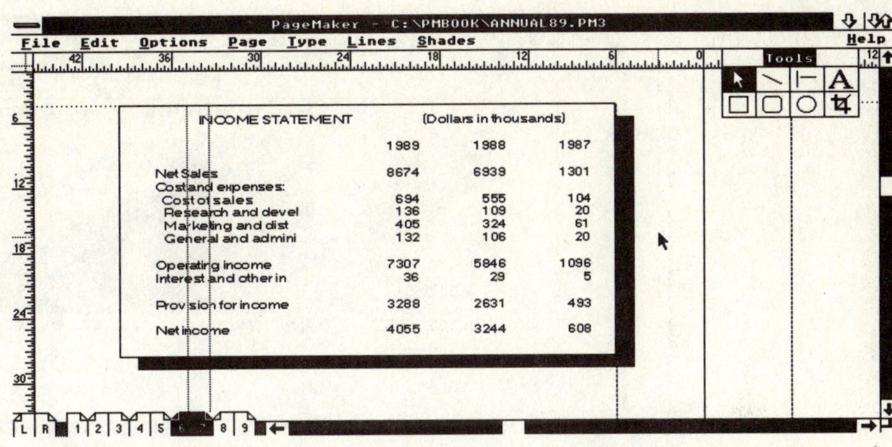

Figure 3-32. The drop shadow, set to a black shade, is placed behind the other elements with the Send to back option.

shadow would occupy (Figure 3-30). Use the arrow pointer tool to switch your selection to the first box (Figure 3-31). Next, use the Send to back option in the Edit menu and the Paper option in the Shade menu to turn the first box into a white box that is located underneath the text. Select the second box, set its shade to Solid (black), and use the Send to back option again. A black drop-shadow box should now appear behind the white box, which is behind the text (Figure 3-32).

If you need to move the entire spreadsheet along with its box and shadow box, first select the spreadsheet element. Hold down the Shift key to select both boxes without deselecting the already-selected spreadsheet. Release the Shift key and click in the center of the group until you see the four-arrow symbol. Now drag in order to move the entire group.

If you want to draw lines inside of the spreadsheet to emphasize rows, use the perpendicular line drawing tool. If you want to underline individual strings of text or numbers, use the text tool, highlight the text to be underlined, and choose Underline from the Type menu.

Adding Charts and Graphs

PageMaker reads the graphic output of some spreadsheet programs, such as the charts and graphs produced by Lotus 1-2-3, Microsoft Excel,

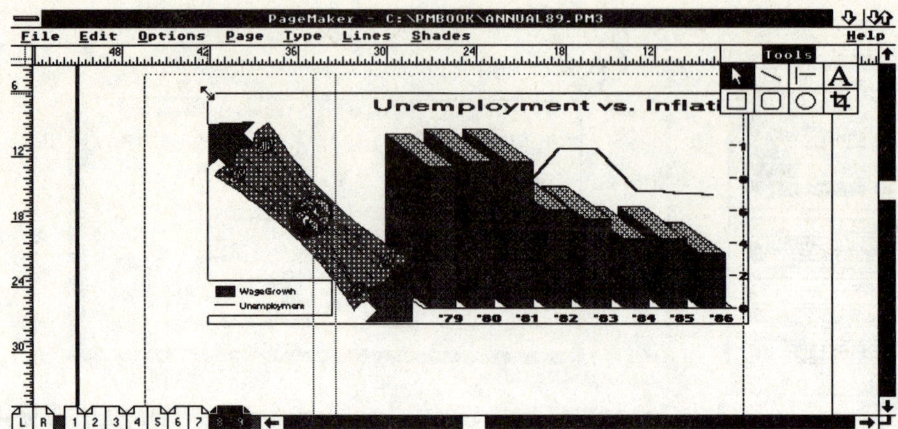

Figure 3-33. Place a chart from Micrografx Windows Graph and then resize it.

Multiplan, and business graphics programs such as Microsoft Chart, Micrografx Windows Graph, Micrografx Windows "Draw!", and Micrografx Designer.

If you use Lotus 1-2-3, transfer the graphics to a better graphics program, such as Micrografx Designer, Lotus Freelance, or Micrografx Windows "Draw!", in order to produce high-quality, high-resolution images with PageMaker. Another alternative is to use Lotus 1-2-3 data with a more powerful charting and graphing program, such as Micrografx Windows Graph (Figure 3-33).

If the graphics file was created by an object-drawing program (as described in Chapter 1), you can resize the graphic as desired without holding down the Control (Ctrl) key. For instance, if the graphics file is an Encapsulated PostScript (EPS) file, a Lotus 1-2-3 .PIC file, or a Micrografx "Draw!" file, just drag a corner of the image (hold down the Shift key to maintain the image's proportions) until it reaches the size that you want. If the file is a bit-mapped image from a program such as Microsoft Windows Paint, hold down both the Control (Ctrl) key and the Shift key while you drag the image.

Some object-drawing programs let you select Windows standard fonts or graphics fonts for typing text, and these fonts are carried over into PageMaker. Graphics fonts are reduced or enlarged with the image when you resize the image, but they usually do not correspond directly to laser printer fonts that are defined for use with Windows. The Windows standard fonts, however, correspond directly to the laser printer fonts for the target printer, but these fonts do not change size when the image changes size (unless they are PostScript fonts).

You can place just the graphics in PageMaker without the text, and then add text with PageMaker. This method gives you more control over text size and font styles within a text block. If you want text to run vertically alongside a vertical axis, or in any other orientation other than the usual horizontal orientation, use a graphics program to define the text because PageMaker does not offer the ability to rotate text.

You can also draw an entire chart or graph by using PageMaker's line-drawing, box-drawing, and circle-drawing tools and gray shades. PageMaker's Snap to guides feature makes it easy to line up several distinct boxes to form a bar chart. You can draw perfect circles by holding down the Shift key while dragging with the oval/circle tool, or make perfect squares by holding down the Shift key while dragging with the box tool.

Spreadsheet and business graphics programs perform calculations and then produce a bar chart, a pie chart, or an x-y graph that is accurate in proportion to the calculations. It is therefore better to use the output of these programs, at least as a template for the purpose of tracing new shapes that are accurate. You can bring the template into a program such as Micrografx Windows "Draw!" or else directly into PageMaker, draw your own shapes based upon the template, and then delete the template.

Printing the Report: Using Different Devices

If you use the same printer with PageMaker and Windows that you used with your graphics program, you will obtain optimal results. If you created graphics with text formatted for a different type of printer, you may have problems when you attempt to print that text.

For example, assume that you composed a pie chart with text that uses the standard fonts in Micrografx Windows "Draw!", and that the default Windows printer was set to the Hewlett-Packard LaserJet Plus. Assume also that you have installed a PostScript laser printer and typesetter, and that you want to print the final version of the report on the PostScript devices.

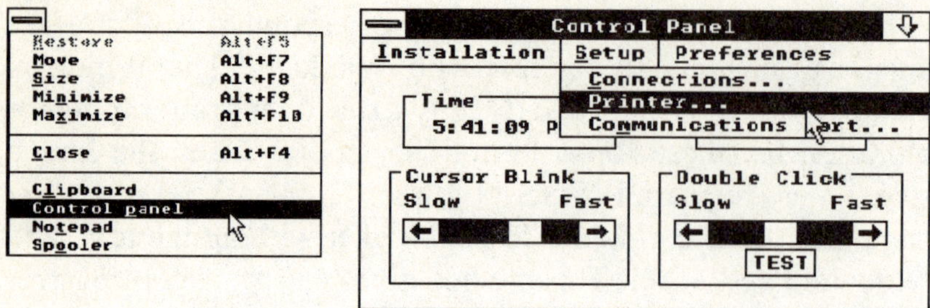

Figure 3-34. After starting the Control program (or choosing the Control panel from the System menu), choose the Printer command from the Setup menu in order to change the default printer that will be used with Windows applications.

Before you place the Micrografx Windows "Draw!" file, use the Windows Control Panel program to change the default printer to the PostScript printer (such as an Apple LaserWriter printer or an Allied Linotype Linotronic typesetter).

The Control Panel program can be launched in two ways. When the DOS Executive window is displayed, you can double-click the CONTROL.EXE file in the \WINDOWS directory. In PageMaker (before opening or after closing a publication file), you can choose the Control panel option from the System menu above PageMaker's file menu. Then, from within the Control Panel window, select the Printer option from the Setup menu (Figure 3-34). This option displays a dialog box that lists each type of printer driver installed on your system (Figure 3-35).

If you select a PostScript printer, another dialog box that contains more settings for PostScript printers appears (Figure 3-36), along with print options that pertain to the selected printer. You can change the dpi resolution (up to 300 dpi for the TurboLaser/PS), the orientation (landscape or portrait), the source of paper (manual feed or the paper tray), and the number of copies of each page to be printed. After clicking OK to accept the default printer setting and options, you can use standard PostScript fonts. Other options include whether or not to send the PostScript header with each job, how long the system should wait for a print job to finish (usually zero, which prevents a time-out), and whether or not to change the margins to compensate for printing factors.

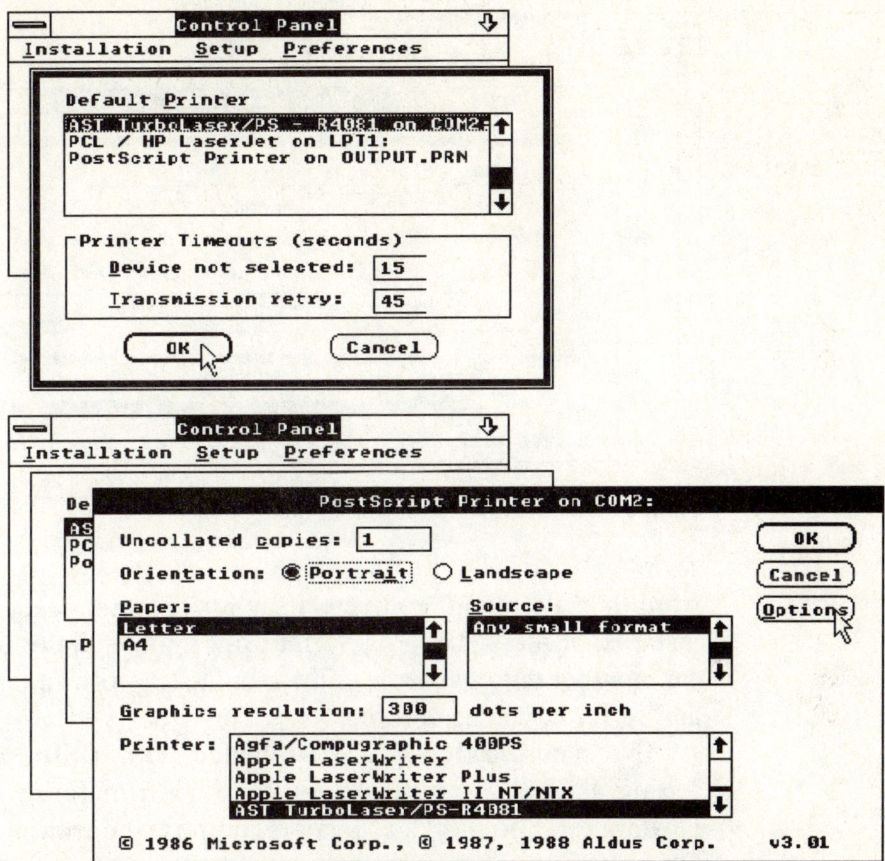

Figure 3-35. Select a PostScript printer (the AST TurboLaser/PS).

PageMaker sends the PostScript header with every file that you print, unless you specify otherwise. The printer needs the header, but if the printer already received a header from a previous print job, you don't need to send another header with each job. (There is no harm in sending a new header with each job.) It is essential to send a new header if the printer has been turned off, or initialized with a different printer driver. The time that you save by not sending the header is about 30 seconds.

Once you open the PageMaker document, the default printer (also called *target printer*) may have to be changed if you first composed the pages with another printer setting. Choose the Printer setup command

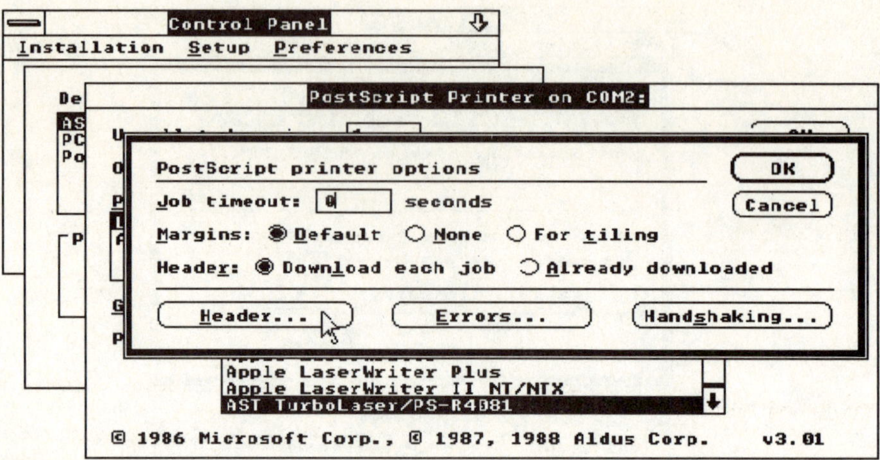

Figure 3-36. The PostScript printer dialog box.

from the File menu, and select the appropriate printer from the list of installed printers. The PostScript print options dialog box appears. You can now set options, such as the resolution, portrait or landscape mode, and so forth, just as before.

If the publication file was created with a different target printer setting, PageMaker will ask you for a confirmation when you choose a new printer: Should PageMaker recompose the entire publication? Click OK to confirm the recompose operation, because PageMaker must use the new printer's font information to perform proper kerning, justification, and spacing. The recompose operation should not take longer than a few minutes (or a few seconds for a short publication), but it may change the line length of some of the text.

To print the report, simply choose the Print command from the File menu, to display the printing dialog box (Figure 3-37). The printing dialog box also allows you to specify the number of copies of each page, whether to print a range of pages rather than the entire publication, the order of the page printing, and the percentage of scaling for the pages (if any). Scaling is useful when you design a page that is larger or smaller than the final size, and you want to print the page in its final size. You can also print a page at 200%, for example, and then reduce the printed page with a camera to

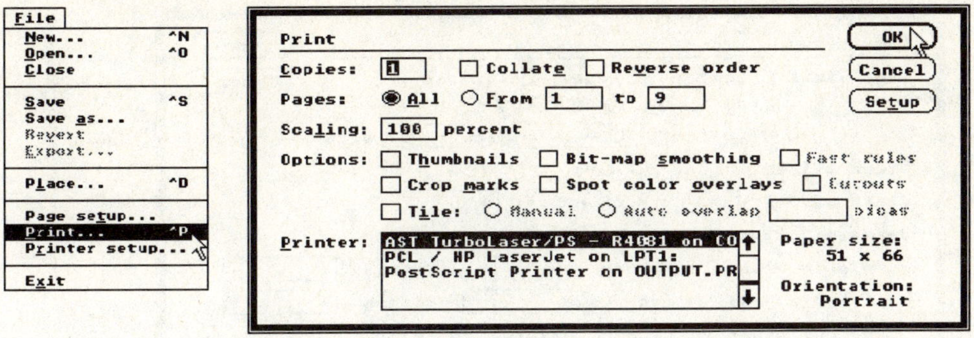

Figure 3-37. When printing the report, you can select a number of copies, or select a range of pages to print rather than the entire publication.

regular size in order to gain twice the resolution. Tiling is also available when an oversize image is printed on a standard laser printer with an overlap, so that you can line up and overlap the pages to form the large page. You can even specify the amount of the overlap.

A change in the resolution affects the appearance of graphics. The lower the resolution, the faster the publication file prints—but the graphics will be coarser, and hairlines may not print at all below 288-dpi resolution. In addition, fonts selected for use with graphics will not reproduce well at lower resolutions.

Technical Manual

The technical manual is an example of a lengthy publication that can be published with PageMaker. The Aldus PageMaker manual was produced with PageMaker, as was this book (the process of designing the pages is discussed later). The following example, however, is simpler in design and in execution. The idea is to produce a publication in which all the pages have a similar format, yet contain certain differences such as illustrations, photos, or footnotes. It is very important to keep the design simple for two reasons. First, you need to attract and hold the reader's attention without too many distractions or arresting items. Second, you

Page setup
Page size: ○ Letter ○ Legal ○ Tabloid
○ A4 ○ A3 ○ A5 ○ B5
◉ Custom: 38 x 51 picas
Orientation: ◉ Tall ○ Wide
Start page #: 1 # of pages: 4
Options: ☒ Double-sided ☒ Facing pages
Margin in picas: Inside 3 Outside 3
Top 6 Bottom 4
Target printer: Postscript printer on LPT3:
OK
Cancel

Figure 3-38. The Page setup for a technical manual that is about the same size as the PageMaker manual.

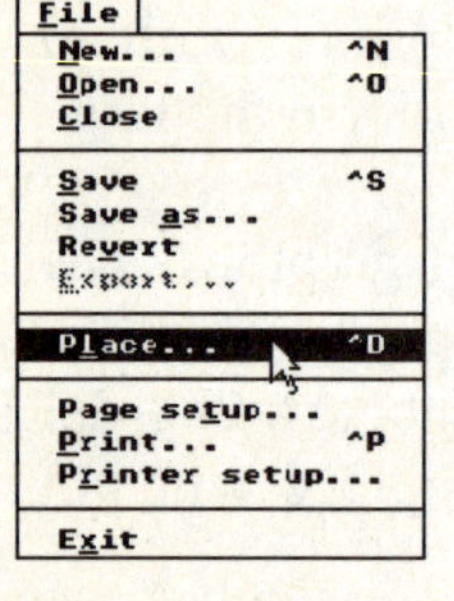

Figure 3-39. Scale the graphics image of the title for the first page of the manual. Fancy titles can be prepared separately in a graphics program and then placed on the page.

have to streamline the production process to be able to produce many pages quickly.

To compose sections of the technical manual, you can use the text and graphics files supplied in the PageMaker tutorial directory, PMTUTOR.

Designing the Pages

Follow the procedures to start a new publication. Change the default settings for the page setup menu to the dimensions of the pages that you will produce: a custom page that is 38 picas wide by 51 picas high, with tall (portrait) orientation and double-sided pages. The image area is defined by margins that are 3 picas in from the binding, 3 picas in from the edge of the page, 6 picas down from the top of the page, and 4 picas up from the bottom (Figure 3-38).

In the master pages, specify a two-column format with 1 pica space between the columns. The column guides indicate the location of the middle of the page. On Page one, place a title logo (the file LOGO.PCX in the PMTUTOR directory, supplied with PageMaker). To scale the title properly, hold down the Control (Ctrl) key and the Shift key while you drag a corner of the image (Figure 3-39).

Preparing Text and Graphics

The text for the manual should be preformatted so that italic and bold styles and tabs are already set. In this way, you can bring tables and formatted text into PageMaker with the styles intact by using the Retain format option in the Place dialog box. Microsoft Word has the closest relationship to PageMaker, because PageMaker can recognize all Word formatting settings, and selected text can be exported from PageMaker pages into Word files. The export feature makes the updating process a lot easier if you make last-minute changes to the text in PageMaker.

Tables of data should be prepared so that the same number of tabs are used between columns of a table. Set the tabs so that the table columns line up in the word processor, with one tab between each column item. In PageMaker, you can change the tab settings to fit the column format, or else use the tabs that were already set in the word processing program. PageMaker can't handle more than 20 tabs on a single line.

Use a tab to indent the first line of each paragraph (or, in Microsoft Word, you could use the first line indent for a paragraph format). PageMaker recognizes the left margin setting as a starting point, but disregards the right margin. Instead, PageMaker breaks lines according to the column settings. PageMaker also recognizes the first-line indent of a paragraph in Microsoft Word and other word processors (see Appendix

A), whether that indent is positioned to the left of the left margin (a *hanging indent*) or to the right (a *regular indent*).

If your text is not preformatted, you can still do some preparation work (even in the case of a simple ASCII text file) to help speed up the process: Use *carriage returns* (when you type Enter in a word processor, you generate a carriage return) only at the ends of paragraphs and fixed lines. Delete any extra spaces (such as the extra space that is usually inserted by typists after a sentence).

Text brought in without formatting settings takes on the characteristics of the Type specs dialog box (in the Type menu). Choose the text font, size, style, and leading before you place the text. If you place the text first, choose the text tool, click somewhere in the text, and employ the Select all command (Control A) to highlight all of the text. Next, make changes in the Type specs dialog box.

Technical manuals usually require many illustrations that chiefly consist of line art, rather than paintings with gray scale. (Drawings of equipment and schematics are *line art* because they consist of lines, curves, and geometric shapes, without rough edges and blurred details.) Use a drawing program, rather than a painting program, so that the fine lines and curves will be reproduced with the highest possible resolution (and, therefore, the highest quality). Draw the graphics at the size that is most comfortable for you and that offers the most accurate detail. After they are drawn, draw-type graphics can be scaled in PageMaker to any size.

Technical manuals may also need photographs, which can be scanned into the computer using a desktop scanner. Existing line art can also be scanned to be turned into electronic form. Scanned images are paint-type graphics, and are subject to the same restrictions as paint-type graphics (as described in Chapter 1). You will get the best results from scaling scanned images if you use PageMaker's built-in scaling percentages by holding down the Control (Ctrl) key while scaling).

Placing Text with the Autoflow Option

The quickest way to place text is to use the Autoflow option. PageMaker lets you mix automatic text flowing with manual text flowing, so that you always have control. Even when text is flowing automatically from page

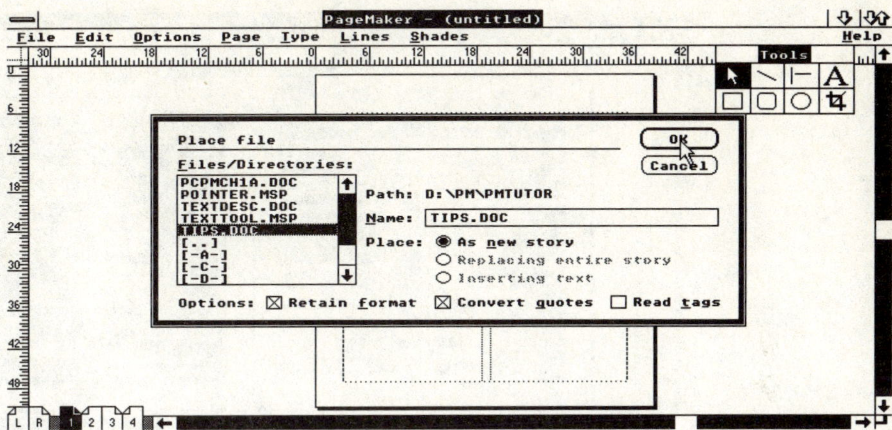

Figure 3-40. Select TIPS.DOC from the PMTUTOR directory for automatic text pouring into the manual.

Figure 3-41. The automatic text pouring icon for placing text.

to page, you can stop the process immediately by pressing the mouse button.

Begin this example by placing text on Page 1, using the method described earlier. First, check to be sure that the Autoflow option in the Options menu is off (no check mark), and then choose the TIPS.DOC file

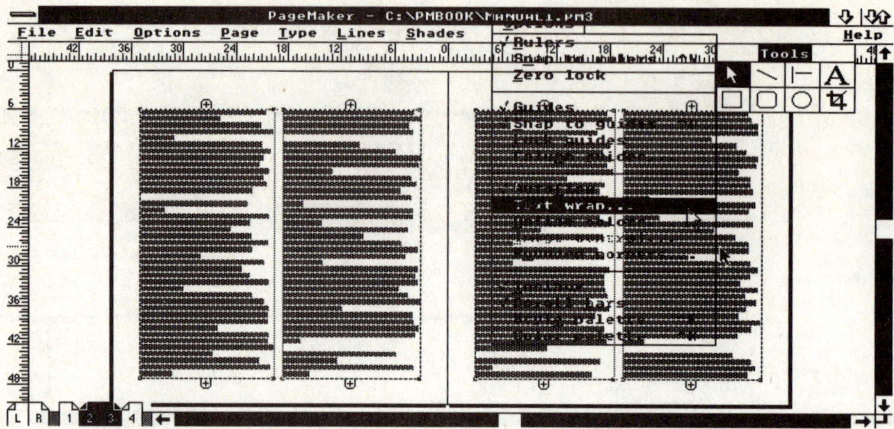

Figure 3-42. The Autoflow option causes text to be poured from column to column, page to page, automatically (and creates pages if necessary in order to fit the text).

(Figure 3-40). Place the text in both columns on Page 1.

Next, select Autoflow in the Options menu in order to turn this option on. Click the bottom + sign in the second column to continue placing text. The text icon turns into the automatic text pouring icon (Figure 3-41). Click the page number icon to move to Page 2 and start placing text at the top of the first column. PageMaker automatically pours text from column to column and page to page (Figure 3-42), stopping when it runs out of text in the file. You can also stop the process by clicking the mouse.

When the Autoflow option is on, PageMaker jumps over existing text and graphics, and continues to pour text. You can switch to manual text flow by pressing the Control (Ctrl) key. To switch to semiautomatic text flow, press the Shift key. When semiautomatic text flow is active, PageMaker stops at the bottom of each column and leaves the icon on the screen, ready for you to place the next column. To switch back to automatic text flow, release the Shift key.

Placing Graphics

Large publications (such as manuals and books) usually contain references to illustrations and photos. Typically, you want to place the illustrations and photos as close to their text references as possible. But

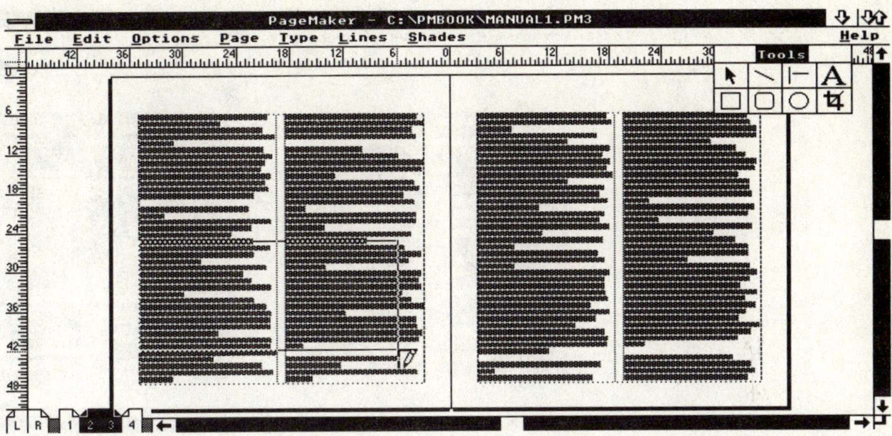

Figure 3-43. Place and resize a draw-type graphic by dragging while placing.

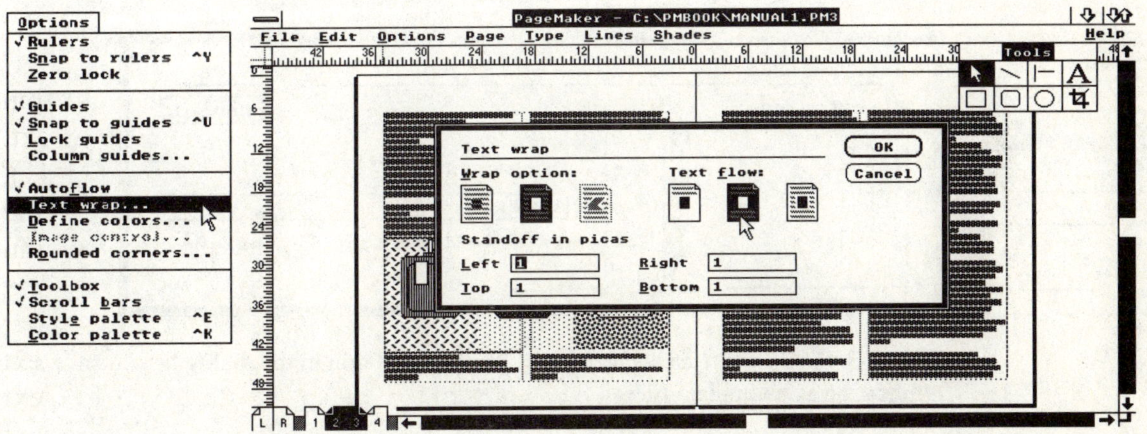

Figure 3-44. Choose the Text wrap option. Select a rectangular wrap and text flow that jumps over the graphic.

how do you know where the references will occur without placing all of the text? Although you would start a short publication (such as a newsletter, brochure, or magazine article) by placing the graphics first, you probably would not begin the design of a manual or book in that way.

PageMaker's Autoflow and Text wrap features make it easy to place

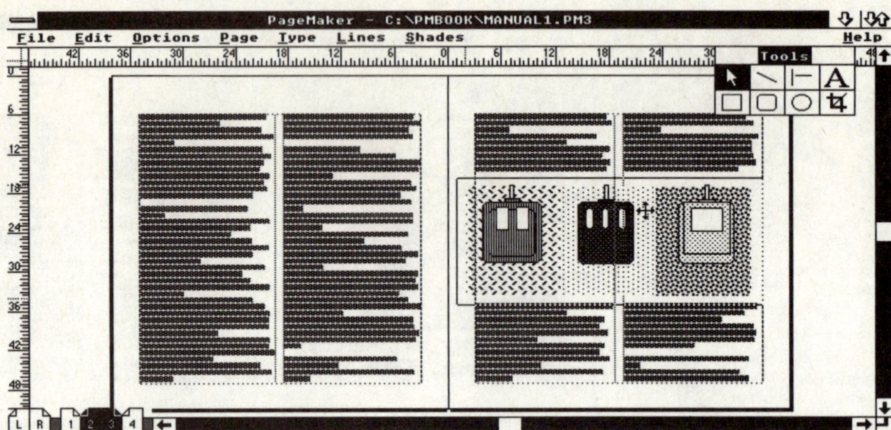

Figure 3-45. Drag the graphic image to another location in the text. The text automatically flows around it.

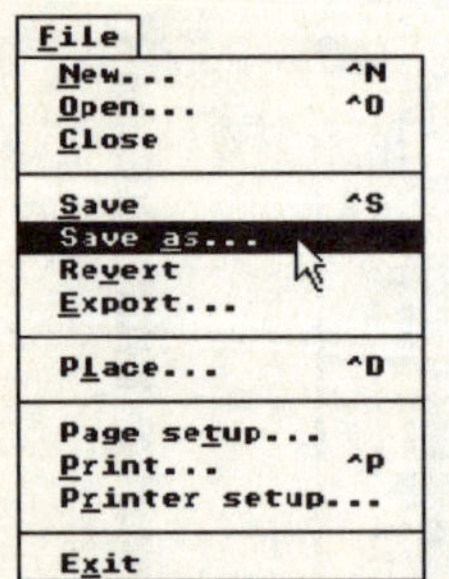

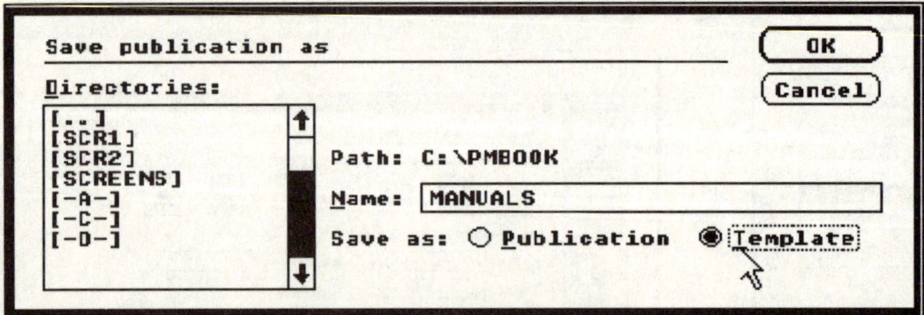

Figure 3-46. Use Save as and select the Template option in the dialog box to save a publication as a template file.

all of the text first and then go back and adjust the text to accommodate illustrations and graphics. You don't have to adjust the text—simply place the graphic image and select Text wrap from the Options menu.

When you position draw-type graphics, you can take a shortcut and resize the graphics at the same time. While you are placing the graphic, drag the placement icon across the area that is to be filled by the graphic (Figure 3-43). This step is a quick technique for filling an area with text or draw-type graphics. Paint-type graphics should be resized by holding

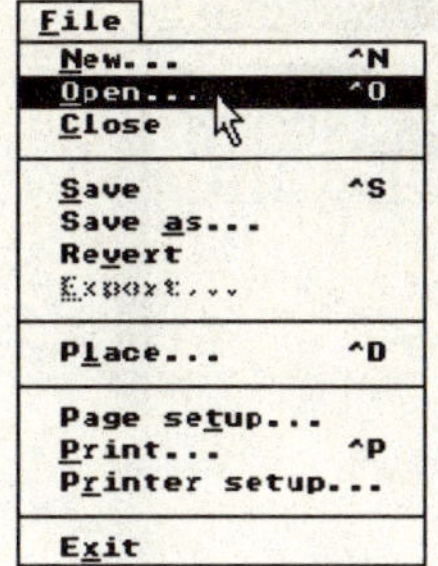

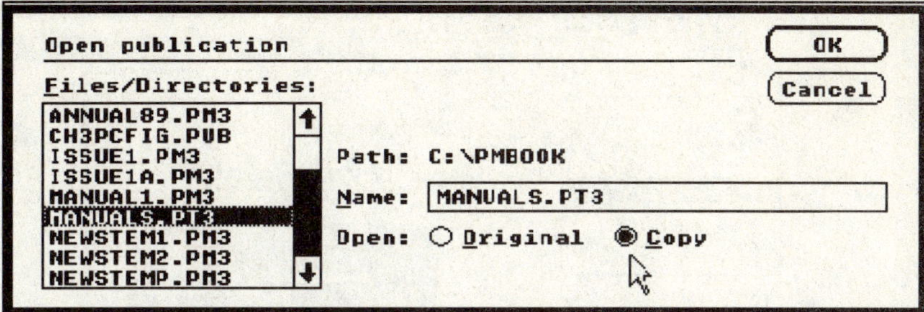

Figure 3-47. You can open any publication file as a copy rather than opening the original, then create a new untitled document and leave the original intact. A template file can be automatically launched from MS-DOS Executive as a copy.

down the Control (Ctrl) key in order to obtain PageMaker's best scale factors.

After placing the graphic image, and while the image is still selected, choose the Text wrap option (Figure 3-44). Set the wrap to be rectangular by selecting the middle wrap option. Indicate that the text is to jump over the graphic by selecting the middle text flow option. After the Text wrap for the graphic object is set, you can drag the object to another location in the text (Figure 3-45) or resize the object. The text continues to flow around it automatically.

Saving and Using Templates

PageMaker offers the ability to save a publication file as a *template* file, which can be used to define new publications simply by replacing the contents of the template file with new contents.

You can create a template file with any publication. First, use the Save as command to save the publication under a new name as a template file, rather than as a publication file (Figure 3-46). PageMaker adds the extension ".PT3." From that point on, you can double-click the template file from the MS-DOS Executive window and launch PageMaker. The template file also automatically opens as a new, untitled document, and leaves the original template file intact and untouched. (You can, of course, use the Open command and dialog box to open a copy of any publication

Figure 3-48. Select the first story to replace, and then choose the Place command.

as a new, untitled document, and leave the original publication intact, as shown in Figure 3-47.) The creation of a template file makes this operation automatic, so that you can double-click the filename in MS-DOS Executive and launch PageMaker with a copy of a file rather than with the original file.

The use of a template to create a publication is perhaps the easiest way to produce a publication. Open the template as an untitled file, and select the first column of the first story. Select the Place command (Figure 3-48) and choose the file that contains the story that will replace the selected story. Select the option to replace the entire story (Figure 3-49). PageMaker replaces the text of the old story with the text of the new story in the correct place on the page, using the same layout. Thus, if the text from the old story wrapped around a graphic image on Page two, the new text also wraps around the graphic image (if there is enough new text to reach that point in the layout).

You can use this technique to publish such publications as a weekly newsletter. The first issue can be used as a template for the second issue: Simply save the first issue as a template under a new name (such as NEWSTEMP), and then open a copy of it to make another issue. Use the Place command to replace text and graphics with new text and graphics. When you replace a graphic element, the new graphic element occupies

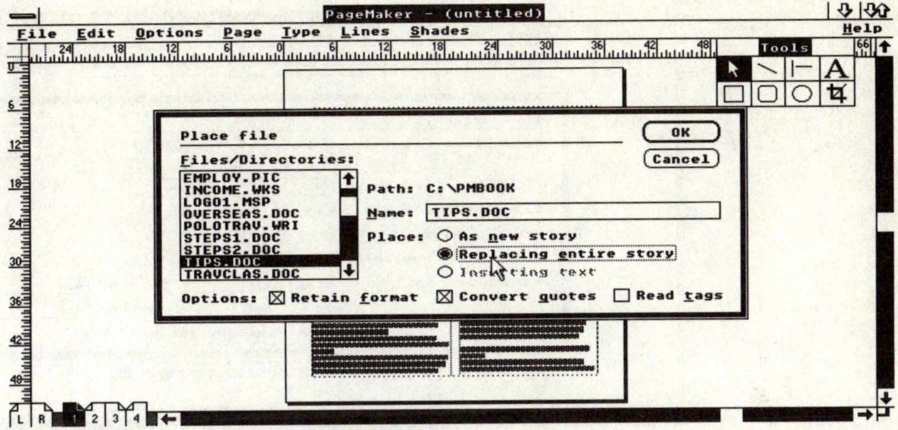

Figure 3-49. Place the new text with the Replacing entire story option turned on, so that the new text completely replaces the old text in the layout.

exactly the same space that the replaced element occupied, and is automatically distorted if necessary. To adjust the image to be proportionately sized, hold down the Shift key while you resize the image.

The size of the text file that can be used to replace another story is limited: it must be less than 64K. If your text file is larger than 64K, place it as a new story. Delete the old story first by selecting each column and pressing the backspace key to leave blank columns for pouring new text. Use the Autoflow option to automatically flow the new text into the layout.

A Complete Book

It is not only possible to produce a book with PageMaker, it may be the preferred method so that the layout of the book's pages can be flexible. A book that is visually more interesting and more readable can be produced, especially in the case of a book that contains many illustrations.

A book is like a manual in that both involve the use of long text files, which are usually separated into chapters, and the use of a single column on each page (although some large books are laid out with two columns).

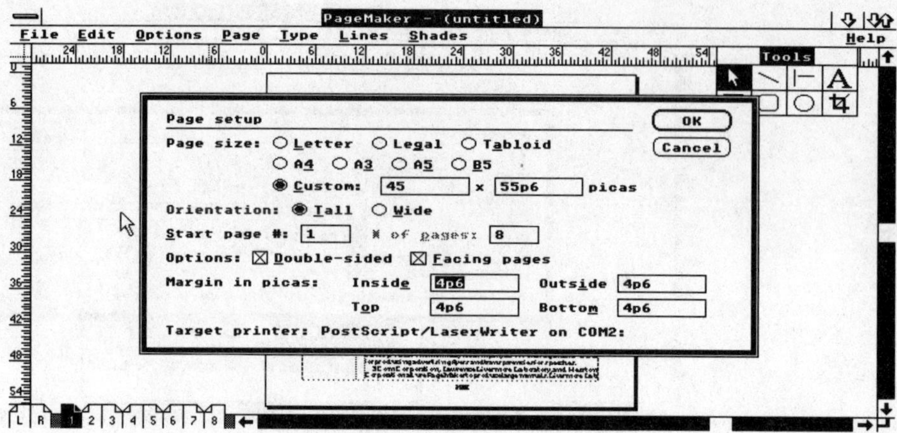

Figure 3-50. Page setup for this book, which was produced with PageMaker.

A book is usually completely written before it is produced. In the case of some books, there is a considerable need to update the pages at the very last minute and to save those changes in the text files.

PageMaker has a close relationship to Microsoft Word: PageMaker recognizes Word's formatting, and also recognizes Word's style sheet definitions. In addition, PageMaker can export text, including style sheet definitions, to Word files. Microsoft Word was used to create the manuscript of this book, and styles were assigned to sections of the text before the text was placed in PageMaker. The style sheet definitions could then be edited in PageMaker. The style sheet definitions include the font, the type size, the type style (italic, bold, etc.), leading, paragraph spacing, tab settings, indents, and even color. When you change a style sheet definition, all of the sections of text that are defined by that style sheet change automatically to adopt the new definition.

PageMaker does not generate an index or table of contents, but they can be created by using a number of different programs or your word processor. After you produce the PageMaker pages, use your word processor to put page breaks into the text files to match the page breaks in PageMaker. You can then use the word processor text file with an indexing program (such as ProIndex from Elfring Consulting).

Microsoft Word was used to prepare the text files and to produce the index for this book. After the Word text files were placed onto PageMaker pages and last-minute changes were made, the text was exported to Word files. Page breaks were inserted using Word to match the final pages, and the index entries were marked.

Word was also used to create *glossary entries* (abbreviations that represent an index entry, markers, and delimiters) so that the authors could move quickly through the electronic manuscript, marking index words and phrases. Word then compiled an index from separate chapter files, with page numbers based upon the page breaks in those files. The table of contents for this book was created by using another code for the table of contents entries in the same text files.

Designing the Pages

Most books are not 8 1/2 inches by 11 inches, which is the standard page size for letters, newsletters, and some technical manuals. A smaller book size (such as 6 1/2 inches by 9 inches) can be laid out on pages that are standard size (8 1/2 inches by 11 inches), and margin settings can be adjusted to create an image area that is the size of the book's pages. It is much better, however, to change the page size, so that you can print crop marks on the 8 1/2 inch by 11 inch paper. *Crop marks* are recognized by the volume printer or print shop as the marks that define the edges of the page. They are printed automatically by PageMaker if you select them from the Print dialog box.

Begin a new publication for each of the book's chapters. Change the default settings for the page setup menu to contain the dimensions of the book pages: a custom page that is 45 picas wide by 55 picas and 6 points high, with tall (portrait) orientation and double-sided pages. The image area is defined by margins that are 6 picas in from the binding, 3 picas in from the edge of the page, 4 picas and 6 points down from the top of the page, and 4 picas and 6 points up from the bottom (Figure 3-50).

In this example, a horizontal guide has been placed on the master pages for placing text at the top of the page, and for placing a different page number header for the left and right pages. The page layout has also been set up to be one column, but with one vertical rule guide placed on the left master page at the 33-pica marker, and another vertical rule guide placed on the right master page at the 12-pica mark. To get the vertical rule

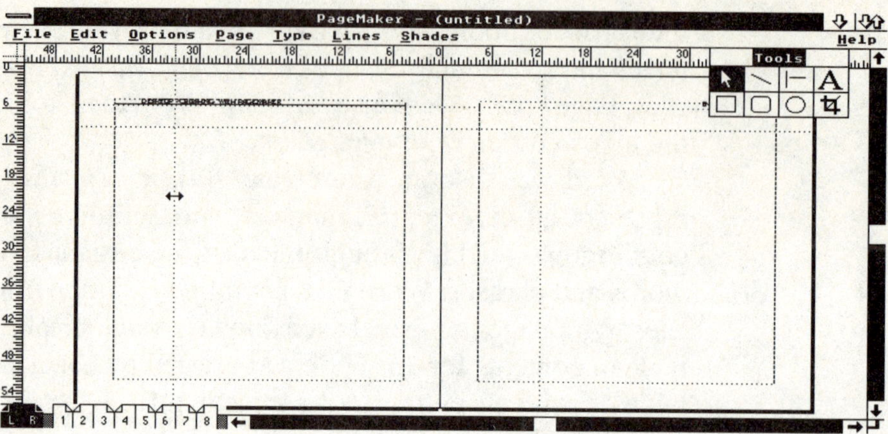

Figure 3-51. The one-column layout for this book, with a vertical ruler guide that defines the body text indent, and narrow space for icons and menus.

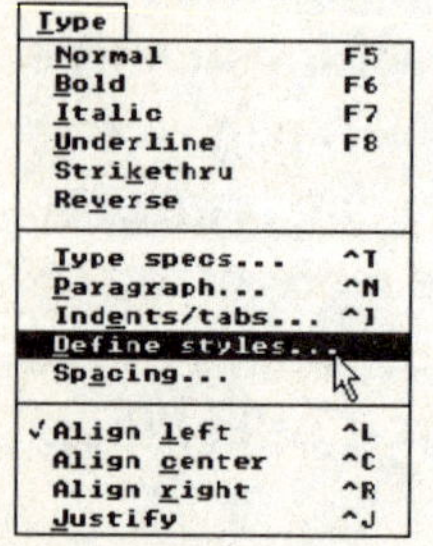

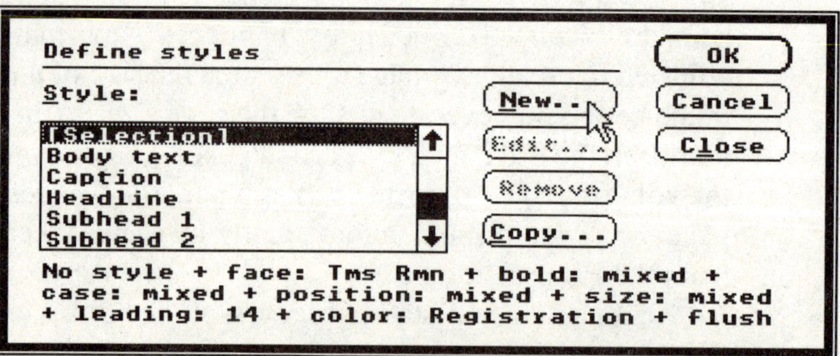

Figure 3-52. Define a style for a section of text.

guides, drag from the vertical ruler. These guides will help you place icons next to the body of the text, which will be indented. Both master pages should now have the same layout (Figure 3-51).

All of the guides on the master pages display on each page. You can modify them separately on each page without affecting the master page guides or the guides on other pages. (To restore guides on a page back to the guides used on the master pages, use the Copy master guides command in the Page menu.)

Set the Type specifications for the chapter title (Times Roman bold italic at 36 points, with 40 points of leading) and choose Justify from the Type menu. The text will be justified using the minimum and maximum word spacing percentages in the Spacing dialog box, as well as the desired word spacing percentage, which is the only percentage used in ragged-right columns.

You may want to save a version of the publication as a template so that you can start new chapters with blank pages, but with the page layout and ruler guides in place.

Preparing Text and Graphics

If your word processor is one that offers a style sheet feature, use your word processing program to preformat the manuscript to use style sheet definitions with names such as **subhead1**, **subhead2**, **caption**, **body**, etc. The style names should define the text font, the type size, the type style, and leading, and should include tab settings, indents, and any other formatting characteristics that are appropriate. The simple assignment of style names to appropriate sections of text is all that you need to do. You can edit the style definitions in PageMaker, but the more style definitions you set in advance, the faster the production process. Use the Retain format option in the Place dialog box to bring formatted text into PageMaker with the style sheets included.

If your word processor does not offer style sheets that are recognized by PageMaker, do not format the text in your word processor, because you want to control all of the formatting for this example by using style sheets. You can create the style sheets in PageMaker later and then place unformatted text, so *don't* use the Retain format option. To speed up the process, use carriage returns only at the ends of paragraphs and fixed lines, and delete any extra spaces (such as an extra space between sentences) in the text file before placing it into PageMaker.

PageMaker can export selected text, including style sheets, back to files in the Microsoft Word format. You will be able to make last-minute text and style sheet changes and then export the text back to Word files for your archive or for use in other Word documents.

If you are not working with Word, use the Clipboard to copy and paste selected text into Microsoft Windows Write. Books can be archived in

PageMaker publication files, as well as in word processing files.

It can be useful to type captions as numeric footnotes in Word files, so that when PageMaker places the files, the captions (which are acting as footnotes) end up at the end of the story. You can then click the text element handles to reposition the captions alongside the figures. The numbered references in the text remain intact, as do the numbered captions. An alternate method is to store the captions in a separate file and then place that file alongside the page in the empty pasteboard area. After you place an illustration that requires a caption, drag the captions block and click its handle to leave only one caption in place. Next, place the rest of the caption block back where it was located on the pasteboard. Continue this process with each figure until you have used up all of the captions. Either method is fine because both avoid the insertion of many small stories (separate text blocks) in the publication file. This is an important benefit because the more small stories in the file, the more disk space is taken up by the file.

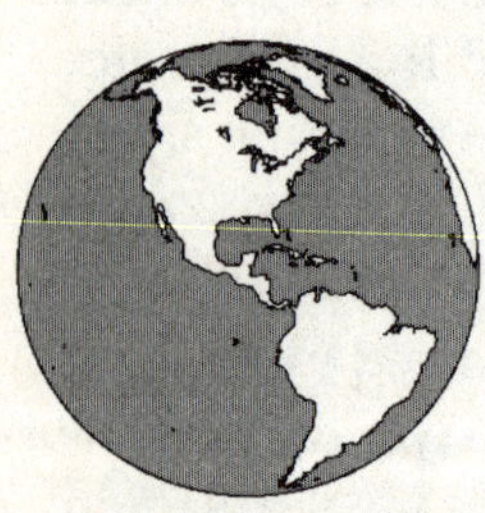

Books sometimes require line art (draw-type graphics) or paint-type graphics. You may also want to add artistic flourishes or cartoon characters to book pages. You can create such art yourself by using a paint program, or you can use (and possibly modify) electronic clip art from various clip art libraries on disk. You could place clip art such as the sample next to this paragraph, and resize the images to fit the narrow column next to the text. Remember that with all paint-type graphics, you should hold down the Control (Ctrl) key while you resize the graphic, in order to use PageMaker's built-in optimal sizes (also hold down the Shift key to preserve the graphic's proportions).

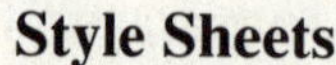

Style Sheets

Be sure to select the Convert quotes option in the Place dialog box. This option instructs PageMaker to convert any instance of a double-hyphen to an em dash (—), and to convert quotation marks and single quote marks into the proper open and close quote symbols.

When you place text without the Retain format option, the text takes on the characteristics of the Type specs dialog box (in the Type menu). The Type specs have already been set for the chapter title, so you must change them after typing the chapter title. For the body of the text, choose

Times Roman or another serif font, at 10 or 12 points with 12 or 14 points of leading, respectively. Choose these specifications in the Type specs menu before you place the text. If you place the text first, choose the text tool, click somewhere in the text, and employ the Select all command (or press the Control (Ctrl) key and type the letter A) to highlight all of the text. Next, make changes in the Type specs dialog box.

If you use style sheets, place the text with both the Retain format option and the Convert quotes option turned on. Do not turn on the Read tags option, because that option requires the use of tag names in the text. (Tag names are discussed later in this book.)

You can place the text of a chapter rapidly. This is especially true if you use the semiautoflow feature, which lets you place text into the wide column of each page without having to click the bottom handle. (To use the semautoflow feature, select the Autoflow option and hold down the Shift key when you place the text.)

The text should be placed so that it fills the entire width of the page. By changing the definition of the body text to include an indent, the body of the text can be edited while first-level headings remain flush with the left margin. Second-level headings can be defined to be indented along with the body text.

If you did not define style sheets in your word processor (or if PageMaker does not recognize your word processor's style sheet definitions), select the text in PageMaker and define a style sheet for it. To define a style for a section of text, choose the section and then choose Define styles from the Type menu (Figure 3-52). You can then assign an already-defined style sheet to the section of text, or else create a new style sheet definition by clicking New. When you create a new style sheet definition, PageMaker asks for the new style definition's name. You can base the new style's definition upon another style (Figure 3-53). For example, you can create a style sheet called Special, and base it on the Body style sheet. When you change the font in Body, the same font change also occurs for Special.

You can edit a style sheet definition at any time. The styles shown in Figure 3-52 were brought into PageMaker from Word. To indent the body of the text, select the Body style and click the Edit button. A dialog box appears that contains buttons for the style sheet definition (Figure 3-54).

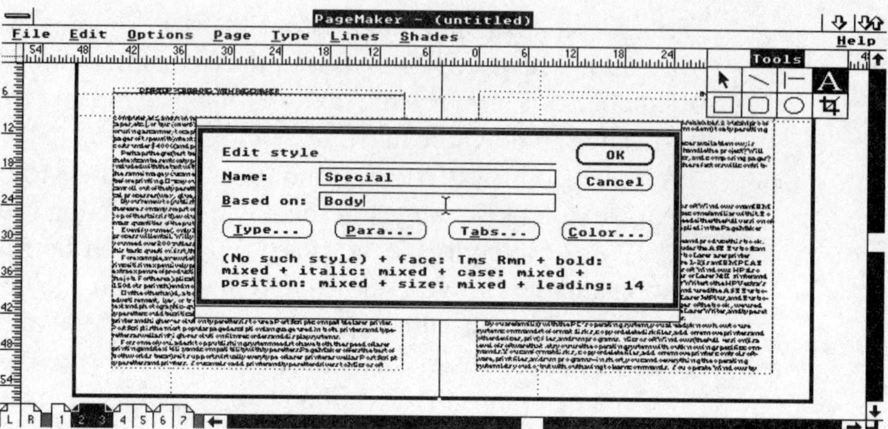

Figure 3-53. Create a new style sheet, called Special, based upon the Body style sheet.

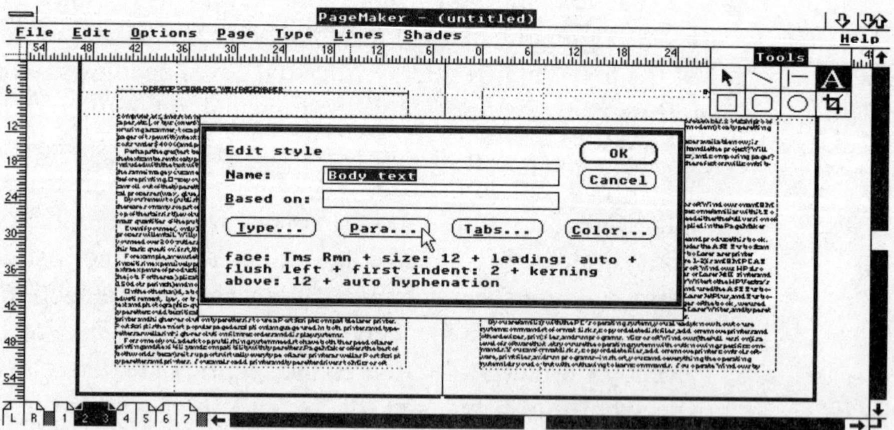

Figure 3-54. Edit an existing style sheet definition, Body, in order to indent the body text of the book.

Select the Para button to edit the paragraph indent specification (Figure 3-55). After you click OK in the definition box and in the final style sheet box, the body text is indented throughout the entire book.

During the process of assigning style sheet names to the text, it helps to display the *style palette* (a toolbox of style names). To do so, select the

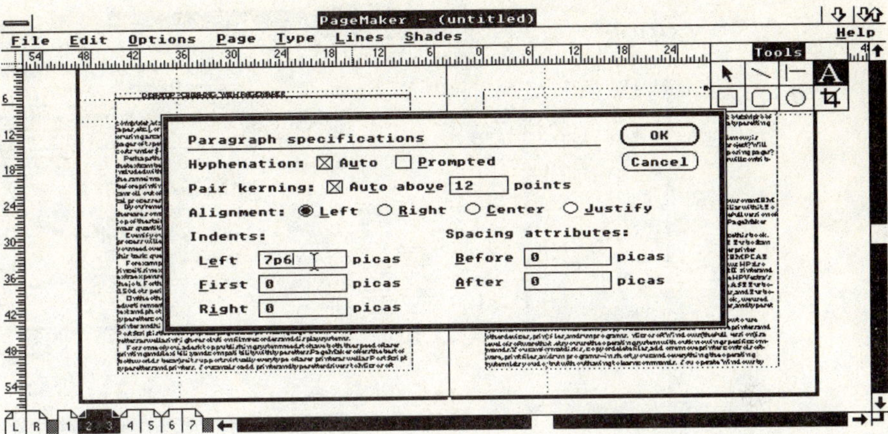

Figure 3-55. Change the paragraph indent for the Body style sheet so that body text is indented by 7 picas and 6 points throughout the book.

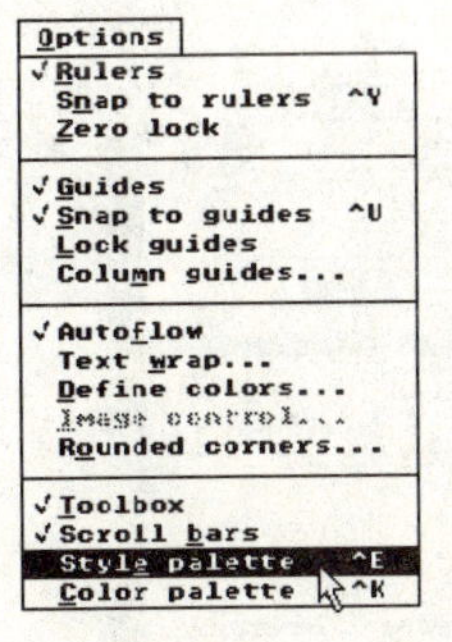

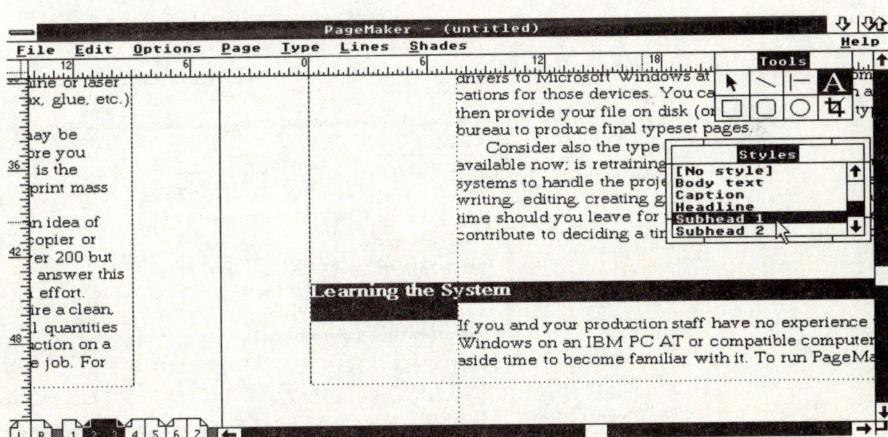

Figure 3-56. Select the Subhead style so that level 1 subheadings are not indented with the body text.

Style palette option in the Options menu, or type Control-E. The style sheet names appear in a scrollable box on the page. Select text with the text tool, and then select a style name (Figure 3-56). In this manner, select the subheadings and assign them to the Subhead style sheet, so that they are not indented with the rest of the body text.

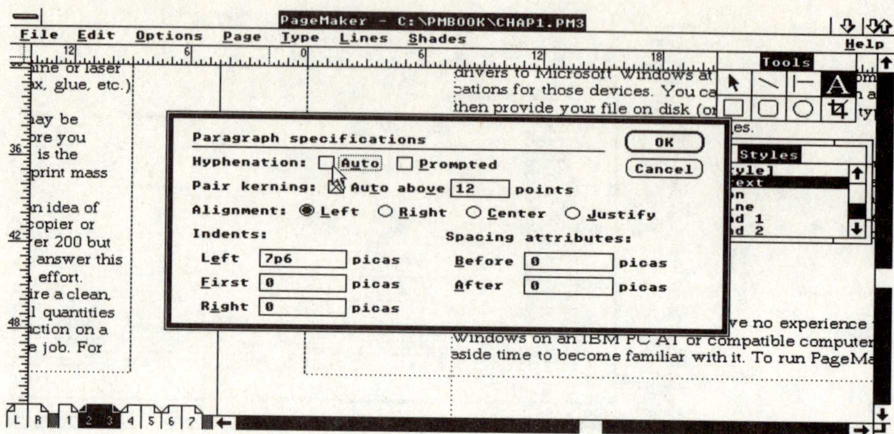

Figure 3-57. The Paragraph dialog box has an option for turning the automatic hyphenation feature on or off. Turn this feature off for a section of text if you don't want the hyphenation.

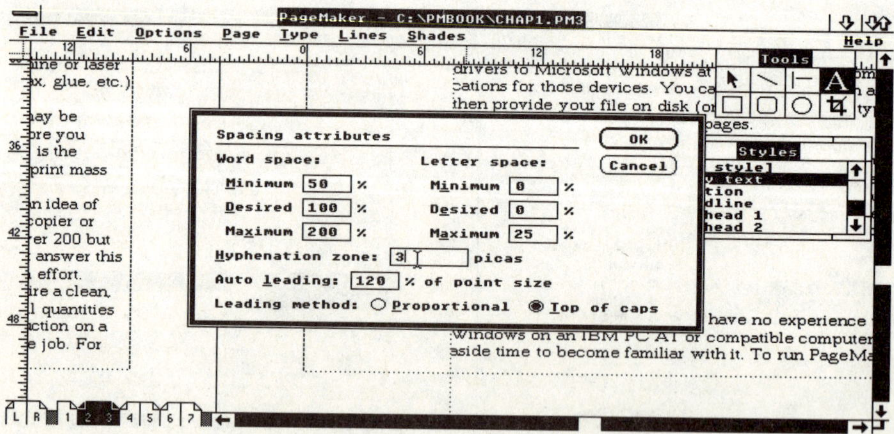

Figure 3-58. Change the hyphenation zone for ragged-right text.

Style sheets are an important innovation because you can change the formatting settings of the entire publication by changing a few style sheet definitions. The use of style sheets is another reason why a template file is valuable—a template file contains predefined style sheets that can be assigned to incoming text without any need to remember the specifications of a design.

Hyphenation

To avoid the creation of an *orphan* (a single word or a very short line by itself at the bottom of the page) or a *widow* (a word or a very short line by itself at the top of the page), turn off hyphenation for the section of the text that is highlighted with the text tool. To do do, select the text and then choose the Paragraph command from the Type menu (Figure 3-57).

When automatic hyphenation is turned on, PageMaker decides how to hyphenate words by checking its 110,000-word dictionary (based on software from Houghton Mifflin). You can change from automatic to prompted hyphenation, so that PageMaker prompts you with a dialog box when it encounters a word to hyphenate. You can then accept PageMaker's guess at the correct hyphenation, or else type a hyphen exactly where you want it. You can also add hyphenated words to a supplemental dictionary so that PageMaker remembers how you wanted the word hyphenated.

Another way to control hyphenation is to limit the hyphenation zone with ragged-right text (this method does not work with justified text). The Spacing dialog box (Figure 3-58) lets you change the zone measurement from the right margin to a new measurement, such as 3 picas in from the right margin. When automatic hyphenation is turned on, PageMaker checks if the hyphenated word breaks within the specified zone. If it does not break within the zone, PageMaker does not hyphenate the word. Instead, it carries the word over to the next line.

You can also change the word spacing that is used to justify the text. The spacing values apply to the entire story or chapter (or text file), however, not just to the area selected with the text tool. The new setting may cause undesirable changes to occur elsewhere in the chapter. For optimal spacing for justified text, leave automatic hyphenation on and set the word spacing range at 50% for minimum, 100% for desired, and 200% for maximum. Leave the letterspacing at 0% and 25% for minimum and maximum, respectively.

Printing Chapters

Publication files are limited to 128 pages each, so it makes sense to separate a book into chapters and to store each chapter in a separate publication file. Set the starting page number of a publication file in the

Page setup dialog box. PageMaker can automatically number pages up to 9,999 (starting with whatever number you want), using arabic and composite page-numbering systems.

If you turn on crop marks in the Print dialog box, crop marks are printed at the page boundaries and used as trim marks. You can also print the book's pages in reverse order for use with printers that send pages out face up (and backward in sequence).

Summary

The information presented in this chapter enables you to successfully produce an annual report, a technical manual, and a book. The examples demonstrated how to use PageMaker to perform several steps in the publishing process. A summary of the steps follows.

First, set up master pages with footers, page numbers, and a logo. Move and resize the logo for the master pages, and place the logo on Page 1 because the master items display option is turned off for Page 1.

Next, place text on Page 1, using a dropped initial for the first letter in the column, and then cut and paste a headline into the margin. Draw a rule and finish placing text. Check for and fix any widows or orphans by adjusting the word spacing. Draw a rectangular framed placeholder for a photo, and then force text to wrap around it. Add more graphics, and use the cropping tool to hide portions of a graphic image.

Place data from a Lotus 1-2-3 spreadsheet by using the installed PageMaker filter. This allows you to place part of a spreadsheet by using a named reference, or to place the entire print area of a spreadsheet. Create boxes and drop shadow effects to add dimension to the spreadsheets and charts.

The method that you should use to add charts and graphs depends upon the program that you used to create the charts or graphs, and whether the graphics were stored in a paint (bit-mapped) or draw (object or vector) type of file. Charts and graphs can be placed, cropped, and resized, and any text they contain can be adjusted or replaced with new text. When you work with bit-mapped charts and graphs, type new labels and text with PageMaker in order to obtain the best results.

Before you print the report, check if the fonts that you used are available in your printer. For instance, if your chart or document includes fonts that are not available in your printer, then you need to change the default printer or else recompose your document for a new target printer. Other printing options include the ability to change the printer resolution, the orientation of pages (landscape or portrait; note that this setting also affects the availability of fonts to your printer if you use PCL font cartridges), the number of copies, the range of pages to be printed, and so on.

Design the pages of a technical manual, and pay special attention to the ability to flow text quickly by using the Autoflow option. Use the Text wrap feature to allow text to jump over the illustrations, and to leave an equal amount of space between the text and the illustration.

Design the nonstandard pages of a book (with crop marks for the printing press), and create and use template files. Define style sheets and use them to set formatting settings for captions, body text, and subheadings.

4 Graphic Design

Coffee-table books contain pages that have a well-designed, polished appearance. Page advertisements and flyers are designed purposely to attract a reader's attention. Magazine pages are designed to be both visually exciting and to have a clear hierarchy that begins with the article's title and department heading, and extends to text subheadings and captions for photos or illustrations.

Only a few clear rules need to be followed during the process of designing pages. For example, don't mix more than three fonts (italic and bold styles of a font count as the same font) on a page, and don't crowd the page with text and graphics. For the most part, design decisions are subjective. If you are not a designer, and you are not employing a designer to design a template for you, use one of the templates supplied with PageMaker. They are all examples of the application of excellent design techniques.

PageMaker excels at providing tools for moving elements on the page and for customizing layouts. You can mix two or more column styles on one page (for example, use a two-column format at the top of the page and a three-column format at the bottom), wrap text around irregularly shaped objects, put reversed (white) type onto a black background, begin a paragraph with an enlarged capital letter, and so on. You can also move

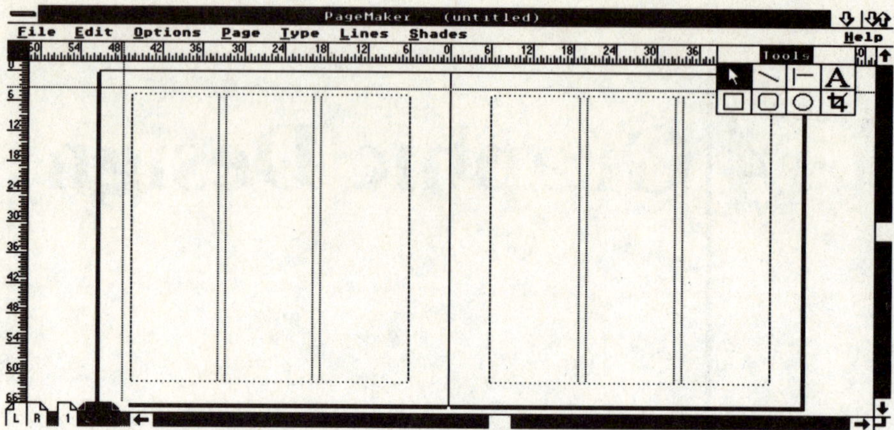

Figure 4-1. Drag the zero point from its former position on the top left edge of the page to the top left margin.

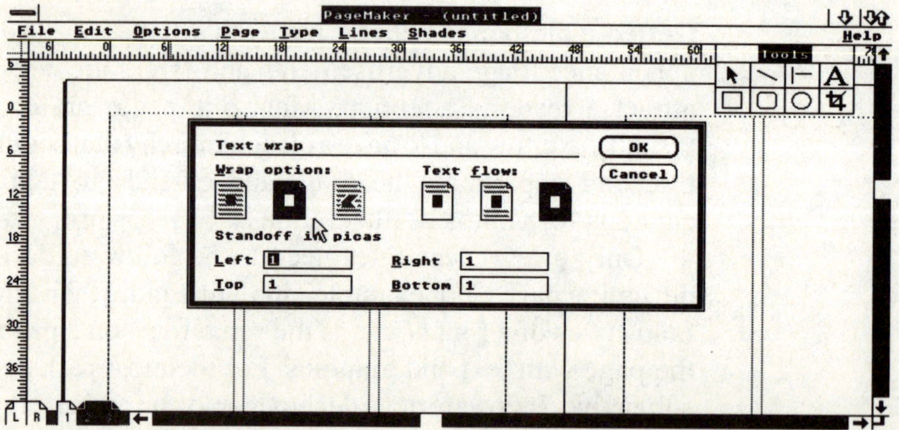

Figure 4-2. After selecting Text wrap from the Options menu, choose the middle wrap option, which automatically selects the right-hand text flow option.

letters closer together by using a manual kerning function. These kinds of enhancements give your pages a designed appearance.

The trick to producing custom pages is to design the elements (such as fancy line styles and boxes, or reversed-type-on-black headlines) first, and then copy them for use on different pages. For example, if you design

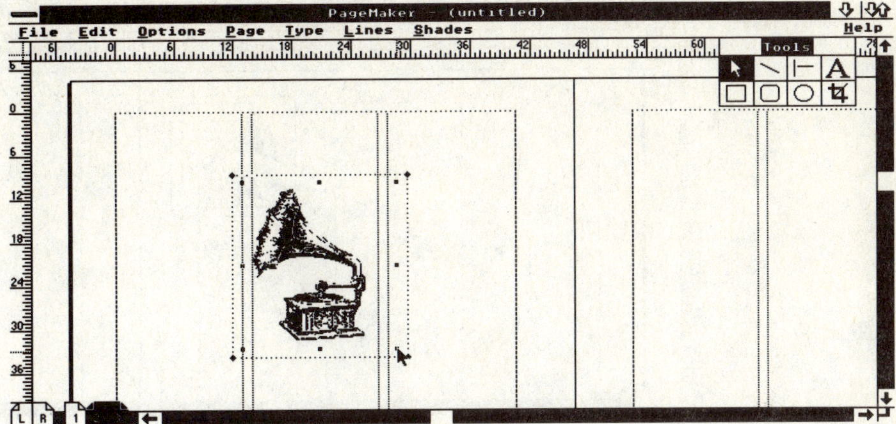

Figure 4-3. When you select the Text wrap option after choosing to place a graphics file, PageMaker displays a wrap boundary for wrapping text around graphics.

a black panel with reversed (white) text for use on many different pages, copy the panel and text and paste them onto another page. Type new text and resize the panel to fit the new text. The original elements remain the same, and you can copy and paste them again.

The following special effects and techniques are by no means the only effects that can be achieved with PageMaker, but they serve as a representative sample of the application of PageMaker's tools. This chapter also shows how to change the contrast and brightness values of scanned images by using the Image control command.

Ruler Zero Point

One aspect of PageMaker's rulers makes them even more useful for measuring distances on layouts. The rulers start at a zero point that corresponds to the top left edge of the page, so that you can measure to the right of the left edge or down from the top edge. This zero point does not change as you move around the page so that distances are measured from a specific point. In a double-facing page display, the zero point is the point on the edge between the pages (the top left edge of the right-hand page); otherwise, each page has its own zero point.

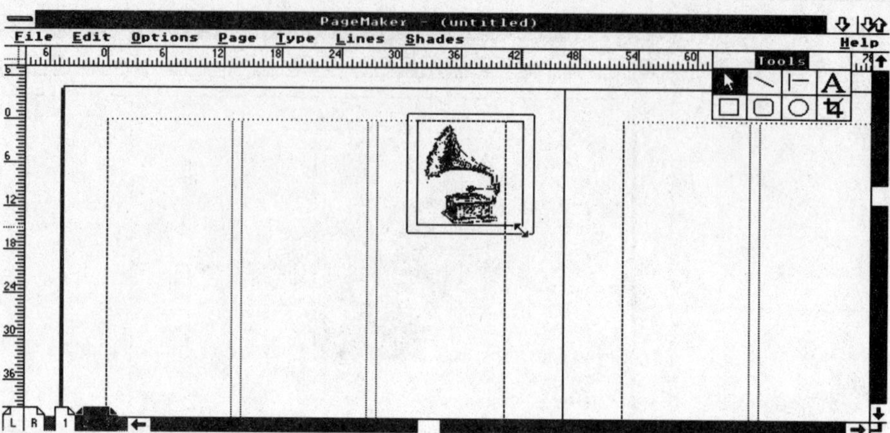

Figure 4-4. The wrap boundary scales with the graphic image.

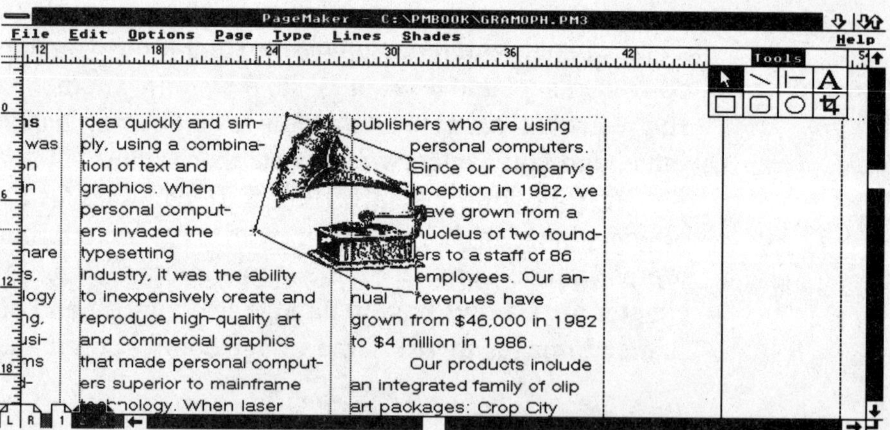

Figure 4-5. Drag a point along the wrap boundary to adjust the boundary's shape, and thereby adjust the white space between the graphic image and the text.

Move the zero point to any location on the page in order to measure distances across or down the page. Many designers prefer to move the zero point to the top left margin of the page, rather than to the top left edge. To move the zero point, point on the two dotted lines that cross in the upper left corner of the display (Figure 4-1). Drag the two dotted lines diagonally in order to change both rulers. To change one ruler, drag the two

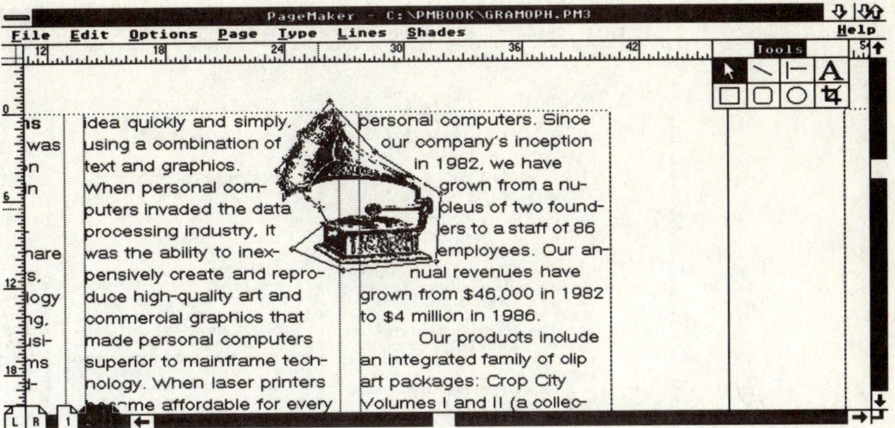

Figure 4-6. After adding points by holding down the Alt key while clicking on the boundary line, you can fine-tune the wrap boundary.

dotted lines either horizontally or vertically. The zero point is the base for both rulers.

After you place the zero point where you want it, lock it into place with the Zero lock option in the Options menu so that you don't accidentally move it later. When you begin a new publication, the zero point is unlocked and you can either change it or lock it.

Wrapping Text around Graphics

PageMaker offers a very flexible method for wrapping text around graphics. Select the graphic image and choose the Text wrap option from the Options menu (Figure 4-2), PageMaker displays a dotted line that acts as a wrap (or *text standoff*) boundary for wrapping the text around the graphic image (Figure 4-3). If you move or resize the image, the wrap boundary line moves or scales with it (Figure 4-4).

To adjust the boundaries of the wrap, drag the dotted line with the mouse. This step allows you to control the amount of white space between the text and the image (Figure 4-5). To add points to the wrap boundary, press the Alt key when clicking on the boundary line. You can then adjust the shape of the text wrap even further (Figure 4-6).

Figure 4-7. The enlarged initial capital letter, cut from the text body and pasted next to the text (or simply retyped).

The wrap boundary provides the flexibility to wrap text around part of an image while overlaying text upon another part of the image. The wrap boundary also permits the amount of white space between the image and the text to be altered. If you make editing changes later, the text will flow naturally around the graphic image, following the wrap boundary.

Enlarged Initial Capital

Magazine articles usually begin with a single enlarged capital letter (called an *initial capital*) that leads in the first sentence of the article's text. Usually the letter is in the same font as the article's title, but the letter's size is two or three times as large as the size of the letters in the rest of the text. Sometimes an initial capital is also placed at the beginning of a new section of the text.

If the enlarged initial capital letter is in the form of a graphic image (that is, composed with a graphics program or a font design program), simply place the graphic image as you would any other graphic image. Use the Text wrap boundary (as previously described) to wrap text around the image's irregular shape. If you want to simply type the letter as another

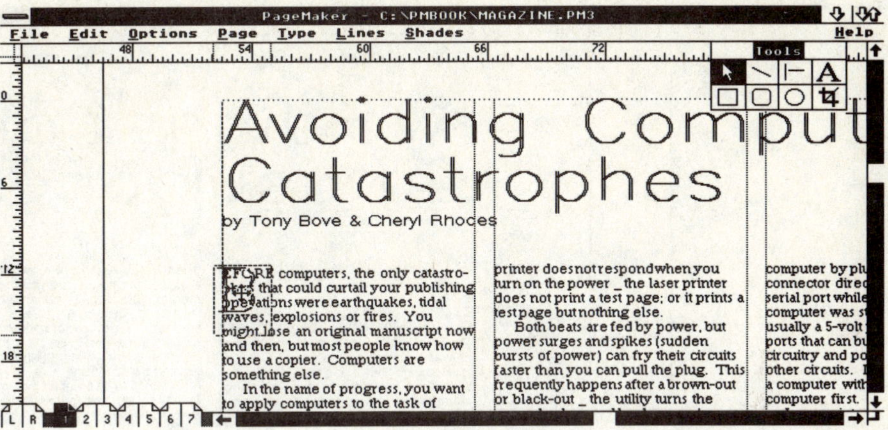

Figure 4-8. Drag the enlarged initial capital letter into its position on top of the text body.

piece of text, don't use the Text wrap option because that option doesn't work with text blocks.

Assume that the capital letter is designed to be located inside of the boundaries of the opening text block (so that the letter does not stick out of the column at the top or on the side, as in the example in Chapter 3). Type the letter in an area next to the text body and delete that letter from the opening of the article. Alternatively, use the Cut command to cut the letter from the opening, and then use the Paste command to paste the letter into an area next to the text body. Click an insertion point immediately after the enlarged letter and press the Enter key to ensure that the line length of the character is accurate.

Use the text tool to highlight the letter, and then set the letter's type specifications. The letter should be at least two or three lines deep in comparison to the size of type in the regular text, or else the letter will not stand out. The letter should not be bigger than the letters that are used in the article title.

If the regular text is 10 points with 12 points of leading (as in the first example), choose a font that matches the font in either the text body or the article title. (The sample initial capital letter is set in the title font at 48 points, which is the same size as the title font's size).

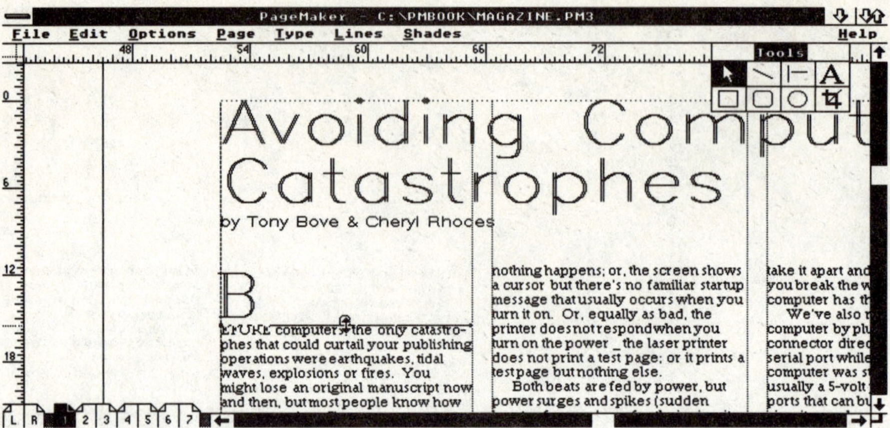

Figure 4-9. Push down on the text block and line the text up with the neighboring column.

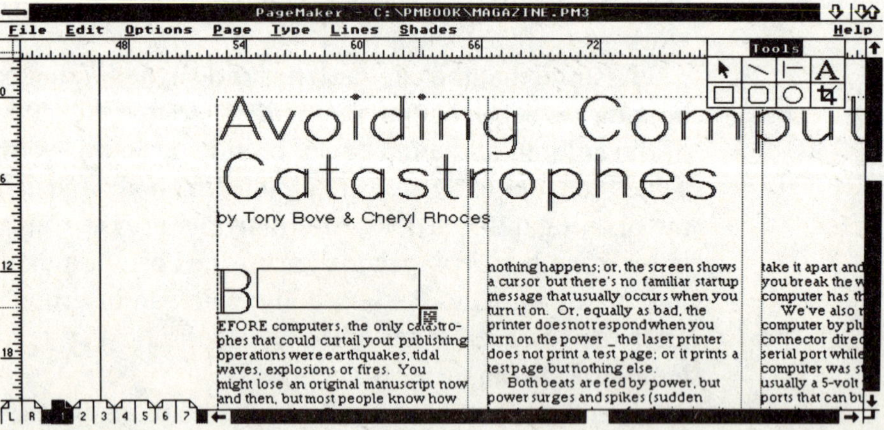

Figure 4-10. After clicking the top handle of the text block, drag-place the text next to the initial capital.

Figure 4-7 shows the enlarged initial capital after it has been pasted or typed next to the text body across from the actual position that the letter will occupy, and then set to the proper point size. You may also want to change the characters in the first word in the text block to capital letters, as shown in the figure.

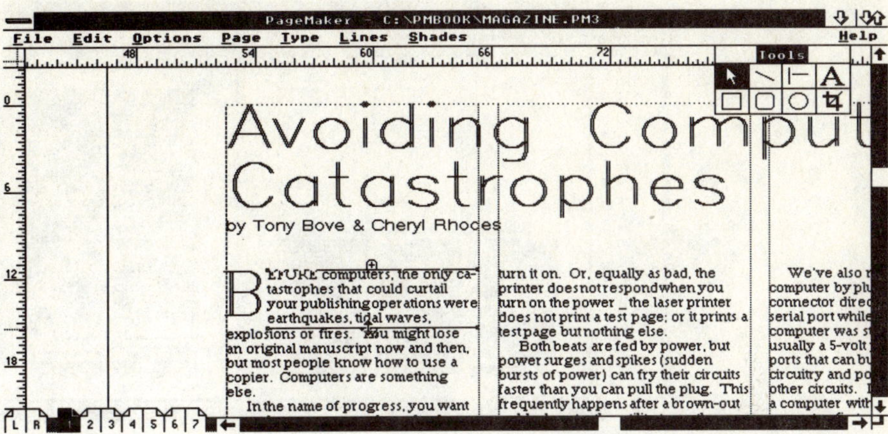

Figure 4-11. Adjust the new text block to line up with the other text.

Drag the initial capital in the text body to the letter's appropriate position (Figure 4-8). Choose the Send to back option from the Edit menu so that the letter is positioned behind the text body.

Push down on the text body (Figure 4-9) far enough to line up the text located below the initial capital with the text of the neighboring column. Click the handle on top of the text body, and drag-place the top part of the text body next to the initial capital (Figure 4-10). Finally, adjust the new text block located next to the initial capital so that the text lines up with the other text (Figure 4-11).

Mixing Column Layouts

You can combine one type of column layout (such as a two-column layout) with any other type of column layout on the same page. It is easier to combine column layouts after you first separate them with a rule or with white space, so that readers are not confused about the flow of text.

A typical combination of layouts may be a two-column layout at the top of a page, and a three- or four-column layout at the bottom of the page. The publication file should contain master pages that are set to the predominant column layout (in this case, the three-column layout). Draw a line to separate the layouts (Figure 4-12), and then change the number

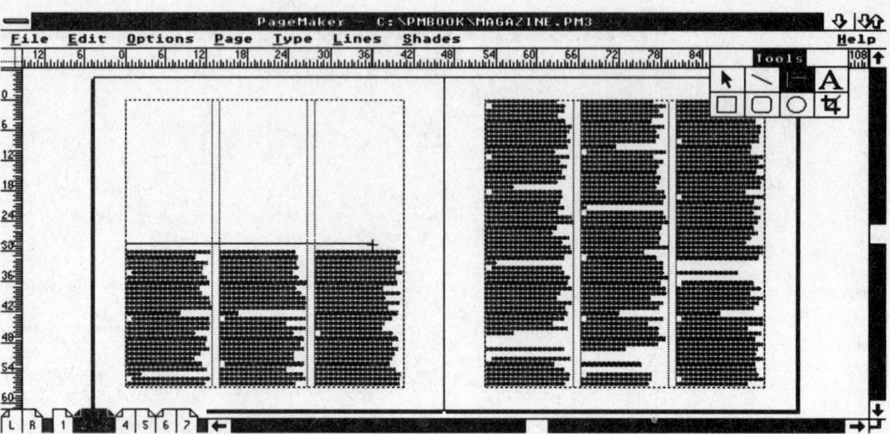

Figure 4-12. Draw a line across the three-column page after placing the three-column text, but before placing the two-column text.

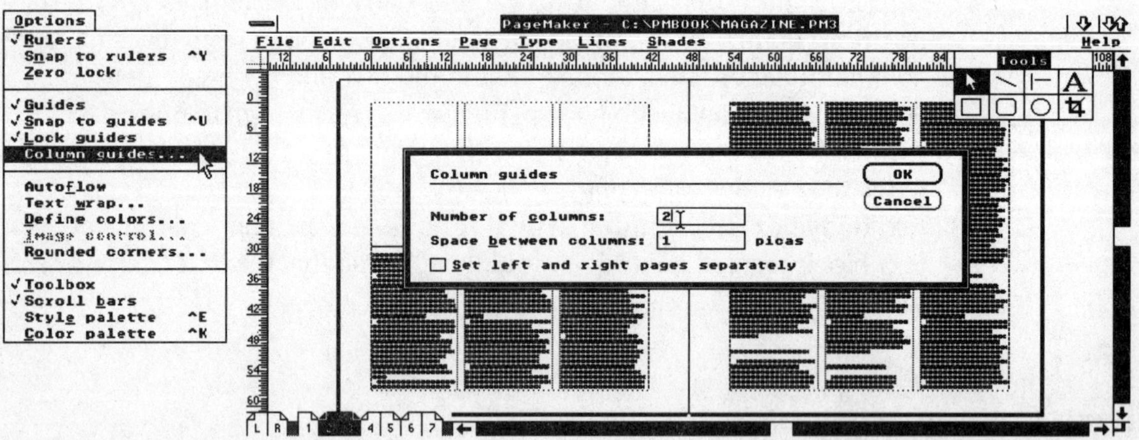

Figure 4-13. Change the number of columns for this page after pouring the three-column text.

of columns by using the Column guides option (Figure 4-13). (Changing the column layout has no effect on already-placed text.) You can now place the two-column text (Figure 4-14). Leave the same spacing between columns. (Use less spacing if the columns are very narrow.)

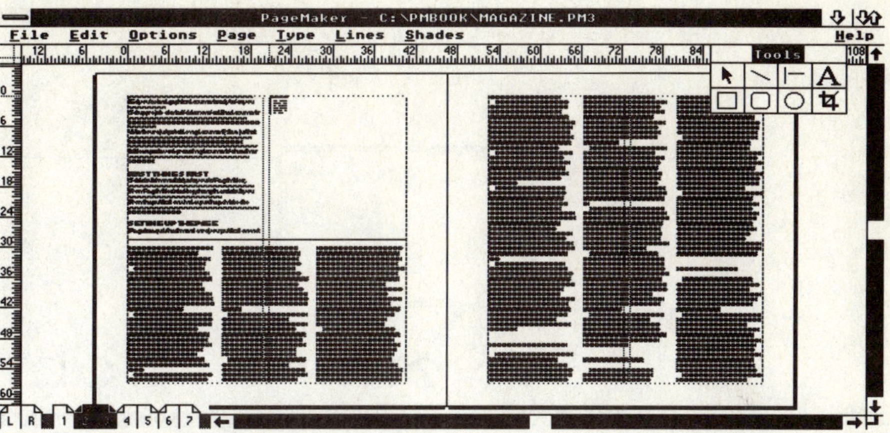

Figure 4-14. Place the text in a two-column layout after changing the layout.

Continue placing the text in the two-column layout. When you are finished, delete the separation line and replace it with a stylized border. Alternatively, draw a box around the three-column layout to separate it from the two-column layout.

Reverse Type

One popular effect (which originated from the design of menus on computer displays) is *reverse* (white) type on a black or gray background. Use reverse type in a black background or in a background with a 60% or an 80% gray shade, because these contrasts provide the best results. If you want to reverse type from a patterned background, experiment to see which pattern creates the best results.

The example is the first page of a magazine department, which includes a department heading box. Draw the box (Figure 4-15), and assign to it the line style of a double-line.

The box bleeds off the top of the page, and the part of the box located above the page trim mark will not print. Select the box, then select Black from the Shades menu.

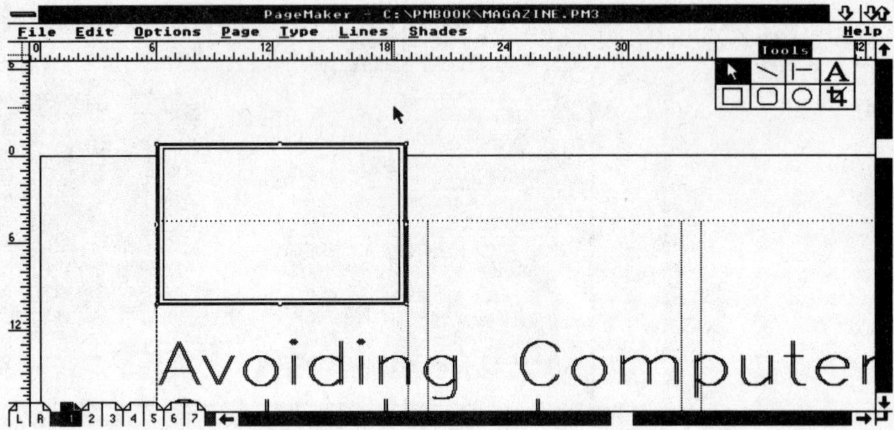

Figure 4-15. Draw a box with the double-line style, and shade it black.

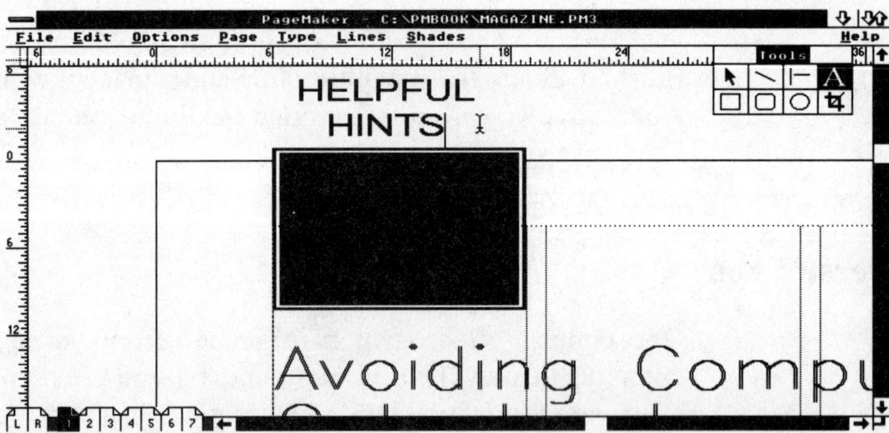

Figure 4-16. Type the text for the black box (before selecting Reverse type).

Next, switch to the text tool. Select a font, point size, and leading value in the Type specs dialog box. Type the text for the panel in the area outside of the panel (Figure 4-16). Note that a sans serif font, such as Helvetica, produces a crisper white type. You can use a very light or italic font reversed against a black background, but don't use reverse italic type in a gray-shaded box. Also, always check that your print shop can reproduce

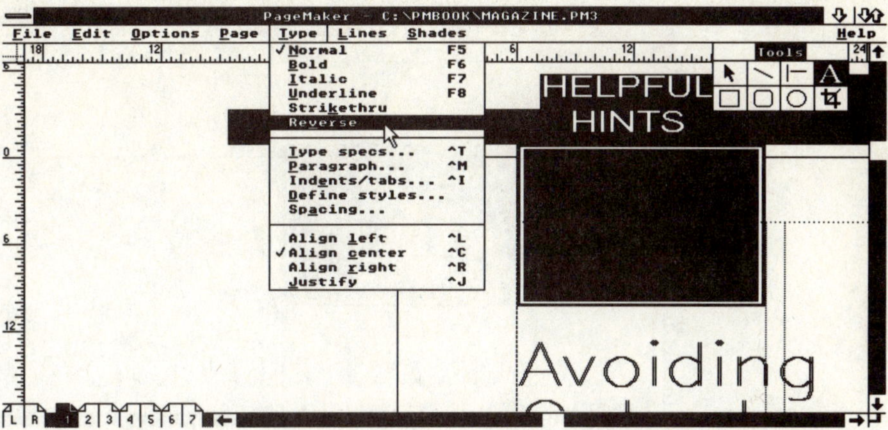

Figure 4-17. Highlight with the text tool and select Reversed type.

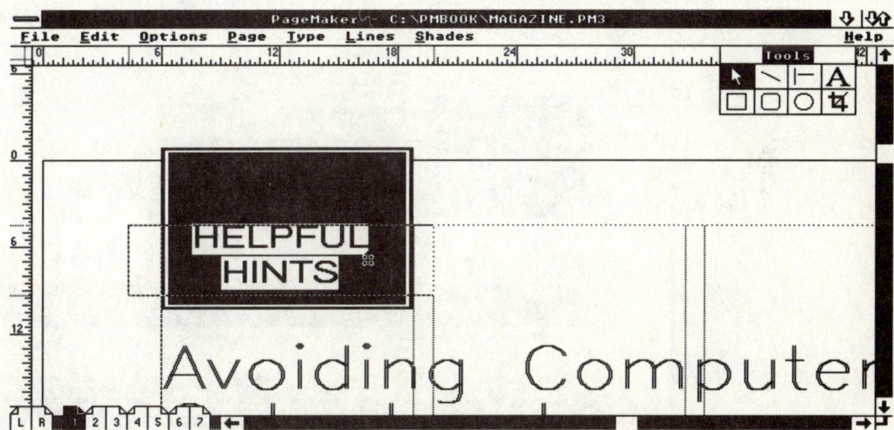

Figure 4-18. Drag the text into the panel.

your master page for the press without breaking the type or plugging the type up.

Drag across the text and select Reverse type from the Type menu (Figure 4-17). The text disappears because it is still placed on a white background.

Switch to the pointer tool, point in the middle of the text block, and

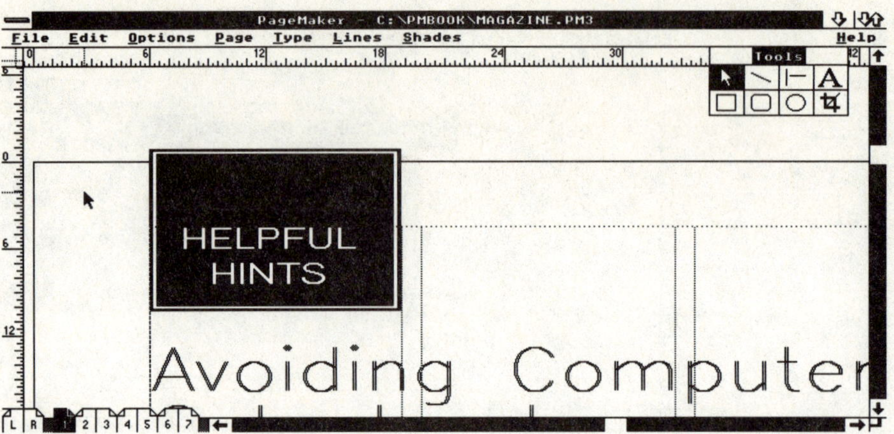

Figure 4-19. The final result is white text on a black background.

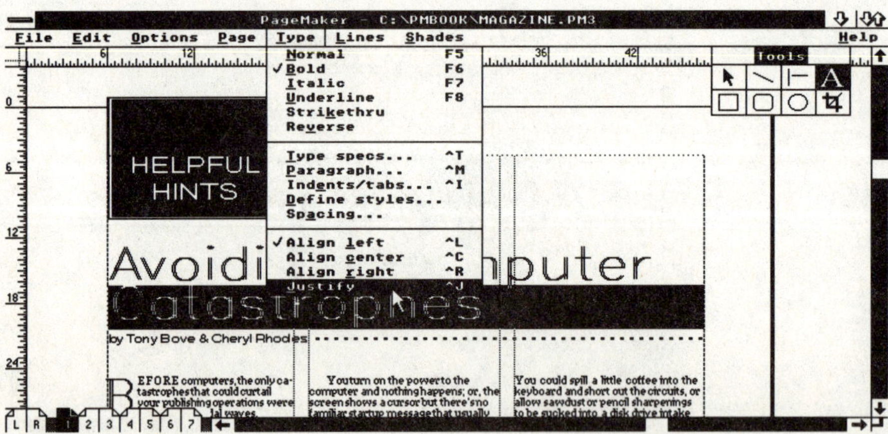

Figure 4-20. After cutting and pasting the second part of the title as a separate text block, set it to be justified.

drag the text into the black box (Figure 4-18). The final result should be white text in a black background (Figure 4-19). Now that you can see the white text against the black background, switch to the pointer tool. Point in the middle of the text and drag the text in order to center it properly in the panel.

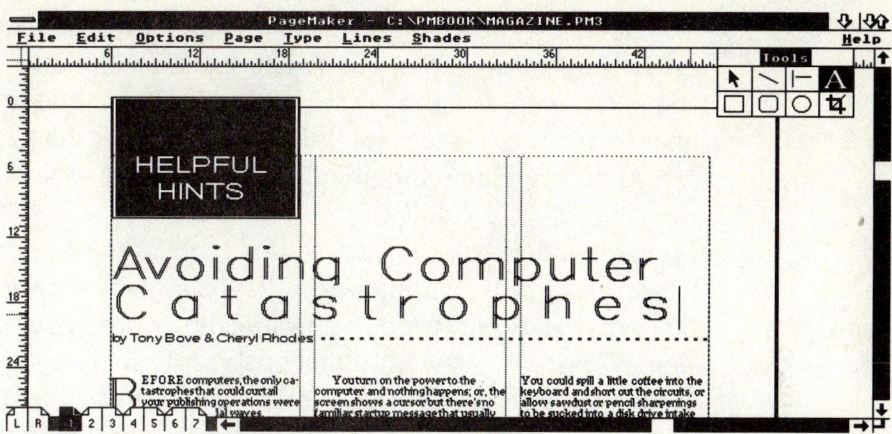

Figure 4-21. Add regular spaces between letters, two spaces between words, one space at the end, and finally, enough nonbreaking spaces to fill the line.

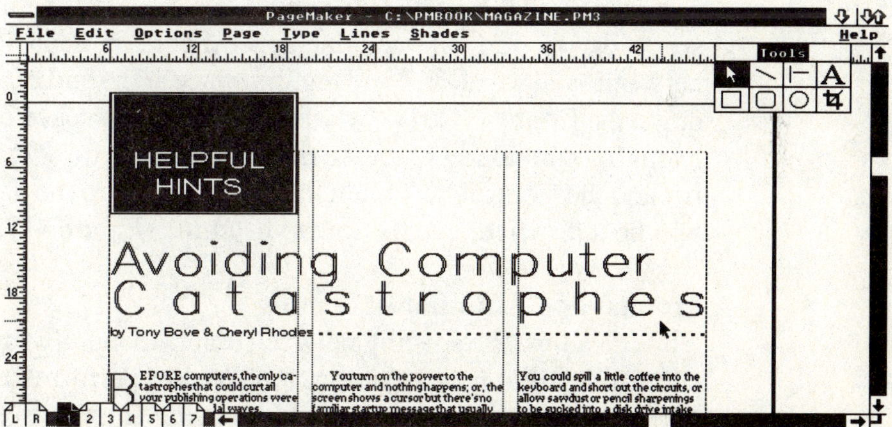

Figure 4-22. An evenly spread headline justified to both margins, with a reverse type panel for the department title.

Fancy Titles and Headlines

Two very common methods that are used to create fancy headlines and article titles are the technique of spreading a headline (by adding space between the letters) and the technique of kerning the letters in a headline so that they are closer together. The second technique is useful when the first letter in the headline is set in plain or bold style text and the second letter is italic, or if the size of the title is greater than 18-point type size. PageMaker can handle both effects, plus many others.

Spreading Text

To add space to a headline, simply type a space between each character. You can type an em space by pressing the Control (Ctrl), Shift, and = keys (or the Control + keys) simultaneously. Alternatively, type a nonbreaking space by holding down the Control key when you press the space bar.

To spread a headline so that it fills a specific width, first isolate the headline as a separate text block. Cut the headline from the rest of the article text and paste it elsewhere on the page, or simply type the headline separately. Set the headline's font, size, and leading. Select Justified as the paragraph style (Figure 4-20) and move the headline into place. Use the space bar to add one regular space between each letter, two spaces between each word, and one regular space at the end of the headline. Hold down the Control (Ctrl) key while pressing the space bar in order to add enough nonbreaking spaces to fill the line (Figure 4-21). Release the space bar and the Control key when the cursor jumps to the next line. The result will be a justified, evenly spread headline (Figure 4-22).

Manual and Automatic Kerning

You can adjust the spacing between letters manually (by kerning), or else control the automatic spacing. PageMaker performs automatic kerning with selected pairs of characters by using information supplied by the designer of the printer font. The degree of automatic kerning depends both upon the printer and upon the font that you use. (Some printers do not support pair-kerning.)

The pair kerning option is usually turned on for all of the text that is above 12 points in size. You can change this setting in the Paragraph dialog box (Figure 4-23). Note that if automatic kerning is used for text point sizes smaller than 12 points, the text flowing and placement functions slow down. You can turn on automatic kerning for selected

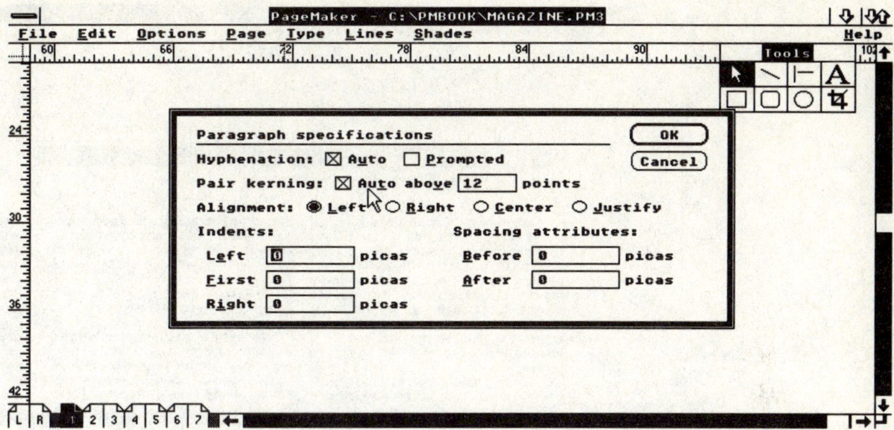

Figure 4-23. The Paragraph dialog box, which lets you specify settings for automatic pair kerning, as well as for automatic hyphenation, paragraph indents, alignment, and interparagraph spacing.

areas of the text, rather than kerning the entire text.

Kern the letters in headlines manually. Decrease the space in order to tighten any two letters, and increase the space in order to create breathing room between any two letters. Use the text tool and click an insertion point between the two characters. Press the Control and Backspace keys to delete the automatic kern. Next, press the Control and Backspace keys, or the Control, Shift, and Backspace keys, to begin manual kerning. To decrease the spacing, hold down the Control key and press the Backspace key. To increase the spacing, hold down the Control and Shift keys and press the Backspace key.

The unit of measurement for manual kerning is about 1/24th of the em space for that particular font—exactly 1/24th of the point size of the character to the left of the insertion point. For example, if the font size is 24 points, the spacing is increased or decreased by 1 point. in the case of 12-point type, the spacing is increased or decreased by 1/2 point. You may not notice the space between letters increasing or decreasing on your computer display (although at 200% viewing size, the change is almost always apparent), but the printed page should contain properly kerned letters.

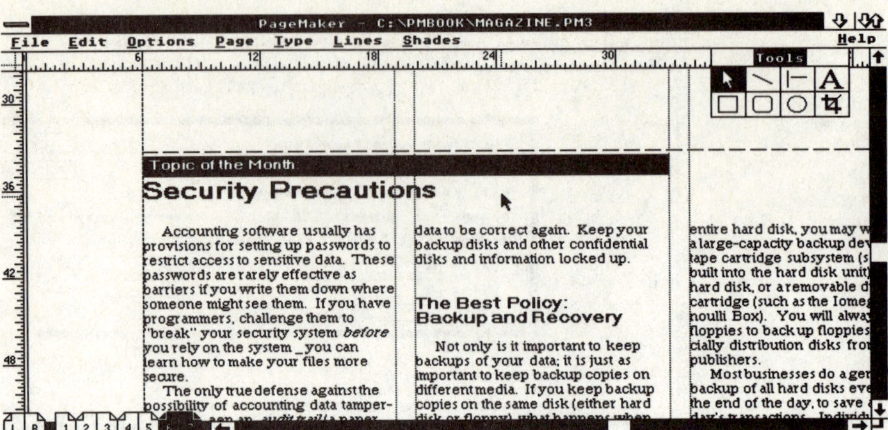

Figure 4-24. A thick rule with reverse type (a banner) and a dotted rule separator.

Rules, Borders, and Boxes

The judicious use of *rules* (horizontal and vertical lines on a page), borders, boxes, and line styles can make your page design more interesting. These elements can also serve as helpful separators that preserve the hierarchy of headings, subheadings, text body, sidebars, pull-quotes, and other elements.

Use a rule to divide one kind of text from another (such as a headline from text), one article from another, or an article from a sidebar. Vertical rules are often used to separate columns of text, especially when the text is aligned on the left margin and ragged on the right margin. Thick rules are often used to identify department headings in a magazine, or to create black banners for reversed type. Figure 4-24 shows a thick rule used as a text banner, and a dotted rule that separates articles.

Use the appropriate thickness for the rule. For example, don't use a thick rule to separate text in the same article—use a thin rule instead (perhaps a hairline rule). To draw attention to a headline, use a thick rule. Double rules tend to resemble picture frames, so use them only when they add emphasis to a headline or graphic, or serve as an appropriate frame. Above all, be consistent with the use of rules in a publication.

Different line styles can enhance the appearance of the page. The

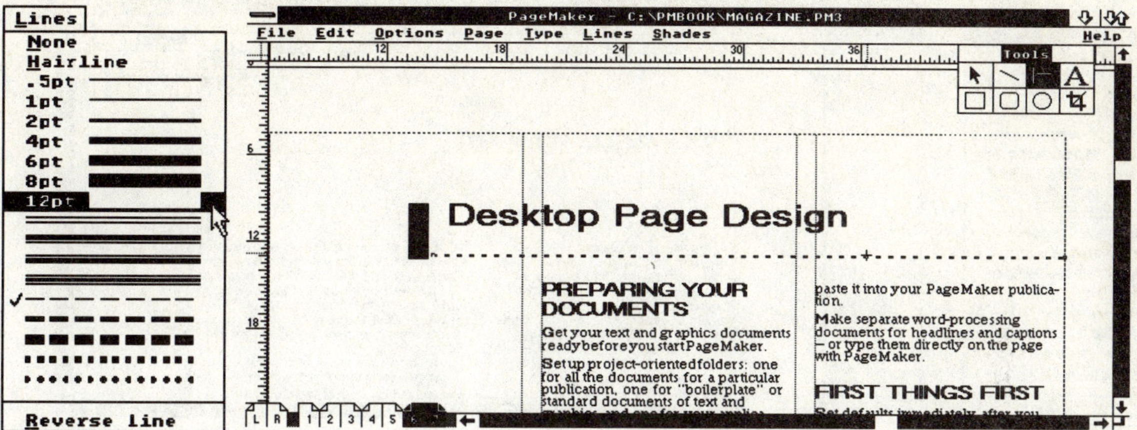

Figure 4-25. Line styles, such as a line of dots, can improve the appearance of the page.

dotted line is used in some popular magazine styles, as is the line of dashes. Figure 4-25 shows how a 12-point line (which looks like a solid, vertically oriented box) and a dotted line can be used in the same article title.

If you want to use a line style that is not available in the Lines menu, create a box that is only one line wide and use an appropriate pattern. For example, you can create a much thinner line of dots by first selecting the box tool, choosing no line style, selecting parallel lines for the box shade, and then drawing a box that is the length of the line (Figure 4-26). The next step is to resize the box. Overlap the long edges of the box (Figure 4-27) until they disappear from the display. The result is a thin vertical line of dots (Figure 4-28).

A box can be useful as a border around text that is separated from the main article, or as a border around an entire page that is different from other pages because it has a different column layout. Use thin line styles for borders around text, graphics, or a photo, with an equal amount of white space on all sides from the edge of the graphic or text to the box. To put a box inside a column, line the box up with the margins of the column. Resize the text block inside the box to be narrower than the column width (Figure 4-29).

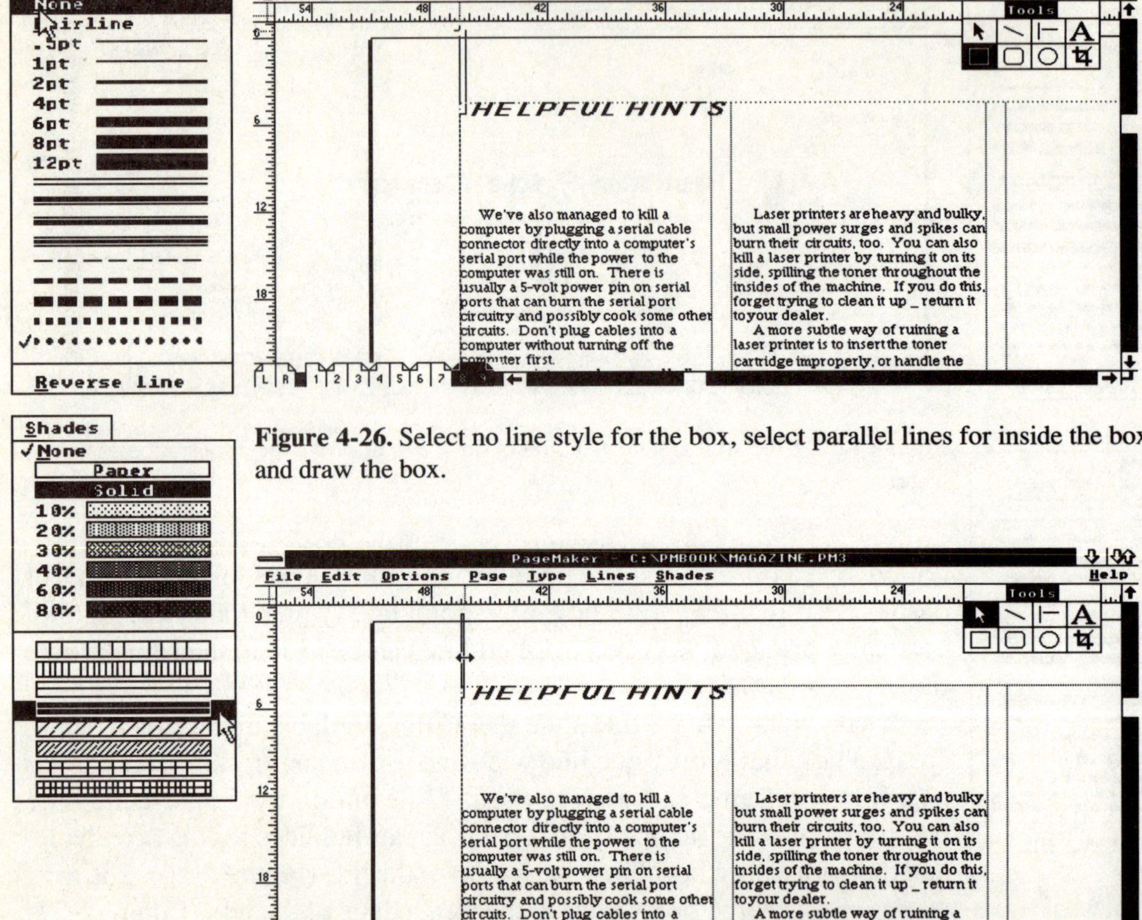

Figure 4-26. Select no line style for the box, select parallel lines for inside the box, and draw the box.

Figure 4-27. Change the width of the box to be only as wide as a line.

Image Control

PageMaker not only lets you place a scanned image onto the page—it also lets you adjust the brightness, contrast, and halftone screen characteristics of the image. PageMaker can print scanned images at actual size or at reduced or expanded sizes with excellent results, if you use the automatic

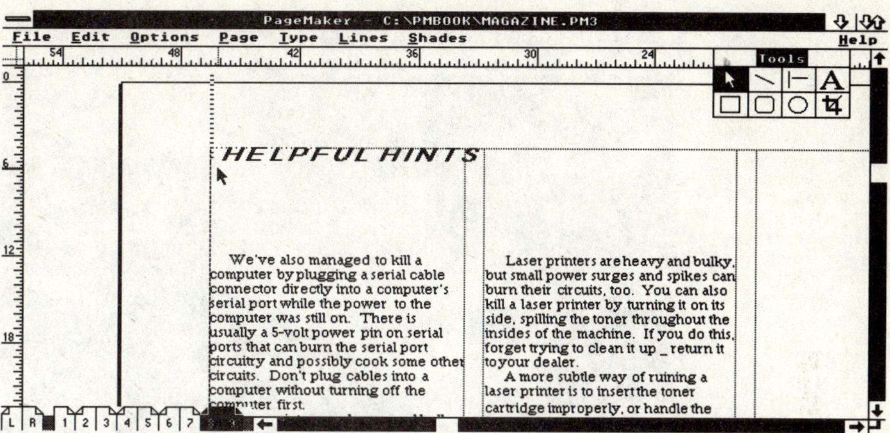

Figure 4-28. By selecting the parallel-lines pattern, you change the very thin box into a very thin line of dots.

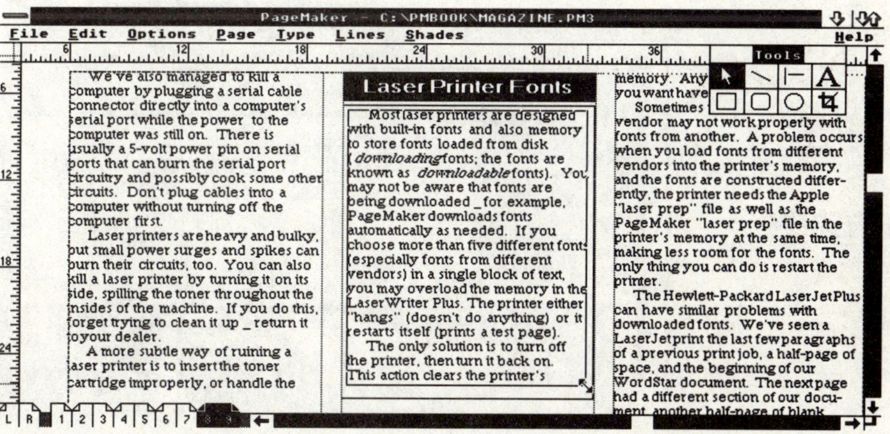

Figure 4-29. Resize the boxed text block inside the column.

resizing feature (by holding down the Control (Ctrl) and Shift keys while resizing).

A *halftone* is a continuous tone image that is converted by the use of a screen into dots, or *halftone cells*, that simulate gray shades on a black and white printer. The *screen density* (the frequency of cells measured in lines per inch, or lpi) determines the size of the halftone cells in the image.

Figure 4-30. Placing a scanned image on the page from a TIFF file. (Image courtesy Comstock Desktop Photography, Copyright ©1988.)

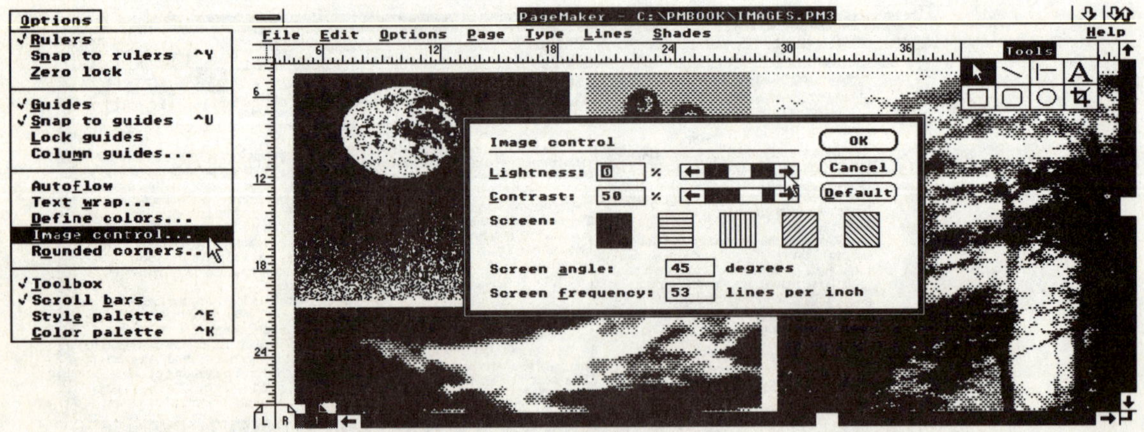

Figure 4-31. The Image control dialog box with default settings.

Newspapers typically need a 65-line or 85-line screen. For advertisements, commercial work, and magazine pages, use screens with 120, 133, 150, or more lines per inch. (Specifying too fine of a line screen for the type of paper or press method used can result in a muddy image if the ink plugs up between the dots on press. Specifying too coarse of a line screen can result in a less clear definition of the image.)

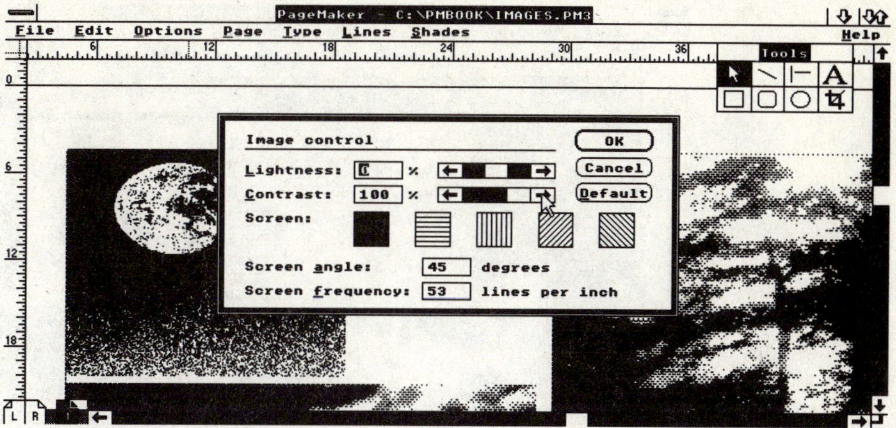

Figure 4-32. Adjust the contrast value to 100 percent and the lightness value to zero percent in order to create a high contrast (no gray scale) image.

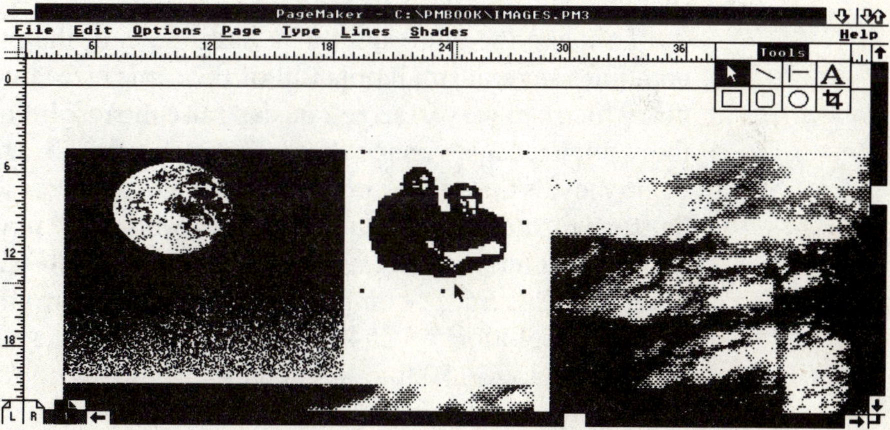

Figure 4-33. The result of increasing the contrast value to 100 percent while reducing the lightness value to zero percent: a black and white image with no gray scales.

PageMaker initially screens gray-scale images at 53 lpi, which is a density that works well with 300-dpi laser printers. The Image control feature allows you to change the screen frequency to anything that you want, including 90 lpi or greater for printing on high-resolution devices

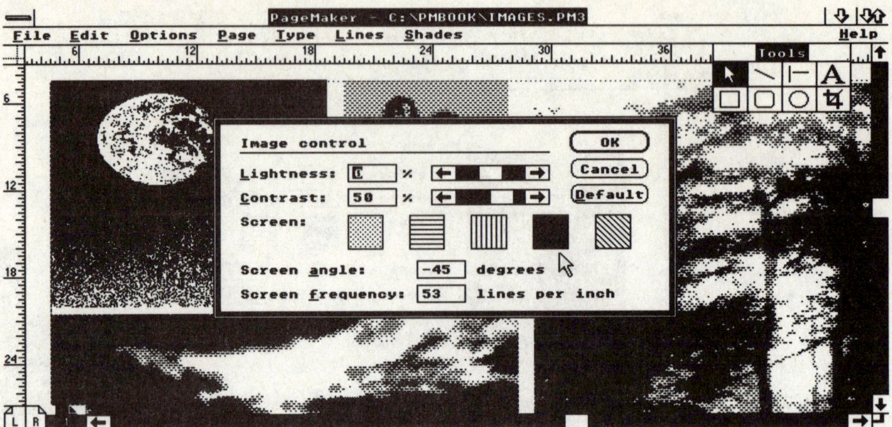

Figure 4-34. Adjusting the screen angle and frequency. (These values are changed to optimize the printed results for different types of printing presses and papers.)

such as the Linotronic 100 or 300.

To make the equivalent of a halftone cell, the printer or typesetter combines several small dots (all of the same size) into one halftone cell dot, which can vary in size. You can raise the resolution of the image, but the result is a denser image with less gray levels. To determine the number of gray levels that will be printed, divide the printer resolution (dpi) by the halftone resolution (lpi), and raise the result to the power of two. Thus, a 300 dpi printer can print a 50 lpi halftone with 36 (simulated) levels of gray. The PostScript-compatible Linotype Linotronic 300 Imagesetter (with a resolution of 2540 dpi) can reproduce a commercial-quality halftone at up to 150 lpi with at least 256 levels of gray.

PageMaker's Image control command gives you control over the frequency and angle of the line screen for halftoning, and over the lightness and contrast values. Remember, however, that the more gray levels you specify (the higher the frequency), the more slowly the image will print.

To use Image control, first place the image on the page. (Figure 4-30 shows several TIFF files placed on a page oriented to be wide, rather than tall.) Select one image, and choose the Image control command from the Options menu. PageMaker displays the Image control dialog box (Figure 4-31), which provides scroll-bar controls for lightness and contrast, and icons for different types of dot and line screens. You can also specify a screen angle and frequency. To use the scroll bars, click the arrows in order to reduce or increase the amount of lightness and contrast, or drag the elevator box.

The *lightness value* lightens or darkens the image, and the *contrast value* lightens or darkens areas of the image in relation to their surrounding backgrounds. For example, you can adjust the contrast of an image to 100 percent and reduce the lightness to zero percent (Figure 4-32) in order to obtain a high-contrast image with no gray scales (Figure 4-33).

The type of screen (the default is dot) can be changed for special effects. The screen angle changes according to the type of screen that you select. You can modify the screen angle further, as well as modify the frequency (Figure 4-34), which is measured in lines per inch (such as 53 lpi). The screen angle and frequency are changed to optimize the printed results for different types of printing presses and papers.

Layouts with Color

PageMaker lets you apply colors to text, to drawn objects on the page (such as boxes and lines), and (to a limited extent) to graphics. PageMaker does its best to display colors from color graphics programs, but it prints graphics in only one color. (More than one color cannot be applied to graphics placed on the page.) You need a color monitor in order to see colors displayed on the computer screen. The displayed colors do not accurately match the printed colors.

Colors can be assigned directly to objects (text, boxes, lines, or graphic images) by selecting the object and choosing the Color palette option from the Options menu. PageMaker displays the color palette (Figure 4-35). The color palette can remain displayed so that you can assign colors to other objects. You can resize the color palette, just as you can resize any window.

When you apply a color to a shaded box, the shade pattern changes color but remains a pattern. Boxes, circles, and ovals can be filled with a color. The bounding line of the color-filled object takes on the same color

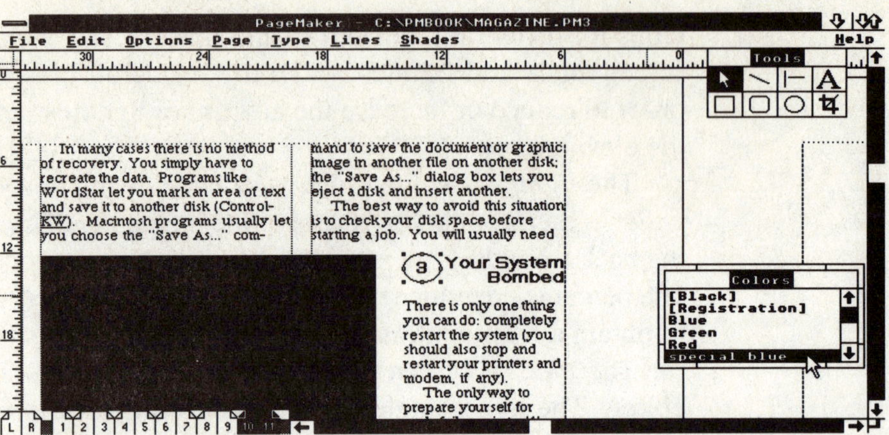

Figure 4-35. Assign a spot color to a circle on the page.

as the filled area. You can also apply color to text or to the black portions of a graphic image.

The colors for a publication are defined in a *color sheet*, which is like a style sheet that holds the names of colors, and is saved with each publication. You can copy colors from another publication (just as you can copy style sheet definitions), and then edit color definitions, as well as remove them. Each color has an associated name and value. The value is expressed either in percentages of cyan, yellow, magenta, and black (CYMK); or in percentages of red, green, and blue (RGB); or in percentages of hue, lightness, and saturation (HLS).

The Define colors option in the Options menu provides a dialog box for defining colors in any of these models (Figures 4-36 and 4-37). The colors that you define appear in the color palette by name, so that you can assign colors on a black-and-white monitor. Click the New button to define a new color, click the Edit button to change a color's values. Click the Copy button to copy colors from another publication. You can also remove a color from the color sheet for the open publication.

When you edit a color, you change the color of every object in the publication that to which that color name is assigned. For example, if the **special blue** color is edited to be a different tone, the color of all items tagged as **special blue** changes to the new tone.

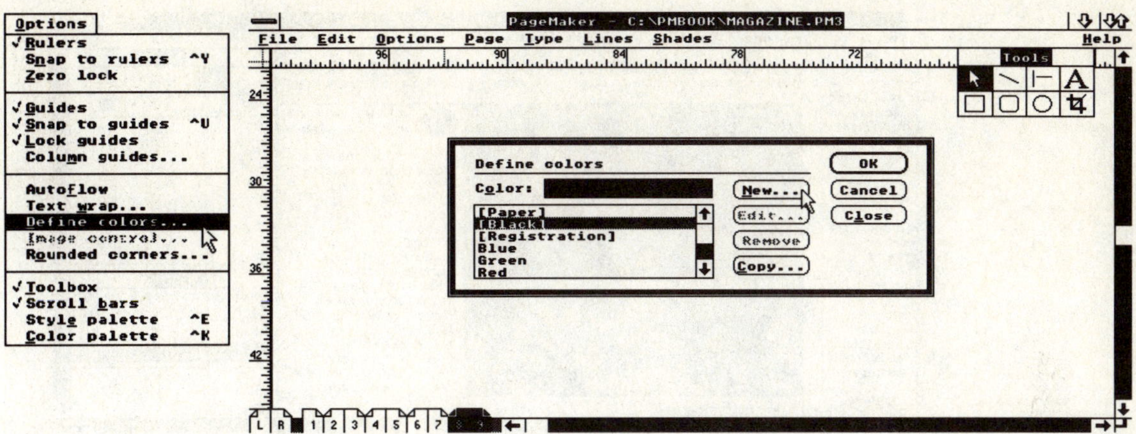

Figure 4-36. Click New to define a new color for a publication's color sheet.

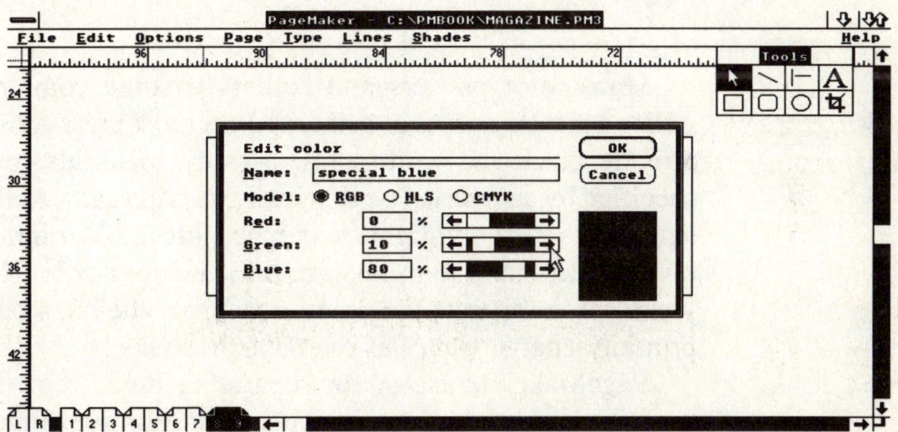

Figure 4-37. Use the RGB (red, green, blue) model to define the color.

You can apply a color to a selected object from the Define colors dialog box. If you are applying the color from the color palette, you may modify the color's definition before applying the color. To do so, hold down the Control (Ctrl) key while you click the color name. PageMaker displays the Edit color dialog box for you to make changes, and then returns the color palette to the screen. To close the color palette, select Color palette again in the options menu, or type the Control and K keys.

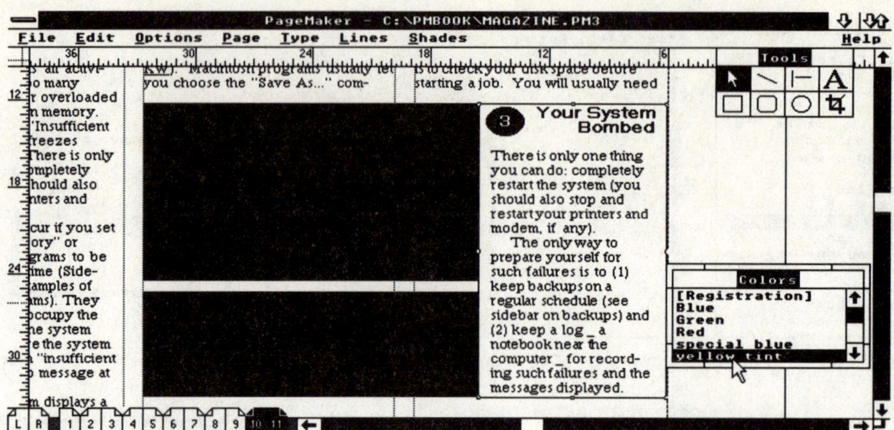

Figure 4-38. A layout with four-color images and captions that uses a yellow tint in the caption background and reverse type within spot-blue circles.

Until color printers and copiers become commonplace, you will utilize a printing press or print shop for most press runs. You will need to provide black-and-white camera-ready materials, with colored areas specified by an overlay page with instructions attached. For *spot color* (a single color that highlights text or graphics), *color tints* (a single color or mix of colors used for a background), and *four-color* (full-color) images, you have to separate the color areas from the black-and-white areas by printing separate pages as overlays or masks.

PageMaker is useful for separating tinted areas of a page, or for separating spot-colored elements. For example, Figure 4-38 shows a magazine page with a three-column layout customized to include four-color photographs and stylized captions, with a color tint and spot color circles for caption numbers.

To create overlay pages that contain colored objects, choose the Print command. Select the Spot color overlays option in the Print dialog box (Figure 4-39). PageMaker automatically prints color registration marks (which are used for lining up overlays) and the name of each color on the overlay. A different overlay is printed for each color.

You may also select Cutouts in order to create a blank spot on the bottom (black) overlay where the colors overlap. The color objects are cut

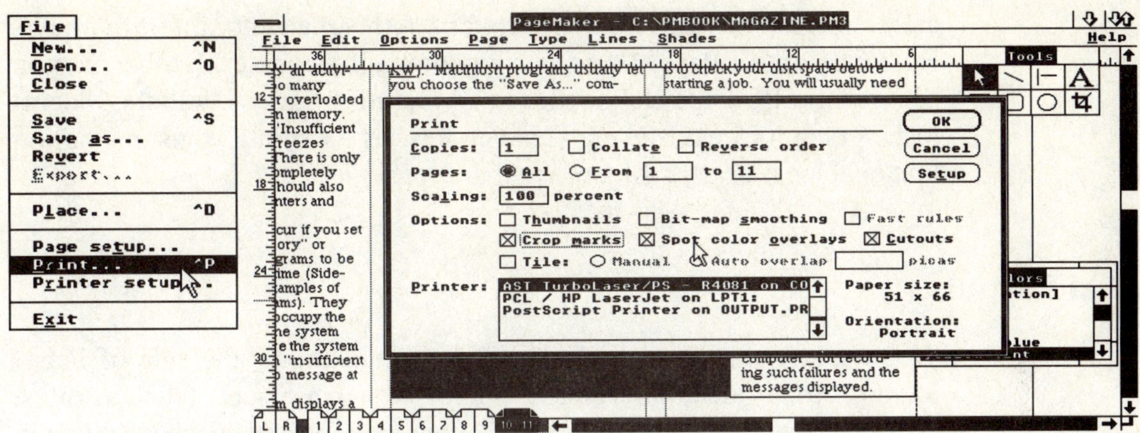

Figure 4-39. Select to print spot color overlays from the Print dialog box.

out on each overlay according to the order in which they are stacked on the page. (This order is defined by using the Send to back command.) If you work with printing press operators who want to create their own cutouts to solve registration problems, leave this option unchecked. Be sure to check the Crop marks option if you print pages that are smaller than the normal 8 1/2 by 11 inch size. Crop marks only print if the paper (or film, in the case of typesetters) is larger than the page size defined in PageMaker.

You may want to use copier-certified acetate sheets to print the spot color overlays and then print the black elements on paper. This method lets you easily overlay the paper with the acetate sheets by matching registration marks. Your printing process will determine the steps that you should take. Check with your printer to determine if the final artwork should be printed on separate sheets of paper, or if acetate sheets can be used instead. If your printer can work from both paper and acetate, check the text areas of your pages. Look closely at the type to see whether paper or acetate provides the crispest characters, and then use the best medium.

PageMaker is not a graphics painting or drawing program, and the separation of four-color images must be precise. Programs such as Micrografx Designer, Adobe Illustrator, and Aldus FreeHand for the Macintosh, as well as PageMaker on the Macintosh, can separate line art and some graphics into color separations, rather than into simple overlays. Both versions of PageMaker are file-compatible with each other, so you can transfer PC PageMaker files to a Macintosh for use with the Macintosh version of PageMaker. This version has a Color Extensions option that enables it to perform color separations.

Special Layouts

When special layouts are designed for publications, the role of PageMaker is to provide boilerplate graphics, design elements (such as rules, boxes, and reverse text panels), and repeatable formats (such as indented paragraphs, dot leaders, and stretched headline or title blocks). Save all of the designed elements in a separate template file that can be opened whenever you need those elements. You may also copy the elements to your publication via the Clipboard and the Copy and Paste commands, and then save some of them on master pages to be repeated as necessary. Save the column layout of each page without text and graphics, so that you can place new text and graphics without redrawing the column rules and reinventing other design elements.

Magazine Page

The previous color layout example shows a magazine page with a three-column layout that was customized to include four-color photographs and stylized captions. To prepare this page, place the left column of text first, and then place the top of the middle and right columns. Push the text up to the top. Place the graphic images or use black-filled placeholders. Draw separate boxes around the caption space and the photo area, with the boxes overlapping on one edge (use a 1-point line for the box). To overlap an edge, draw one box over the other box so that the edge disappears in the computer's display.

Next, drag-place the caption text into the space provided next to the black-filled boxes or graphic images. Design each caption by drawing a circle and then wrapping the text around the circle by aligning the subheading text to the right. Select a color for the circle and drag a number that you typed in a sans serif bold font into the circle in order to complete

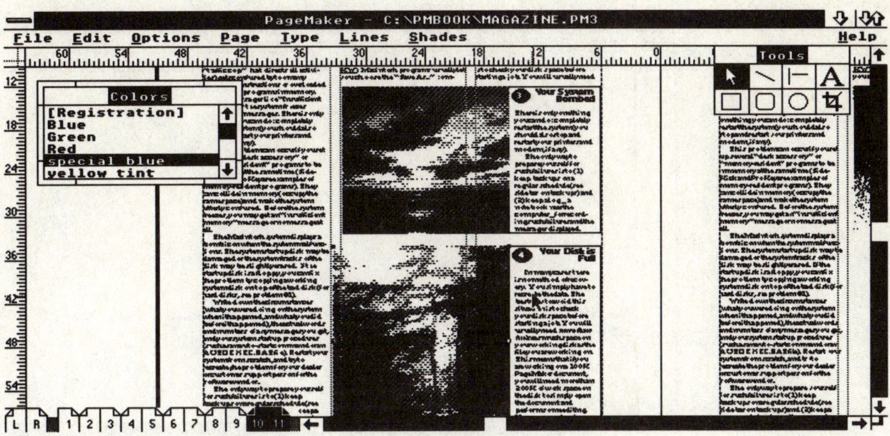

Figure 4-40. A sample magazine-style layout with photos.

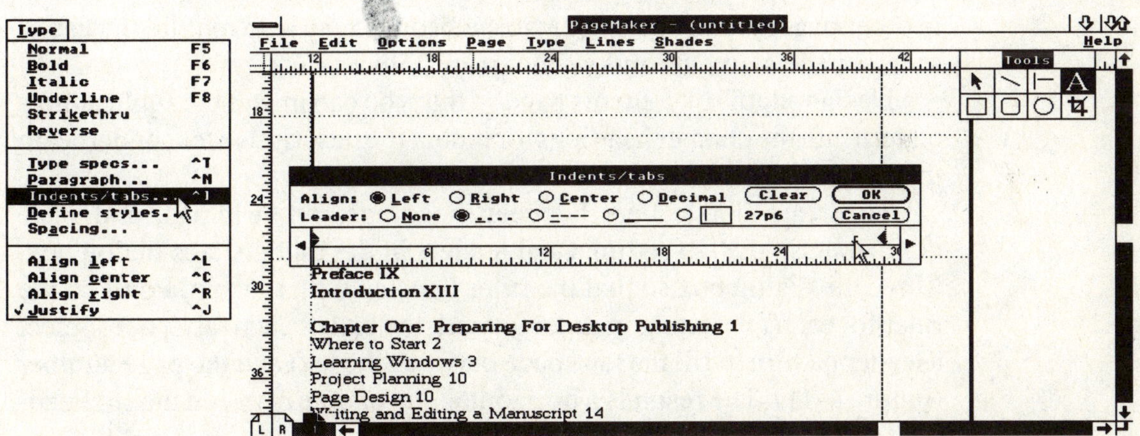

Figure 4-41. After setting the tab space, choose the dot Leader option to typeset a horizontal line of very small dots in the tab space.

the caption's circled numbers. Select Reverse type for the number, and assign the tint color to the caption box (Figure 4-40).

Table of Contents Page

Publications usually include special pages, such as a table of contents or an index page, that require a special layout and contain elements not used

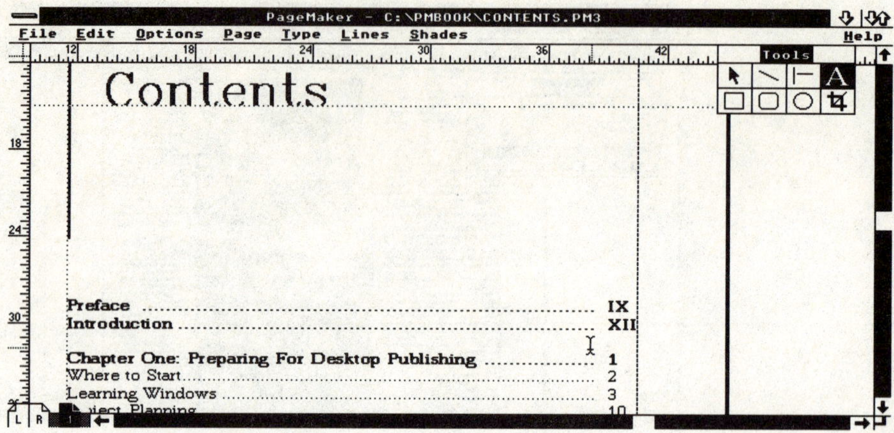

Figure 4-42. The tab space is filled with dot leaders.

in other pages. Catalogs and database listings may also require the use of special page elements and very narrow columns.

Design a table of contents page so that you can indent the subheadings underneath the chapter headings, or indent the descriptive text underneath the article titles.

To create dot leaders between headings, subheadings, and page numbers, use the tab settings and leaders in the Indents/tabs dialog box. Move the dialog box so that the ruler lines up with the text. Point on the ruler for each tab setting in order to mark the end of each tab space. Select a leader pattern to fill the tab space between the text and the page number (Figure 4-41). The result is a horizontal line of dots between the subheadings and the page numbers (Figure 4-42).

You may specify a different character to be used for a leader, or else use the dotted- or dashed-line leaders. You may also control the alignment of the characters within a tab space. (The arrows in the ruler define the endpoint of a tab space.) The tab spaces in the sample table of contents are left-justified.

Catalog Page

A catalog page may contain many small items and one large item. Figure 4-43 shows a page from a publisher's catalog. To prepare this page, use a four-column layout and drag-place the opening text blocks over two

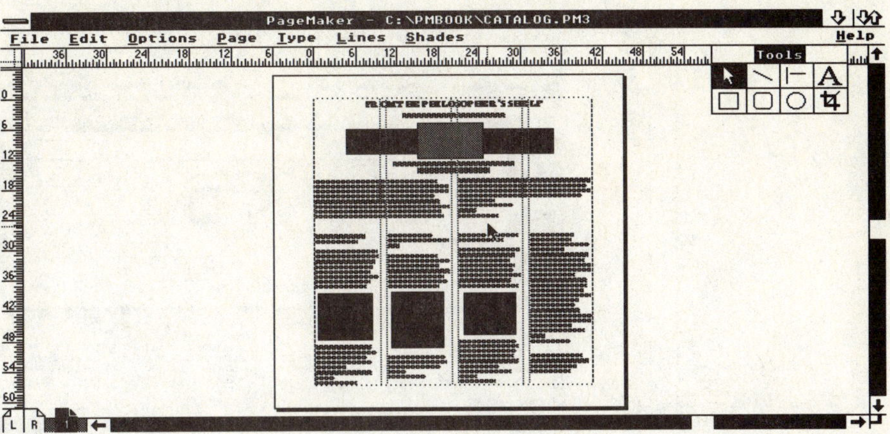

Figure 4-43. A page of a publisher's catalog that uses a mixed column layout, dotted rules, and placeholders for four-color images.

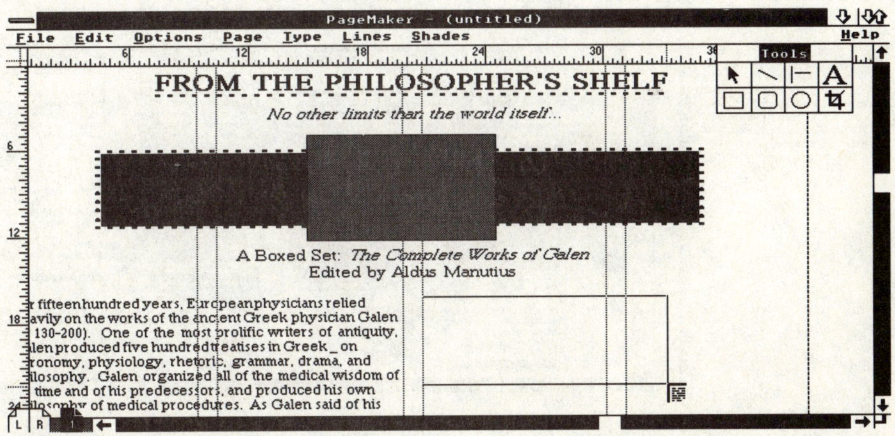

Figure 4-44. Drag-placing the text block over two columns at the top of the page.

columns at the top of the page. (Leave the space between columns unchanged.) Add the headings and photo placeholders. Balance the two columns by dragging down on both handles and pushing up on the left column until the columns are balanced (Figure 4-44). Next, place the other text and photo placeholders in the four-column layout (Figure 4-45). Choose the Wrap text option and specify that text should jump over the

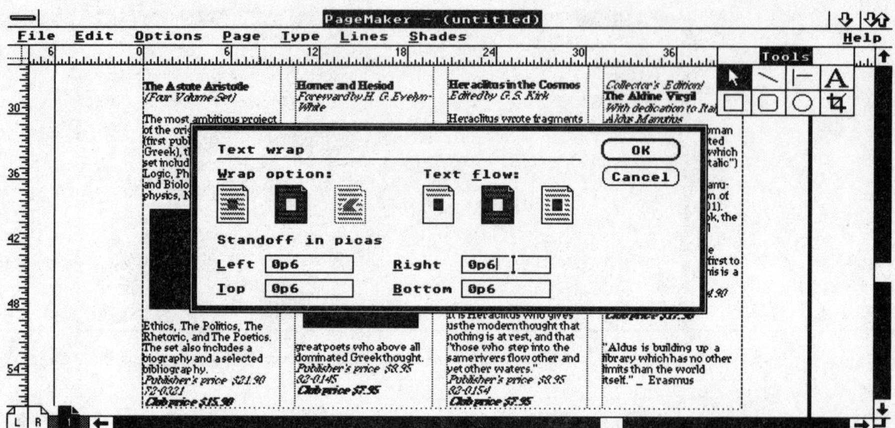

Figure 4-45. Place and customize the text and graphics in the four-column layout.

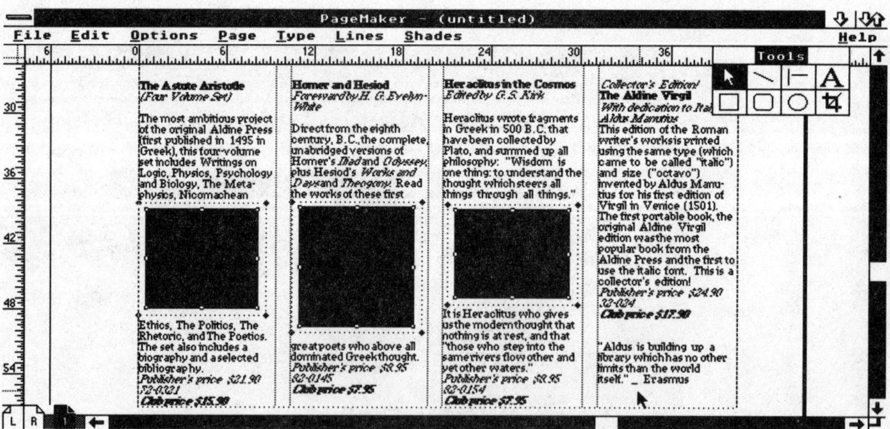

Figure 4-46. Use Text wrap to force text to jump over the placeholders, leaving six points of space between the text and each placeholder.

placeholders. Leave six points of space between the text and the placeholders (Figure 4-46).

Flyers, Brochures, and Advertisements

A flyer or handout is usually a standard size of 8 1/2 inches by 11 inches, and is designed to look like a one-page advertisement. Brochures can be

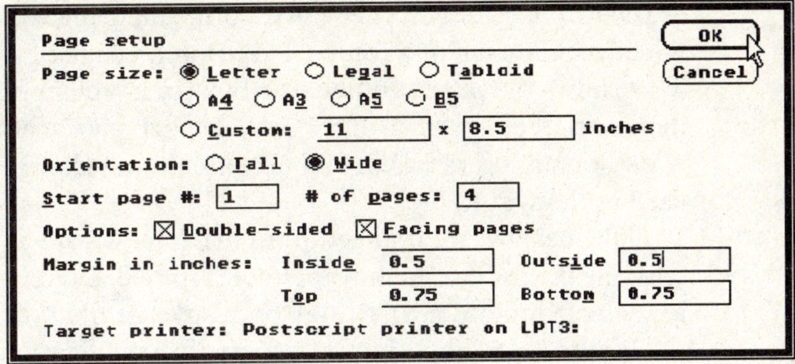

Figure 4-47. Page setup for a gate-folded brochure.

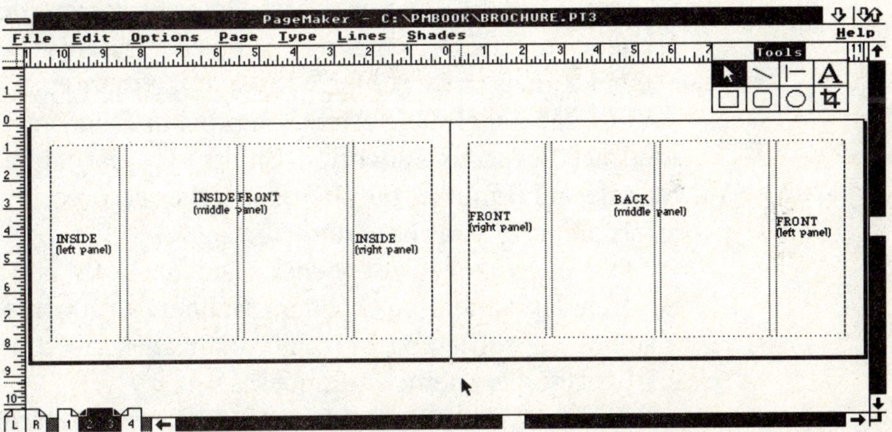

Figure 4-48. Pages 2 and 3 are used to define the brochure pages in landscape mode, using 8 1/2 by 11 inch folded paper.

almost any size and shape, depending upon how they are folded. The simplest folding methods are used with paper that is 8 1/2 inches wide by 11 or 14 inches long.

Obtain paper samples from a printer before deciding which paper size is best to use. Choose a type of fold that can be handled by the printer's machines, because the process of hand folding is expensive.

There are many different ways to lay out information for a brochure or flyer. It is most helpful to first define the page setup so that it reflects the measurements of a folded and trimmed page of the brochure. Figure 4-47 shows the page setup dialog box for a typical gate-folded brochure that is printed on standard 8 1/2 by 11 inch paper, and defined to have a wide orientation rather than a tall orientation (the 11-inch dimension is used as the width).

The margins are reduced from the default sizes in order to avoid text crossing the fold when the brochure is folded. Double-sided facing pages are selected in order to display both sides of the brochure.

Figure 4-48 shows how two pages in a publication file can be laid out for a gate-folded brochure so that the panels are ready for folding. Graphics and text can bleed across the middle panels on the front and back of the brochure. (Experiment with page mockups on your printer before beginning real production work—laser printer models vary. Most laser printers can't print to the very edge of standard-sized paper, and leave about 1/8 inch or so of blank paper at the margins.)

Use special graphic effects on brochures and advertisements in order to attract the reader's attention. Enlarged initial capitals, dotted line styles for rules, and four-color photos or other colored images can enrich the information in your brochure.

Use a small font size for charts and diagrams, and a larger font size for headlines and attention grabbers. Banners with white or black type (with black or a specified background tint, as described previously) are especially useful as attention grabbers.

There are few rules for designing effective advertisements, but plenty of guidelines are published in advertising and design magazines and newsletters. These publications contain regular feature columns by design experts who critique advertising. It helps a great deal to read about actual ads that worked or flopped.

Advertisements take up costly space in magazines, and direct-mail promotions are expensive to create, mail, and manage. Promotions and advertisements should directly generate income for your business.

Consult with a communications or design expert before finalizing your ad design, in order to make sure that your ad looks as good as it possibly can.

Summary

This chapter, presents some design rules and techniques for achieving various special effects with PageMaker.

Text can wrap around a rectangular shape or around an irregular shape, if you specify the Text wrap option for the box or shape (Options menu). Although there is more than one way to wrap text around an object, Text wrap is the best method, unless you are wrapping text around text (such as around an enlarged initial capital). In such cases, resize the text block to fit alongside the other text block.

Articles with different column layouts can be combined on the same page. To help with automatic or semiautomatic page pouring, for example, first set the page to contain three columns. (This step can be performed either directly on the page, or in the master pages.) Place all three-column text. Next, change the number of columns to two, and position the two-column text, which will not disturb the three-column layout. Alternatively, whenever you need to place a text element without regard to column rules, drag-place (drag the text flow icon) over the area to be filled with text.

Reverse letters, lines, and shapes can provide special effects. Although usually black type is set on a white background, you can reverse white type or rules out of a black box or band, and reverse colored text on another colored background.

The letters in story titles can be spread in order to fit a particular width by using fixed spaces. You can also perform manual kerning and control automatic kerning. To perform manual kerning, click an insertion point with the text tool and press the Control (Ctrl) key and the Backspace key to delete the automatic kern. Now perform manual kerning by pressing the Control and Backspace keys again to decrease the space, or by pressing the Control, Shift, and Backspace keys to increase the space.

This chapter also presented some techniques for the effective use of rules, lines, and boxes. Custom rules can be designed by using very thin, shade-filled boxes with no lines (a box can be as thin as one line).

PageMaker offers Image control—the ability to adjust the brightness, contrast, and halftone screen characteristics of a scanned continuous-tone image (a photograph). The Image control command also gives you control over the type of screen, the screen frequency, and the angle of the line screen. By default this command uses a dot screen at 53 lines per inch.

The lightness value lightens or darkens the image, and the contrast value lightens or darkens areas of the image in relation to their surrounding backgrounds. To determine the number of gray levels that will be printed, divide the printer resolution by the halftone resolution, and raise the result to the power of two.

PageMaker automatically creates spot color overlays, and lets you assign colors to text, drawn objects (such as lines, boxes, and ovals), and the black portions of graphic images. The Color palette displays the names of defined colors in the color sheet and lets you assign colors to objects.

The Define colors option lets you define color names for the color sheet, which is stored with each publication. When you edit a color name's definition, the color of every object in the publication to which that color name is assigned changes.

To create a different overlay page for each color, choose Print and select the Spot color overlays option. PageMaker automatically prints color registration marks and the name of each color on the overlay. Select Cutouts to create a blank spot on the bottom (black) overlay where the colors overlap. Objects are cut out on each overlay according to the order in which they are stacked on the page.

Crop marks are available in the Print dialog box, but only print if the paper or film is larger than the trim size defined in PageMaker.

By storing design elements and boilerplate graphics in PageMaker's publication files, you can the manage production process for magazine pages, catalog pages, and special pages (such as a table of contents). Advertisements, flyers, and brochures can also be created in nonstandard page sizes. Use the techniques presented in this chapter to enhance your page designs. Consider consulting a design expert before you mass-produce your masterpiece, or obtain feedback about the design from the intended audience in order to get the best possible result.

5 Tips and Techniques

This chapter contains important tips, tricks, and techniques for working with PageMaker. Tips have been organized by topic, and the topics are listed in the same logical order in which you are likely to encounter them. This simple organization should provide easy access to the information without having to search through previous chapters.

Should you want more information about a topic, or information about topics not covered here, refer to the index of this book and to the PageMaker manuals.

Very Important!

Before starting a publication, select a target printer. (This selection remains in effect until you change it.) You can change the target printer for a publication at any time. Every time you change the target printer, however, the composition of the publication may be altered, because different target printers use different fonts and options.

PageMaker performs a mini-save whenever you turn the page in the publication file. You may Revert the publication file to its state at the time of the last full save operation. You may also return to the state of the publication at the time of the last mini-save operation by holding down the Shift key when selecting the Revert option.

Preparation

PageMaker allows you to type and edit words on the page. Use a word processor when you write more than a page of text, or you write text that will be used with different programs or in other publications.

You may change fonts, styles, and sizes for the text in PageMaker. To save time, select fonts (if possible), styles, and sizes in the word processor while you write the text (if the word processor is supported by PageMaker). The text is then already formatted for placement onto a PageMaker page, and you can place text on many pages at once in the PageMaker publication file without stopping to select fonts.

If your word processor is not listed in the PageMaker reference manual, then save and place your file with the Retain format selection turned off. In such cases, the text adopts the default font, style, size, leading, and tab settings that are already defined in PageMaker. These default settings can be set before a publication is opened.

PageMaker recognizes tabs in a word processor file and uses them to align text or numbers in tables. The word processor file should already contain the tab characters, and each line of a table should end with a carriage return. You can change tab settings in PageMaker to fit the column width.

In typeset copy, sentences should not be followed by two spaces. Before placing files in PageMaker, use your word processor to search for all instances of two consecutive spaces that follow a period, and replace the spaces with one space.

Captions, footnotes, and other independent elements can be included in some word processor files, depending upon the word processor. (In some cases, these elements are ignored by PageMaker.) Alternatively, put these elements into a separate file and then place that file separately.

To run text vertically alongside a vertical axis, or in any orientation other than the usual horizontal orientation, define the orientation with a graphics program. PageMaker does not offer the ability to rotate text.

Existing text in a template may be replaced with new text. If you first break up very large text files into smaller files of less than 64K each, PageMaker can respond quickly when you adjust the text. To conserve disk space, keep the number of separate stories low. One long story takes up less space than the equivalent amount of text contained in separate stories. The Windows Clipboard allows you to cut, copy, and paste text to another window, but only transfers files smaller than 64K.

Design

You can print thumbnail sketches of the publication's pages from the Print dialog box. Use gray boxes to represent text, black boxes to represent images, and white boxes to represent line art.

To bypass page specifications, either choose the default specs (by clicking OK) or start with a template, which is a predesigned publication file ready for use in page makeup. Replace the text and graphics in the template with new text and graphics via the Place command.

Use about 1/4 inch (0.25) for the column gap (space between columns) in order to open up more space, or use the PageMaker default of .167 inch (1 pica).

Don't mix more than three fonts on a page. Use white space so that the page is not overcrowded with text and graphics.

Reverse (white) type may be used on a black background or on a background with a 60% or 80% gray shade.

Use a thin rule (such as a hairline rule) to separate columns of text. (If your printer can't produce a hairline, a thicker line is substituted automatically.) Use a thicker rule as a separator of page elements (for example, between the two sections of a page that contains text in both two columns and three columns). To draw attention to a headline, use a thick rule. Double rules tend to resemble picture frames, so use them only when they add emphasis to a headline or graphic, or they serve as an appropriate frame. Above all, be consistent with the use of rules in a publication.

Use thin line styles for borders around text, graphics, or photos. Leave an equal amount of white space on all sides from the edge of the graphic or text to the box.

To put boxed text inside a column, line the box up with the margins or column guides of the column. Resize the width of the text block inside the box to be narrower than the column width.

Placing Text

PageMaker offers three ways to place text. To use *manual placement*, click the top of each column, then click the handle on the bottom of each text block. To use *semiautomatic placement*, click the top of each column and do not click the bottom handle. To use the *fully automatic placement* method, select the Autoflow option. This option pours each column and creates pages, if necessary, without your intervention. When placing text manually, you can switch to semiautomatic placement by holding down the Shift key. You may switch to fully automatic placement by holding down the Control (Ctrl) key. You can also turn on the Autoflow option in the Options menu. To stop automatic placement at any time, click the mouse.

If you use the Retain format option when you place a text file, PageMaker uses the formatting settings that are already specified in the word processing file. You may also place a text file without retaining its formatting settings.

PageMaker does not use the right margin setting, page numbers, headers, or footers created by word processors. The program breaks lines to fit its columns, and treats carriage returns as paragraph endings. PageMaker recognizes most fonts, type styles and sizes, line spacing (leading), upper- and lower-case letters, left and right indents, first line indents, and tab settings created by most word processors. (See the PageMaker reference manual for specific information about your word processor.)

If your word processor is not supported by PageMaker, or you want to ignore its formatting settings, place your file without using the Retain format option. PageMaker will apply default type specifications.

If you set a 1-inch indent from the left margin in a word processor file, and you place the file and retain its formatting settings, PageMaker places text 1 inch from the left edge of the column.

PageMaker recognizes (and retains) all first-line indents in a word processor file that are either indented to the right (a regular indent) or are indented to the left of the left margin (a hanging indent). For more information about how PageMaker treats text files from popular word processing programs, see Appendix A.

Tabs, carriage returns, and spaces are recognized when you place text without retaining formatting settings; but no formatting settings from the word processor are used. In most cases, you can bring tables (with tabs) and paragraphs of text into PageMaker without retaining formatting settings and still retain paragraph endings and table column positions. (See Appendix A for more information.)

If you turn on the Convert quotes option, PageMaker automatically transforms a double quote (") that is preceded by a space into an open quote (“), and changes a double quote that is followed by a space into a closed quote (”). The program also changes a single quote (') in the same manner, so that contractions, possessives, and quotes-within-quotes are indicated with the properly slanted punctuation symbols. PageMaker changes a double hyphen (- -) into an em dash (—), and changes a series of hyphens into half as many em dashes to create a solid line.

When you place a spreadsheet file from Lotus 1-2-3 and you've installed the Lotus filter in PageMaker, the program displays named cell, row, column, and range references, as well as the print area. You may place any area of a spreadsheet by placing that area's name. You can also place the entire print area. Save other types of spreadsheets as text-only files and then place them.

Placing Graphics

When a graphics file larger than 64K is placed onto a page, PageMaker creates a lower-resolution version of the image and stores that version in the publication file. PageMaker establishes a link to the original, higher-resolution version of the image and uses that version for printing. PageMaker uses the lower-resolution image for display purposes in order to increase the speed of the program. You can move, resize, and crop the image. PageMaker applies those changes to the original version when that version is printed (although the original file is not changed). In order for PageMaker's link to work, leave the original graphics file in the directory where it was located when you placed it. If PageMaker can't find the original image file at the time when it prints the publication file, the program displays a dialog box that asks for the image file. At that time, you may ignore the original higher-resolution version and print using the lower-resolution version. For the best results, locate the original version in the dialog box and click OK.

Hold down the Shift key in order to retain an image's proportions during any resize operation. Hold down the Control (Ctrl) key to select only those sizes that work well with your target printer. If you do not hold down the Shift key, you can stretch or compress an image or graphic, as well as change its size. If you do not hold down the Control key, you can scale the image to any size, even to sizes that are not optimal for your target printer. (Remember to release the mouse button before you release the Shift and/or Control keys.)

No matter how much an image has been stretched or compressed, you can snap it back to a size that is equal in proportion to the original size. To do so hold down the Shift key while resizing. Hold down the Control (Ctrl) key to snap the image into sizes that work well with the selected printer.

If the graphic is a line drawing (without patterns or a lot of details), you can resize it by dragging a handle until the graphic is the right size for your layout. If the graphic image is a bit-mapped image with a pattern or fine detail, hold down the Control (Ctrl) key to select a size from an array of the optimal sizes for your target printer. In addition, hold down the Shift key while resizing to prevent the possibility of distorting the image by stretching or compressing it from any side.

You can resize any paint-type (bit-mapped) graphics in PageMaker by using the built-in resizing feature to obtain optimal sizes for your printer. If you change printers, resize any paint-type graphics that contain a tight pattern of dots via this built-in resizing feature (to avoid moirés). To do so, select the paint-type graphic image and then resize it by holding down the Control (Ctrl) key while dragging one of the image's corners.

Excellent printed results are possible with paint-type graphics. This is especially true with line art, which can be resized into almost any proportion and size and still look good. Images with tight, regular patterns are not displayed well (they look muddy), but if you use PageMaker's special resizing feature (hold down the Control key) in order to select sizes that print best with your printer, you can get excellent results. The size limitation may force you to use a slightly larger-sized image than you want, but you can use the cropping tool to reduce part of the image.

To reduce the size of a graphics file that contains text that doesn't print well (especially object-oriented graphics), first use the graphics program to delete the text. Place just the graphics first, and then add text with PageMaker for more control over text size and styles within a text block.

Spreadsheet and business graphics programs perform calculations that produce a bar, a pie chart, or an x-y graph that is accurate in proportion to the calculations. You can use these charts and graphs as templates for the purpose of tracing new shapes that are accurate and smooth.

Viewing Pages

To switch back and forth on the display from actual page size to reduced page size, hold down the Control (Ctrl) and Alt keys and click the mouse. To change the display quickly to a full-page view, type Control W (or pick the Fit in Window option from the Page menu).

When you hold down the Control and Alt keys and click the mouse while pointing to a spot on the page, PageMaker changes the display into actual size, and centers the display on the spot you clicked. If you repeat the command, PageMaker changes to full-page view. The command toggles the displays.

Actual size approximates the printed page size. The 200% size (Control 2) presents the most accurate display for positioning text and images. If your mouse has two or more buttons, press Shift and click the secondary mouse button in order to toggle between the 200% and actual size views.

Hold down the Control, Shift, and W keys to see the entire pasteboard. Hold down the Control and W keys to see all of the page or the spread that you are working on, plus some of the pasteboard (Fit in window). If your mouse has two or more buttons, click the secondary mouse button to toggle between the Fit in window view and the actual size view.

Necessary Skills

To move several objects, select them in a row by holding down Shift and selecting with the pointer tool. Point in the middle of the objects, hold down the mouse button until you see the four-arrows symbol, and drag all of the objects at once into position. If a text block, graphic, or box disappears, redisplay it by selecting whatever is covering that element and using the Send to back command in the Edit menu.

Hold down the Shift key while dragging a graphic or text block in order to drag evenly, without moving up or down.

You can either drag text over a graphic, or drag a graphic over text. If you want the text to appear (as text blocks are transparent), select the text and choose the Bring to front command in the Edit menu.

If you want to use a line style that is not available in the Lines menu, create a box that is only one line wide. To do so, overlap the edges of the box until they disappear from the display. While the box is still selected, choose a pattern from the Shades menu.

To delete a text block but retain its text (so that you can reflow the text into a different layout), select the block with the pointer tool. Close the block by dragging its bottom handle up to meet the top handle. Do not delete the starting text block of a story, or you will delete the story. To reflow the text, click the + symbol of a previous block's bottom handle. You can, of course, delete text blocks by selecting them and pressing the Delete or Backspace keys, or by using Cut from the Edit menu.

There are several different ways to select text. Select a single word by double-clicking the word; you can then drag in any direction to select a group of words. To select a single paragraph, triple-click anywhere in the middle of it. To extend a selection from an existing selection, hold down the Shift key and click a new ending point. (You can also use the cursor movement keys rather than the mouse.) Another way to select a large area of text is to click a starting point at one end, then hold down the Shift key and click the ending point at the other end. The easiest way to select all of the text is to click anywhere in the text once, and then choose the Select all command from the Edit menu (or press the Control and A keys).

Changing a Layout

Although text wraps within the column width, you can change the text block's width. Switch to the pointer tool and drag any corner of the block of text to be wider or thinner, and to be longer or shorter.

To make the text block wider than a column width (e.g., for positioning a headline across text that spans two columns), use the pointer tool to click any corner of the new text block that was formed by the Paste command, and drag the text so that it becomes a wider and shorter text block, and the headline fits on one line.

To increase the white space by one line at the current leading, type an extra carriage return (press the Enter key) while using the text editing tool. For a different measure, highlight the line, choose the Type specs command from the Type menu, and change the leading to a larger point size.

Move a text block in the same way that you move a graphic. Point in the middle of the text, hold down the mouse button until the four arrows symbol appears, and drag the text into position. With the Snap to guides option on, you can attach a text block or a graphic to a column guide or a ruler guide.

To mix column layouts on one page, draw a line to separate the layouts. If necessary, change the number of columns with the Column guides option, but leave the same spacing between columns. (Use less spacing if the columns are very narrow.) Start at the top or left-hand section of the page and position the text in that layout first. Then change the column layout again and continue placing text in that layout. The change does not affect the text that you already positioned in the first layout.

To combine multiple text blocks into one block (effectively deleting a layout so that you can start fresh and place the text again), delete the text blocks, but not the text inside them. Start with the last text block of the story and work backward to the first; however, don't delete the first block. Reflow the text by clicking the + symbol of the first block's bottom handle.

Master Pages

Put a page header and footer on the master page so that these elements are repeated with each page. Headers and footers can accommodate a page number that changes for each page. If you want the same column layout on all pages, set the number of columns and space between columns on the master pages.

Save all designed elements in a separate publication file. You can copy them later to another publication via the Clipboard and the Copy and Paste commands. Save elements on master pages if the elements are to be repeated on almost every page (except those elements for which you have selected the Remove master items option). Also save the column layout of each page without text and graphics but with design elements, so that you can place new text and graphics without reinventing the design elements.

The Display master items option in the Page menu, which is usually turned on (a check mark is displayed next to it), indicates that PageMaker copies text and graphic items from the master pages to the selected page for displaying and printing. To turn off the display and printing of master items for a selected page, choose the option again (the check mark disappears).

PageMaker offers the ability to save a publication file as a template file. New publications can be defined simply by replacing the contents of the template file with new contents via the Place command. PageMaker adds the extension ".PT3" when the Save as option is used with the Template option. From that point on, you can double-click the template file from the MS-DOS Executive window to launch PageMaker. The template file automatically opens as a new, untitled document, leaving the original template file intact and untouched.

Style Sheets

Style sheet names define the text font, size, style (italic, bold, etc.), leading, paragraph spacing, tab settings, indents, and color. When you change a style sheet definition, all sections of text defined by that style sheet change automatically to adopt the new definition.

When using style sheets in Microsoft Word, place the Word file with the Retain format option and the Convert quotes option turned on. Do not turn on the Read tags option.

A tag name (a name surrounded by angle brackets, such as <subhead>) can be embedded into any text file in order to define the sections of text that follow the tag name (until another tag name or the end of the file is reached). PageMaker can export text with embedded tag names. The tag names can be placed into other PageMaker files and can retain style sheet names even without the use of the Retain format option. (In Word files, the Retain format option retains style sheet information, so tags are not needed.)

At any time, you can edit a style sheet definition in PageMaker. When assigning style sheet names to the text, it helps to display the style palette (press the Control (Ctrl) and K keys, or use the Options menu).

Typographic Controls

Em spaces are fixed spaces that are the width of a capital "M" in the chosen font. Unlike regular spaces between words, em spaces are not changed by PageMaker. To create an em space, press the Control (Ctrl), Shift, and M keys. En spaces are fixed spaces that are the width of a capital "N" in the chosen font. To create an en space, press the Control, Shift, and N keys. Thin spaces (press the Control, Shift, and T keys) and fixed spaces (press the Control key and the space bar) can also be typed in PageMaker. Em, en, thin, and fixed spaces are all nonbreaking spaces that connect the characters to their left and right sides. These spaces never fall at the end of a line.

If automatic kerning is used for text point sizes smaller than 12 points, text placement and text flow over pages is slowed down. You can turn on automatic kerning for selected areas of the text, rather than kerning the entire text. The degree of automatic kerning depends both upon the printer and the font that you use. Pair kerning is usually turned on for all text that is larger than 12 points in size, but you can change this setting in the Paragraph dialog box.

To kern characters manually, use the text tool to click an insertion point between the two characters. Press the Control (Ctrl) and Backspace keys to decrease the spacing. Press the Control, Shift, and Backspace keys to increase the spacing. The amount of spacing is 1/24th of the point size of the character located to the left of the insertion point.

Justified text is automatically aligned to the left and right margins of a column. You can control justification by decreasing or increasing the space between words (word spacing) and the space between characters (letter spacing). First use the text tool to select the desired text, and then choose Spacing from the Type menu in order to specify the new settings. PageMaker reforms the entire text file—not just the selected block—using the new settings.

To justify text, PageMaker first adds spaces between words (within the specified word-spacing ranges). Next, it adds spaces between characters (within the specified letter-spacing ranges). If PageMaker still can't justify the line, then it expands word spacing as necessary. If your justified text contains more hyphens than you want, change the settings for word spacing and letter spacing. Aldus recommends a word-spacing range of 50 to 200 percent, and a letter-spacing range of 0 to 25 percent. The narrower the range between minimum and maximum spacing, the more PageMaker will hyphenate; the greater the range, the less it will hyphenate, but more space will be present between words (creating looser lines).

Auto hyphenation is also recommended for justified text. The hyphenation zone setting in the Spacing dialog box in the Type menu is not applied to justified text—this setting works only with ragged text. To control the hyphenation of justified text, use the text tool to select the text, and choose Paragraph from the Type menu to turn on auto hyphenation. PageMaker uses a 110,000-word built-in dictionary, plus your supplementary dictionary, to place discretionary hyphens in words that don't fit at the end of lines.

To control the hyphenation of words that are not in PageMaker's built-in hyphenation dictionary, turn on the prompted hyphenation option, as well as auto hyphenation. When PageMaker encounters a word that is not in its dictionaries and doesn't fit at the end of a line, it prompts you to click an insertion point for each place where you want a discretionary hyphen inserted into the word. You can also add the new word to PageMaker's supplementary dictionary so that the word is automatically hyphenated the next time that it is encountered. Adding the word to the dictionary saves time later if the text block is reformatted to be wider or narrower and line endings change. If you choose not to hyphenate the word, PageMaker increases the word spacing and the letter spacing for that line until the line is justified, and moves the word to the following line.

If you are prompted to hyphenate a word that you never want to break, add that word to the supplementary dictionary without any hyphens. PageMaker will never hyphenate it.

To break lines only at hyphens, spaces between words, and discretionary hyphens, and to be prompted for the hyphenation of all words that do not fit at the ends of lines, turn the prompted hyphenation option on, but do not turn on automatic hyphenation. You will then have full control of hyphenation. Each time PageMaker encounters a word that doesn't fit at the end of a line, PageMaker will prompt you to click an insertion point at each spot where you want it to insert a discretionary hyphen. When you are prompted to hyphenate an unknown word, add the word to PageMaker's supplementary dictionary so that you won't have to hyphenate the same word if it is encountered again, or if PageMaker later has to reflow the text, and the line endings change.

If you turn on prompted hyphenation, it is only in effect for the selected text, and it automatically switches off after your text file has been recomposed. Automatic hyphenation is one of PageMaker's default settings, and is always on until you turn it off.

In nonjustified text, you can adjust the word spacing, but not the letter spacing—the built-in letter spacing is used. You can also specify a width for the hyphenation zone, which is in effect when automatic hyphenation or prompted hyphenation is turned on. The smaller the zone, the more often PageMaker hyphenates words. The larger the zone, the less often PageMaker hyphenates words at the ends of lines. In this case, the right margin will be more ragged (line lengths will be more uneven).

When PageMaker encounters a word that falls into the hyphenation zone and is too long to fit on that line, the program examines the preceding word to see if that word also falls into the hyphenation zone. If both words are in the hyphenation zone, PageMaker breaks the line after the first word and moves the second word to the next line. (In other words, a smaller zone allows more type to fit on the line.) If the first word is not in the hyphenation zone, then PageMaker tries to hyphenate the second word. If auto hyphenation is not on, or if the word can't be hyphenated to fit the line, then the line is broken after the first word and the second word moves to the next line. For full control, turn on prompted hyphenation only.

If you turn hyphenation off for nonjustified text and the column width is narrow in relation to the font used, the text will be more ragged than usual. If hyphenation is on but the hyphenation zone is large in relation to the column width, the text will be more ragged than usual.

To quickly change the point size of text, first select the desired text. Press the F9 key to lower the point size, or press the F10 key to raise the point size. Each time you press the key, the point size changes in 1 point increments. The leading is not adjusted. If you intend to raise the point size to be larger than the leading size, change the leading first so that the larger characters are not clipped when they become too large to fit within the leading.

To quickly change leading, style, and other font attributes, as well as the point size of type, first select the text tool. Double-click on a word (to select a word), or triple-click to select a line. Click an insertion point and press the Control (Ctrl) and A keys (or choose Select All from the Edit menu) to select the entire file. To select a range of text, click an insertion point at the start of the range and drag until you have selected the desired area, or else hold down the Shift key and click a second insertion point at the end of the range. After selecting the text, press the Control and T keys to quickly display and change the type specs (font name, size, leading, style, position, and case). Use other shortcuts listed in the type menu to change the text alignment, justify the text, control the indents and tabs, or change the style of the selected range of type. For example, use function key shortcuts to change the style of selected text to normal (F5), bold (F6), italic (F7), or underline (F8).

Font Issues

Fonts used with earlier versions of Windows (prior to Windows 2.0) and earlier versions of PageMaker must be converted into Windows 2-compatible fonts. Windows is supplied with a font conversion program called NEWFON.EXE.

PageMaker remembers the font you choose, even if your target printer does not print that font. PageMaker substitutes the closest font, and then uses the actual font when you switch to a target printer that can print that font.

Some object-drawing programs let you select Windows standard fonts or graphics fonts for text. These fonts are carried over into PageMaker. Graphics fonts are reduced or enlarged with the image as you resize the image. They usually do not correspond directly to laser printer fonts that are defined for use with Windows. The Windows standard fonts, on the other hand, correspond directly to the laser printer fonts for the target printer, but do not change size with the image (unless they are PostScript fonts).

If the publication file was created with a different target printer, the selection of a new target printer causes PageMaker to ask you for a confirmation: Should the entire publication be recomposed? Click OK to the recompose operation because PageMaker must use the target printer's font information to perform proper kerning, justification, and spacing.

The recompose operation changes the line lengths of some of the text, so look over your publication carefully. For this reason, always try to begin a publication with the right target printer in mind.

Keyboard Controls

Any character in the Windows' ANSI character set can be typed by holding down the Alt key, typing a zero on the numeric keypad, and typing the ANSI code. To type the special language characters, hold down the Alt key and type the three-digit IBM PC character code on the numeric keypad.

The left/right cursor movement keys move the insertion point by a single character or space. The up/down cursor movement keys move the point by a single line. Holding down the Control (Ctrl) key when pressing a left or right key moves the insertion point to the beginning of the next word or the previous word. Holding down the Control (Ctrl) key and pressing an up or down key moves the point to the beginning of the next paragraph or the previous paragraph.

Pressing the Home or End key moves the insertion point to the beginning or the end of the current line (or to the next line if the point is already at the beginning or the end of the current line). When the Control key and the Home or End keys are pressed, the point moves to the beginning of the next sentence or the previous sentence. You can also move up or down in the text block quickly by using the PageUp (PgUp) or PageDown (PgDn) keys. If the Control key is pressed along with the PageUp or PageDown key, the insertion point moves to the beginning or to the end of the text that has been placed.

Special Effects

To type a bullet, hold down the Control, Shift, and number 8 keys.

To draw a drop shadow of a frame, copy the frame to the Clipboard and paste the copy back to the page. Move the copy to the shadow position and change its shade to black. To move all of the elements at once, hold down the Shift key to select the frame and the text without deselecting the already-selected black shadow. Release the Shift key and click in the center of the group until the four-arrow symbol appears, and then drag the entire group. Finally, to move the black shadow behind the frame and text, deselect by clicking the pointer tool again, and then select only the black shadow and use the Send to back command.

To wrap text around a rectangular box, select the box and choose the Text wrap option (Options menu). Select the rectangular text wrap (the middle icon), which automatically sets the text flow icon. Text flows automatically around the box, leaving space between the text and the box as defined in the Text wrap dialog box.

To wrap text around an irregular shape, use the Text wrap option as above, and then adjust the wrap boundary by dragging its points. Create more points in the wrap boundary for fine-tuning by clicking the boundary while holding down the Alt key.

To spread a headline to fill a specific width, first isolate the headline as a separate text block. Select Justified as the paragraph style, and move the headline into place. Add one regular space between each letter, add two spaces between each word, and add one regular space at the end of the headline. Hold down the Control key while pressing the space bar to add enough nonbreaking spaces to fill the line and make the cursor jump to the next line. The result will be a justified, evenly spread headline.

Box and Line Tools

You can draw an entire chart or graph by using PageMaker's line-drawing, box-drawing, and circle-drawing tools and gray shades. PageMaker's Snap-to-guides feature makes it easy to line up several distinct boxes to form a bar chart. To draw perfect circles, hold down the Shift key while dragging with the oval/circle tool. To draw perfect squares, hold down the Shift key while dragging with the box tool. To make very thin dotted lines, use the box tool, select a parallel lines shade, and drag the box inward until it is as thin as a line.

Printing

Changing the resolution (dots per inch) of the printer affects the appearance of graphics. The lower the resolution, the faster the publication file prints; but the graphics will be coarser, and hairlines may not print at all.

You can create a print file of the pages, rather than print the pages on paper. The print file can be transmitted to another computer over a modem and telephone line, or transferred by disk. The receiving computer does not have to run PageMaker in order to send the file to the printer, but that computer must have the same target printer. For instructions on how to set up the OUTPUT.PRN file, see the ports section in the WIN.INI file. (Add the sentence **OUTPUT.PRN=** on a line by itself to the [Ports] section of WIN.INI. Next, select the printer and OUTPUT.PRN as the port in the Connections dialog box of the Control Panel. OUTPUT.PRN appears in the PM directory after a print job, and you can rename the file, save it on disk, and send it to a printer.)

To create overlay pages that contain the colored objects, choose the

Print command and select the Spot color overlays option in the Print dialog box. PageMaker automatically prints color registration marks and the name of each color on the overlay, and prints a different overlay for each color.

Use the Cutouts option to create a blank spot on the bottom (black) overlay where the colors overlap. The color objects are cut out on each overlay according to the order in which they are stacked on the page. Use the Crop marks option if your paper (or film, in the case of typesetters) is larger than the page size defined in PageMaker.

You can choose Page setup from the File menu to change the margin settings, but that change affects your layout and makes changes that you may not want. If your printer supports scaling, you can print the completed pages at a smaller size without changing the layout. To do so, scale the publication to less than 100 percent in the Print dialog box, selected from the File menu at print time.

Archive Files

You can use PageMaker publication files as archive files. PageMaker can also export text as text-only files with optional style tag names embedded to retain formatting information, or as Microsoft Word files with full formatting and style sheet information.

Use the Save as command periodically when building a publication, and once again when the publication is completed. The Save as command compresses the publication file so that the file occupies less disk space and loads from the disk faster.

APPENDIX A

Word Processing Programs

PageMaker expects word processor files to have specific filename extensions.

Word Processor Files	PageMaker Filename
DCA files	sample.DCA or sample.RFT
DEC WPS-PLUS	sample.DX
HP AdvanceWrite	sample.AW
IBM DisplayWrite 3/4	sample.DCA
Lotus Manuscript	sample.DCA
Microsoft Windows Write	sample.WRI
Microsoft Word	sample.DOC
MultiMate	sample.DOC
Olivetti Olitext Plus	sample.OTX
Samna Word	sample.SAM
WordPerfect	sample.WP
WordStar 3.3	sample.WS
WordStar 2000	sample.DCA
XyWrite III	sample.XYW
Text-only files	sample.TXT

Microsoft Word (version 3.0 or newer) files and Microsoft Windows Write files are fully supported—PageMaker recognizes character formats, fonts, indents, justification styles, and tab settings. Write allows you to paste graphics within the text, but PageMaker ignores those graphics. Tabs in Write apply to the entire text file and are not changeable from paragraph to paragraph, but PageMaker can change those tab settings. PageMaker also changes the line spacing to automatic leading.

XyWrite III's character modes (but not fonts and sizes), indents, justification styles, and tab settings are also recognized. PageMaker assumes that all measurements are 10 units to the inch (10-pitch), and does not recognize fractional units in XyWrite's embedded commands. PageMaker also assumes that the left margin is 0 units and the right margin is 78 units, and converts the left and right margin commands to left and right indents. XyWrite's character modes (normal, bold, underline, italic, superscript, and subscript) are used, but PageMaker uses its default type specifications for font, size, leading, kerning, and spacing.

MultiMate font styles, sizes, and line spacing settings are recognized by PageMaker, and MultiMate measurements are converted to points. (Aldus includes a conversion table in the PageMaker Reference Manual.) Justification is not recognized—PageMaker places the text according to the setting you choose in PageMaker. Indents in a MultiMate text file that is to be placed in PageMaker have to be set only in the first line of a paragraph, not line-by-line as with MultiMate. To change the indent in a MultiMate file to be used with PageMaker, you must start a new paragraph. PageMaker converts MultiMate tabs to left-justified, and limits the number of tab settings in the first line of each paragraph to 20.

WordPerfect (version 4.1) type styles (but not fonts and sizes), soft (discretionary) hyphens, indents, justification styles, tab settings, and some alignment commands are recognized by PageMaker. You must explicitly use the justify command if you want this command to be used by PageMaker, even though WordPerfect starts with justified text. The flush right and center alignment commands are recognized by PageMaker and lines that end with them are treated as separate paragraphs. Tabs are converted (up to 20 per paragraph) using the pitch setting and according to the number of spaces between tab settings. PageMaker does not recognize WordPerfect's tab align feature. WordPerfect's type styles (normal, bold, underline, italic, superscript, and subscript) are accepted. PageMaker uses its default type specifications for font, size, leading, kerning, and spacing.

WordStar 3.3's indents and type styles are recognized by PageMaker (double-strike is converted to italics), as well as line styles, but its variable tabs are not (except as the indent of the first line of a paragraph). PageMaker ignores justification, but recognizes fixed tabs.

DisplayWrite 3 (version 1.10) files that are saved as revisable form text (also known as DCA, or document content architecture) are recognized by PageMaker. Although bold text, superscripts, and subscripts are recognized, fonts are converted to PageMaker's default settings. PageMaker converts line spacing and lines-per-inch settings to leading, and accepts tabs and first-line indents (in unjustified paragraphs), but not centered text.

Samna Word III's DCA files are recognized, but PageMaker ignores leader tabs, graphics, math functions, hanging indents, and bulleted paragraphs. PageMaker recognizes only justification (but not centered text), regular and decimal tabs, type size, bold and underlined styles, and line spacing.

Volkswriter 3 (version 1) DCA files are recognized, but PageMaker ignores stylesheets and embedded commands. First-line indents, up to 20 tab settings per paragraph (set in the first line), line spacing, and some type styles (subscript, superscript, and underline) are recognized by PageMaker.

WordStar 2000 (version 2) DCA files are recognized, including tabs, standard indents, nested paragraphs (without bullets—add bullets when using PageMaker), type styles (except italic), and font sizes. The default PageMaker font is used for WordStar 2000 (version 2) DCA files.

ASCII: The Standard Character Set for Text

PageMaker reads text-only files, thanks to ASCII. ANSI (American National Standards Institute), the U.S. counterpart of the European ISO (International Standards Organization), has developed ASCII (American Standard Code for Information Interchange). This is a character code for representing a character set (text and symbols) that has been adopted by the ISO, and is known in Europe as the ISO character set.

IBM uses EBCDIC (Extended Binary Coded Decimal Interchange Code) for their character set, which represents most ASCII characters. The 8-bit numerical values assigned by EBCDIC differ from the 8-bit numerical ASCII values. You can translate ASCII to EBCDIC and vice versa with the appropriate software. The IBM PC uses an ASCII character set; the EBCDIC character set is used on IBM's large computers.

APPENDIX B
Graphics Programs

PageMaker expects graphics files to have specific filename extensions.

Graphics Files	**PageMaker Filename**
AutoCAD	sample.PLT
CGM graphics file format	sample.CGM
EPS-format	sample.EPS
GDI metafiles	sample.WMF
HP Graphics Gallery	sample.TIF
HP-GL plotter file format	sample.PLT
In*a*Vision/Windows "Draw!"	sample.PIC
Lotus 1-2-3/Symphony	sample.PIC
Lotus Freelance	sample.DCA
Microsoft Windows Paint	sample.MSP
Mirage	sample.IMA
PC Paint	sample.PIC
PC Paintbrush	sample.PCX
Publisher's Paintbrush	sample.PCX
Tag Image File Format (TIFF)	sample.TIF
Videoshow (NAPLPS) format	sample.PIC
Windows GDI format	sample.WMF

Painting Programs

With paint-type graphics (also called *bit-map graphics*), PageMaker creates a low-resolution version of the image for display, and establishes a link to the original graphics file. Graphics are adjusted to the resolution of the target printer, so if you change the target printer, you should also resize the graphics.

To use the built-in resizing feature that automatically selects the best sizes for printing with your target printer, hold down the Control (Ctrl) key while resizing (dragging a corner of the image). Hold down the Shift key as well if you want to resize the graphic proportionately.

PC Paint lets you create both color and black-and-white graphics, but PageMaker places only black-and-white graphics. Convert all color images to black-and-white with PC Paint to prepare files for PageMaker, or else PageMaker substitutes black for all colors.

PC Paintbrush, which also works with scanners to manipulate scanned images, can produce very large files. Change your graphics mode to monochrome for scanning and for faster response in general. When scanning, measure the area to scan. Using PC Paintbrush, type in the dimensions of the area or mark the dimensions with a mouse. A scanned image can be a very large file, so PageMaker reduces the image to a size that fits inside of your defined image area. Resize the image for your layout.

Microsoft Windows Paint files can be placed directly onto PageMaker pages or else displayed in a window. You can cut or copy an image to the Clipboard, and paste the image onto a PageMaker page.

TIFF (tag image file format) files can be produced by a variety of graphics programs, including Scan-Do (Hammerlab), HALO DPE (Media Cybernetics, through use of CUTTOTIF utility), Gallery (Hewlett-Packard), and PublishPac (Dest). Scanner manufacturers bundle software with the scanner that produces TIFF files.

Scanned images are paint-type graphics, displayed with less resolution than when they are printed. PageMaker prints scanned images at actual size and at reduced or expanded sizes very well if you use the automatic resizing option. The Image control command can adjust the lightness and contrast, as well as the screen angle and frequency for halftoning, for any TIFF image.

Drawing Programs

Draw-type graphics (also called *object-oriented* and *vector graphics*) can be resized freely without distortion, and without the need for the automatic resizing used for paint-type graphics. You can place color drawings with PageMaker, but PageMaker may substitute black for all colors, or substitute a pattern that makes the drawing appear different on the screen than on the printed page. It is best to use black-and-white graphics and specify colors for the print shop to use when running the job.

Object-oriented graphics must not have metafiles that are more than 64K in size, or they will not place in PageMaker. If the metafile is larger than 64K, save the graphic in two separate pieces, then place and rejoin the pieces on the PageMaker page.

Micrografx In*a*Vision, Windows "Draw!", and Windows "Graph!" use the same file format with graphics described in lines, ellipses, and polygons. These programs all include text. In*a*Vision is intended for use in computer-aided design (CAD) applications that call for complex engineering drawings and blueprints. Windows "Draw!" is a drawing program for business graphics and desktop publishing.

All three programs run under Windows, so you can use the Cut or Copy and Paste commands to transfer images from a graphics window to the PageMaker window. Text is transferred to PageMaker but remains part of the graphic. PageMaker substitutes a font used by your target printer if you use screen fonts in the graphic. Both In*a*Vision and "Draw!" let you choose fonts for Windows printers; otherwise, expect another font to be substituted for the screen font, or else remove the text from the graphic and add the text separately with PageMaker. Keep graphics files shorter than 64K, because the Windows clipboard is limited to 64K.

Lotus 1-2-3 and Symphony graphics look exactly the same on the PageMaker page. When you use hatch and fill patterns, the programs store them as line segments. When they are resized, these patterns are more widely spaced than usual. Text placed from Lotus graphics is in a sans serif font, positioned according to information in the file (which could be wrong if it was set for a different target printer). In this case, remove the text from the graphic, and add the text using PageMaker.

Autodesk AutoCAD plotter files, created by plotting a drawing with the ADI plotter driver (shipped with AutoCAD), are recognized by PageMaker. Drawings are straight line segments; circular objects may print with undesirable results. Hatch and fill patterns are stored as line segments. When resized, these patterns are more widely spaced than usual. Text is described in straight line segments, which also produces undesirable results. Use AutoCAD to create graphics without text, and add the text with PageMaker. Keep graphics metafiles under 64K in size.

EPS-formatted graphics files can be used if your target printer is a PostScript device, such as an Apple LaserWriter or Allied Linotype typesetter. EPS files contain PostScript code, and the format is useful for transferring descriptions of very complex line art graphics (such as technical illustrations and logos) to and from different types of computers. EPS files carry information for displaying the graphic as well as for printing it, so you may see an image on the screen. If the EPS file does not contain that information, you will see a text header that describes the image, and a bounding box that marks the boundaries of the image. You can crop and resize the image freely, even though you may not be able to see it.

PageMaker requires that the PostScript code in EPS files be "well-behaved" in the use of certain operators, stacks, global dictionaries, and the graphics state. PageMaker strips out ill-behaved PostScript code. The manual clearly states which operators and conventions to use and how to use them, but this information is only of use to PostScript programmers. For such tasks, you should read Appendix C of the *PostScript Language Reference Manual*. (See Appendix E, which also contains the address for EPSF technical specifications that are written for PostScript programmers.)

APPENDIX C
Special Characters

Character	**Command**
Bullet	Ctrl Shift 8
Close double quote	Ctrl Shift]
Close single quote	Crtl [
Discretionary hyphen	Ctrl -
Em dash	Ctrl Shift =
Em space (nonbreaking space)	Ctrl Shift M
En dash	Ctrl =
En space (nonbreaking space)	Ctrl Shift N
Fixed space (nonbreaking space)	Ctrl Spacebar
Open double quote	Ctrl Shift [
Open single quote	Ctrl [
Page number marker	Ctrl Shift 3
Thin space (nonbreaking space)	Ctrl Shift T

Use the above special character codes in your text file, or add the special characters after you position the text in the PageMaker publication file. (You have to use the latter method if your word processor won't let you create or export the special characters. Read your word processor manual to determine whether this is the case.) The availability of special characters in PageMaker also depends upon your printer. Read your printer manual to determine if your printer can print the special characters.

A nonbreaking space should be inserted when you do not want a line to break between two words. The size of the spaces range from an em space (equal to the point size), to a fixed space (a normal space), to an en space (1/2 the point size), and a thin space (1/4 the point size, or the width of a number).

APPENDIX D

Transferring Publication Files

One reason PageMaker is attractive to service bureaus is because it saves a publication file in a form that can be used on either a PC-compatible computer or a Macintosh. Another feature attractive to almost any user is PageMaker's ability to import files from a variety of word processors (as described in Appendix A) and graphics programs (as described in Appendix B). Therefore, either the PC version or the Macintosh version of PageMaker can be used to publish information derived from PC or Macintosh files.

PageMaker publication files can also be transferred to remote computers for further production work, or for printing or typesetting. You can recompose the publication for the target printer at the remote site. Note that if the printer is different, PageMaker may substitute a default font for printing, but the program remembers the original font choice in case you use the original printer again.

When screen fonts are available for the fonts you choose, PageMaker uses them; otherwise, PageMaker substitutes a generic screen font or a Windows vector font. PageMaker is supplied with two generic bit-mapped fonts, Tms Rmn and Helv, which correspond to popular Times and Helvetica fonts available on most printers.

If screen fonts are not available for the printer fonts that you choose, the Tms Rmn font is substituted for all proportionately spaced serif fonts, and the Helv font is substituted for proportionately spaced sans-serif fonts. PageMaker is supplied with these fonts in the following sizes: 8, 10, 12, 16, 18, and 24. PageMaker also comes with generic versions of Courier and Lineprinter fonts, which are displayed only if you select them for text (they are not used for substitutions).

The Windows vector fonts (Roman, Modern, and Script) are used to display text that is larger than a certain number of pixels set in your Preferences dialog box (usually set to the number of pixels needed to display a 24-point font). To change the threshold number of pixels, change the "Substitute vector fonts" setting in the Preferences dialog box (Edit menu). Since they are vector fonts, these fonts can be used to display any size font. No matter which font PageMaker chooses, the line endings match the line length of the printed version.

PageMaker can remember its target printer font selection information, but if you print a publication designed for another type of printer, PageMaker will try to print the font and size that most closely matches the original font selection. For best results, change the target printer via PageMaker's Printer setup command in the File menu, and click OK to recompose the entire publication for the new printer.

If you transfer a Macintosh publication file to the PC version of PageMaker, special characters from the Macintosh may appear different in the PC version because some characters are not duplicated in both systems. PageMaker remembers the original character that you chose. If you transfer the publication back to the Macintosh, the publication will contain the same characters as before (unless you specifically changed them on the PC).

To use a PageMaker 1.0 publication with PageMaker 3.0, simply open the publication using PageMaker 3.0. The conversion is automatic, and the original 1.0 file is left intact while PageMaker 3.0 creates a new publication file. The new file may be about 20 percent larger than the original 1.0 file, due to new features in PageMaker 3.0. The older 1.0 files have the extension ".PUB" and the new 3.0 files have the extensions ".PM3" for regular publication files and ".PT3" for template files.

To transfer older Macintosh publication files, first use the Macintosh version of PageMaker to convert the files to 3.0 files by opening the files with PageMaker 3.0 on the Macintosh. Transfer the new versions to the PC.

Converting Graphics

PageMaker publication files can be transferred to a Macintosh and used with the Macintosh version of PageMaker, and vice versa. All text and font information is preserved when you transfer the publication to the Macintosh version or to the PC version, but you may not get the results that you expected if you don't use the same printer. For example, EPSF (Encapsulated PostScript Format) graphics print only on PostScript printers.

PageMaker can transfer within a publication file all text, all PageMaker-created graphics and formatting, all master page items, all paint-type graphics (less than 64K in size), all EPSF graphics, and all style sheet information. Scanned images, paint-type graphics larger than 64K in size, and other types of graphics are best handled by first converting and transferring the graphics files separately, and then using the Place command in PageMaker to place the converted graphics back onto the page.

For example, if your graphics came from PC programs such as Lotus 1-2-3 (PIC files), Windows "Draw!", Windows "Graph!", In*a*Vision, or AutoCAD, you have to transfer these graphics separately and convert them to the Macintosh PICT file format, or else use the EPSF as described in Appendix B. You may either place Macintosh graphics (PICT files) directly into the PC version of PageMaker, or else save the graphics first as EPSF files and then transfer them separately.

With scanned images, PageMaker can transfer the low-resolution display version of the image, but not the actual scanned image. You must transfer the image file separately. Use the universally recognized TIFF (Tag Image File Format) for scanned images. Because image files are usually linked to the PageMaker publication file, store the image file in the same directory as the publication file.

Once the graphics files are transferred and converted into the appropriate format, use the PageMaker Place command to position the graphics in the receiving computer's publication file. By replacing the appropriately converted graphics, you gain the benefit of access to PageMaker's automatic scaling for resizing paint-type graphics. The selection of optimal printing sizes depends upon the target printer connected to the receiving computer.

To convert paint-type graphics, you may use various public domain programs, such as MACTOWIN (MacPaint-to-Windows Paint), which converts MacPaint or PICT graphics to Windows Paint files for use with the PC version of PageMaker. The Missing Link (PC Quik-Art, Inc.) handles a variety of paint-type graphic file formats, including MacPaint, Windows Paint, GEM Paint, PC Paint, PC Paintbrush, BLOAD (PIC files), Dr. Halo, EGA Paint, and Publisher's Paintbrush. Hotshot (SymSoft) is another excellent program that offers the ability to convert graphics files.

If there is no way to convert a graphic from its native format to the Macintosh or PC format, a final alternative is to scan the graphic, and then save it as a TIFF file or an EPSF file. TIFF and EPSF files can be imported into any version of PageMaker. You can also create an EPSF file by tracing over a MacPaint or PICT image using Aldus FreeHand for the Macintosh, which is a PostScript drawing program that creates an EPSF representation of the artwork.

Transferring by Disk

You may use a variety of methods to transfer data to and from various PC-compatible computers. The easiest method is to exchange floppy disks. Most computers have disk drives that accept PC-formatted 5 1/4-inch disks that hold 360 kilobytes (360K, roughly 360,000 characters). To transfer information, copy files from one disk to another. You may be able to transfer files on PC AT-compatible disks, which can hold up to 1.2 megabytes (roughly 1.2 million characters). Another method is to use portable hard disk cartridges, portable hard disks, or magnetic tape cartridges for larger files.

For Macintosh computers, you may purchase an optional Apple PC 5.25 Drive from Apple Computer for reading and writing PC-formatted 5 1/4-inch disks (360K each). You can also purchase a similar disk drive from Dayna Communications that can read and write both 360K PC disks and 1.2 megabyte AT disks. You may also transfer files from IBM Personal System's 3 1/2-inch disks (720 kilobytes each) to the Macintosh IIx, IIcx, or SE/30 (which includes at least one 3 1/2-inch SuperDrive floppy disk drive that reads PS/2 disks).

Transferring by Network

A popular method for managing the sharing of information among different types of computers is a local area network, or LAN. A LAN can be comprised of different types of computers linked by twisted-pair or wide-band cable, with files available to some or all computers through the use of a *file server*—a computer with a hard disk that contains the shared files. Some networks are controlled by the file server computer; other networks allow any computer on the network to act as a file server.

PageMaker publication files can be shared over these networks just as easily as other files. You may not obtain high-quality output if you use a printer that is substantially different from the target printer you chose in the Printer setup dialog box. In addition, PageMaker requires that you leave graphics files in the directories where they were located when you placed the files.

The recommended method for organizing files on a network for production and printing is to copy any shared files into a local disk storage device for use with PageMaker. Print the publication from the same computer with which you placed those files onto PageMaker pages.

Several networks are compatible with IBM's SNA network for mainframe computers, and with IBM's Token Ring network for PCs and PS/2 computers. Novell, 3Com Corporation, TOPS (Sun Microsystems), Ungermann-Bass, Apple Computer, and Microsoft offer local area networks that connect PC-compatible computers. IBM offers network choices for its new PS/2 models that can link these desktop machines with IBM mainframe computers.

The AppleTalk network from Apple Computer is an example of a network that can connect several Macintosh computers to each other, to one or more LaserWriters, and to PC ATs and compatible computers. Other choices include interface boxes, called *gateways*, that connect PC networks and other networks to AppleTalk (available from third-party vendors).

Or, you can link PCs and Macintosh computers in an Ethernet network from 3Com Corporation, which can also be used to link PCs and Macintosh computers to minicomputers and mainframes. Novell's Netware lets you connect PCs and Macintosh computers in the same network.

The software supplied with these products allows the transfer of PageMaker publication files (and other types of files) simply and easily from Macintosh computers to PCs and vice versa. 3Com, for example, lets you copy files by choosing a server, which appears on the PC as another disk drive and on the Macintosh as another disk. Another method is to use electronic mail software such as InBox (Symantec) to send publication files, text files, and graphics files as part of electronic mail messages to a user at another computer linked with AppleTalk.

The TOPS network lets you designate a disk drive as "published" so that you can access the drive as if it were attached to your system. With TOPS, you publish a disk or a folder from the Macintosh over AppleTalk, and treat the published item as a separate disk on the PC (such as drive E). Use the COPY command on the PC to copy files from the Macintosh to the PC or vice versa. You may also publish a PC disk or directory and then treat it as a separate disk on the Macintosh that is represented by a special icon; you can then drag a file from that disk to a Macintosh disk. TOPS includes the TOPS Translators utility that lets you convert files to and from specific types of PC and Macintosh file formats.

Transferring by Serial Cable or Modem

The establishment of a direct connection through a serial (RS-232C) cable or the creation of a modem link through a telephone line are the least expensive ways to connect a PC-compatible computer to a Macintosh. These are also the only way methods for transferring files to and from a computer other than a PC (such as a Kaypro, an Osborne, another CP/M-based machine, an Atari, and a Commodore computer).

With a serial cable connection or a modem-to-modem connection, you can use a communications or transfer program such as MacLink Plus (Dataviz). The MacLink Plus package includes a cable that plugs into an asynchronous port on the PC-compatible computer and also plugs into the modem port on the Macintosh. The package also includes PC and Macintosh software that enables the machines to communicate with each other.

MacLink Plus provides a table of file formats on the PC and a matching table of Macintosh formats, so that you can transfer Lotus 1-2-3 files to Microsoft Excel or vice versa. You can translate nearly every popular PC word processing file format into either the Macintosh version of Microsoft Word or MacWrite file formats. You can also translate database information from dBASE II and other structures to Macintosh database structures.

Essential to any file transfer method is the use of communication protocols. Protocols let you transfer information with the secure feeling that no errors will be placed into the data from noisy telephone lines or other electromagnetic interference.

MacLink Plus provides a protocol for transfer, and communication programs usually offer one or more protocols. The best protocols for transferring PageMaker files from one computer to another are Xmodem, Kermit, X.PC, or MNP. In every case, you need to use the same protocol in the programs that are running on both computers.

You can use the Xmodem protocol to transfer files to PCs from Macintosh computers, to Macintosh computers from PCs, and from both types of computers to CP/M, Apple //, and other computers and back again, without loss of data integrity. Almost every communication program for PC-compatible computers offers the Xmodem protocol, including PC Talk III (Headlands Press), Crosstalk Mk.4 (Digital Communications Associates, Inc.), Relay (VMPC), ProComm (PIL Software Systems), MaxiMITE (Mycroft Labs), and public domain programs such as QMODEM.

Transferring to a Typesetting Service

You can send PageMaker publication files to a typesetting service that uses PostScript typesetters and film recorders. Many services also use PageMaker, and you may supply the publication file on disk, or else transfer the publication file via cable or modem as described earlier.

Although the typesetting service may have a copy of PC PageMaker or the Macintosh version of PageMaker, the service may not have the exact fonts that you are using. In such cases, you are better off preparing a PostScript file with the font information included, rather than providing the original PageMaker publication file. Some services require that you prepare a downloadable PostScript file, rather than a publication file. You can use the PostScript driver available with Windows and PageMaker to prepare a PostScript file and save it to disk. To do so, you must first open the WIN.INI file supplied with Microsoft Windows, and then add a filename to represent a port connection for printed output.

To modify the supplied WIN.INI file, double-click the file (in the MS-DOS Executive window), or use a word processor to open and edit the file. If you double-click the WIN.INI file itself, the Windows Notepad automatically loads and provides editing tools.

Scroll the WIN.INI file until you come to the "[ports]" heading. At the end of the list of device names ("LPT1:=", "LPT2:=", etc.), add a file name with the extension ".PRN" followed by an equal sign (as in **OUTPUT.PRN=**). Close the WIN.INI file, saving the new editing changes, and end your Windows session.

From the DOS command line, restart Windows. Start the Control program (or restart PageMaker, and select the Control panel command from the System menu). Choose the Connections command from the Setup menu, and select the appropriate target printer (a PostScript printer if you are sending the file to a PostScript typesetter or other PostScript output device). Select the filename you added to the WIN.INI file (OUTPUT.PRN) as the port. Click OK and close the Control panel.

You can now open a PageMaker publication file and use the Print command to prepare the PostScript file. PageMaker stores this file (OUTPUT.PRN) in the PM subdirectory. After you print one file, change the filename of the resulting file (from OUTPUT.PRN to something else) so that the next file you transmit using this method does not overwrite the current file.

When you are finished, transfer the PostScript files to the typesetting service just as you would transfer a publication file, by using a modem or using a disk. In fact, because the PostScript file is a simple ASCII file, you can transfer it using almost any communications or electronic mail program.

Before preparing a PostScript file for a typesetter from a publication that contains paint-type graphics or scanned images, be sure to edit the WIN.INI file first before printing the publication. Change the resolution factor for the PostScript device description to match the resolution of the typesetter. The PostScript driver section of the WIN.INI file contains a line that usually reads "resolution=300." Change this to read **resolution=1270** for the Linotype Linotronic 100 typesetter, which prints at 1270 dpi. Change the line to read **resolution=2540** for the Linotronic 300 typesetter, which prints at 2540 dpi.

After making the editing changes, save and close the WIN.INI file. End your Windows session, and then restart Windows so that the new settings take effect. Print the file as previously described.

APPENDIX E
References

Books

Adobe Systems, Inc. *PostScript Language Reference Manual*, *PostScript Language Tutorial and Cookbook,* and *PostScript Applications* (3 volume set). Reading: Addison-Wesley Publishing Co., 1985.

Beale, Stephen and Cavuoto, James. *The Scanner Book*. Torrance: Micro Publishing Press, 1989.

Berryman, Greg. *Notes on Graphic Design and Visual Communication*. Los Altos: William Kaufmann, Inc., 1984.

Bove, Tony and Rhodes, Cheryl. *Desktop Publishing With PageMaker: Macintosh*. New York: John Wiley & Sons, 1989.

Bove, Tony; Rhodes, Cheryl; and Thomas, Wes. *The Art of Desktop Publishing 2nd Ed.* New York: Bantam Computer Books, 1987.

Felici, James and Nace, Ted. *Desktop Publishing Skills*. Reading: Addison-Wesley Publishing Company, 1987.

Garcia, Mario R. *Contemporary Newspaper Design 2nd Ed.* Englewood Cliffs: Prentice-Hall, Inc., 1987.

Holt, Robert Lawrence. *How to Publish, Promote, and Sell Your Own Book.* New York: St. Martin's Press, 1985.

International Paper Company. *Pocket Pal, A graphics arts production handbook.* New York: International Paper Company, 1983

Laing, John. *Do-It-Yourself Graphic Design.* New York: Macmillan Publishing, 1984.

Lem, Dean Phillip. *Graphics Master 3.* Los Angeles: Dean Lem Associates, Inc., 1985.

Nace, Ted and Gardner, Michael. *LaserJet Unlimited, 2nd Ed.* Berkeley: Peachpit Press, 1989.

Parker, Roger C. *The Aldus Guide to Basic Design.* Seattle: Aldus Corp., 1987.

Poynter, Dan. *Publishing Short-Run Books 4th Ed.* Santa Barbara: Para Publishing, 1987.

Poynter, Dan. *The Self-Publishing Manual.* Santa Barbara: Para Publishing, 1984.

Shibukawa, Ikuyoshi and Takahashi, Yumi. *Designer's Guide to Color, Designer's Guide to Color 2,* and *Designer's Guide to Color 3.* San Francisco: Chronicle Books, 1983, 1984, and 1986.

Solomon, Martin. *The Art of Typography.* New York: Watson-Guptill Publications, a division of Billboard Publications, Inc., 1986.

Strunk, William and White, E. B. *The Elements of Style.* New York:

Macmillan Publishing Co., 1972.

University of Chicago Press. *A Manual of Style*. Chicago: University of Chicago Press, 1979.

Venolia, Jan. *Write Right!* Berkeley: Ten Speed Press, 1982.

White, Jan V. *Designing for Magazines*. New York: R.R. Bowker, 1982.

White, Jan V. *Editing by Design*. New York: R.R. Bowker, 1982.

White, Jan V. *Graphic Idea Notebook*. New York: R.R. Bowker, 1981.

White, Jan V. *Mastering Graphics*. New York: R.R. Bowker, 1983.

White, Jan V. *Using Charts and Graphs*. New York: R.R. Bowker, 1984.

Wilson, Adrian. *The Design of Books*. Salt Lake City: Gibbs M. Smith, Inc., Peregrine Smith Books, 1974.

Magazines, Journals, and Newspapers

American Printer. 300 West Adams Street, Chicago, IL 60606. $35 per year.

Electronic Composition & Imaging. Youngblood Publishing Company, Ltd., 200 Yorkland Boulevard, Willowdale, Ontario, M2J 1R5 Canada. $45 per year in U.S., $25 per year in Canada.

Folio, the Magazine for Magazine Management. P. O. Box 4006, 125 Elm Street, New Canaan, CT 06840. (203) 972-0761. $58 per year.

Graphic Perspective. Ashley House, 176 Wicksteed Avenue, Toronto, Ontario, M4G 2B6 Canada. (416) 422-1446. $40 per year.

Graphics Arts Monthly and The Printing Industry. Technical Publishing, 875 Third Avenue, New York, NY 10022. (212) 605-9548. $50 per year.

Inside Print (formerly *Magazine Age*). MPE Inc., 125 Elm Street, New Canaan, CT 06840. (203) 972-0761. $36 per year.

Magazine Design and Production. Globecom Publishing Ltd., 4551 West 107th Street #343, Overland, KS 66207. $36 per year.

PC World. PCW Communications, 501 Second Street, San Francisco, CA 94107. (415) 546-7722. $29.90 per year.

Personal Publishing. Hitchcock Publishing Company, 25W550 Geneva Road, Wheaton, IL 60188. $24 per year.

Printing Impressions. 401 North Broad Street, Philadelphia, PA 19108. $50 per year.

Printing Journal. 2401 Charleston Road, Mountain View, CA 94943. $16 per year.

Publish! PC World Communications, 501 Second Street, San Francisco, CA 94107. (415) 546-7722. $39.90 per year.

Publisher's Weekly. R. R. Bowker, 245 West 17th Street, New York, NY 10011. $89 per year.

Small Press, the Magazine of Independent Publishing, R. R. Bowker, 245 West 17th Street, New York, NY 10011. $18 per year.

Step-By-Step Graphics. Dynamic Graphics, 6000 N. Forest Park Drive, P.O. Box 1901, Peoria, IL 61656-1901. (800) 255-8800. $42 per year.

TypeWorld. TypeWorld Educational Association, P.O. Box 170, Salem, NH 03079. $30 per year.

VERBUM, Journal of Personal Computer Aesthetics. P.O. Box 15439, San Diego, CA 92115. (619) 463-9977. MCI Mail: VERBUM. $28 per year.

Newsletters

Bove and Rhodes Inside Report on Desktop Publishing and Multimedia. Tony Bove and Cheryl Rhodes, P.O. Box 1289, Gualala, CA 95445. (707) 884-4413. $195 per year.

Brilliant Ideas for Publishers. Creative Brilliance Associates, 4709 Sherwood Road, Box 4237, Madison, WI 53711. (608) 271-6867. Free to publishers.

CAP (Computer Aided Publishing) Report. InfoVision Inc., 52 Dragon Court, Woburn, MA 01801. (617) 935-5186. $195 per year.

The Desktop Publisher. Aldus Corp., 616 First Avenue, Suite 400, Seattle, WA 98104. (206) 441-8666. Free to registered users of Aldus software.

microPublishing Report. 2004 Curtis Avenue #A, Redondo Beach, CA 90278. (213) 376-5724. $175 per year.

Quick Printer's Guide. Lambda Company, 3655 Frontier Avenue, Boulder, CO 80301. (303) 449-4827. $75 per year.

ReCAP. Boston Computer Society, Desktop Publishing User Group, One Center Plaza, Boston, MA 02108. (617) 367-8080. $28 per year.

Seybold Report on Publishing Systems. Seybold Publications, Box 644, Media, PA 19063. (215) 565-2480. $288 per year. *Seybold Report on Desktop Publishing*. $192 per year. ($396 combined subscription to both reports.)

SWADTP. Southwest Association of Desktop Publishers, 1208 West Brooks, Norman, OK 73069. (405) 360-5554.

Writers Connection. Writers Connection, 1601 Saratoga-Sunnyvale Road, Suite 180, Cupertino, CA 95014. (408) 973-0227. $12 per year.

User Groups

Boston Computer Society. One Center Plaza, Boston, MA 02108. (617) 367-8080. $35 per year membership includes these publications: *Boston Computer Society Update*; *re:CAP, the publishing/computer-aided publishing newsletter*; and *Graphics News*, plus other newsletters available to members at $4 each per year.

National Association of Desktop Publishers. PO Box 508, Boston, MA 02215-9998. (617) 437-6472. $95 per year.

New England PageMaker Users Group, c/o WordWorks, 222 Richmond Street, Providence, RI 02903. (401) 274-0033. Also represented by MCM Associates, 22 1/2 Lee Street, Marblehead, MA 01945. (617) 639-1548.

SouthWest Association of DeskTop Publishers. 1208 West Brooks, Norman, OK 73069. (405) 360-5554, 682-8541, and 364-2751.

Technical References

Encapsulated PostScript (EPS) format was developed and placed in the public domain and is maintained by Altsys Corporation. It was originally designed as a standard for mixed PostScript and QuickDraw files. A copy of the specification is available for $1 postage from Altsys Corp., Attention: Jim Von Ehr, 720 Avenue F, Suite 108, Plano, TX 75074. (214) 424-4888. MCI Mail: ALTSYS.

Tag Image File Format (TIFF) was originally developed and placed in the public domain by Aldus Corporation, in cooperation with several scanner and printer manufacturers. It was designed as a format for digital data interchange, and is independent of specific operating systems, filing systems, compilers, and processors. For a copy of the latest description of TIFF and further information, contact Aldus or Microsoft.

For questions about PageMaker, FreeHand, Persuasion, and TIFF, address queries to: Aldus Corp., 411 First Avenue South, Seattle, WA 98104, or call (206) 622-5500.

For questions about Microsoft Windows or Microsoft Word, address queries to: Microsoft Corp., 16011 NE 36th Way, Box 97017, Redmond, WA 98073-9717, or call (206) 882-8080.

Index

Book 204

M-7